The Dr. Seuss Catalog

The Dr. Seuss Catalog

*An Annotated Guide to Works
by Theodor Geisel in All Media,
Writings About Him, and
Appearances of Characters and Places
in the Books, Stories and Films*

RICHARD H.F. LINDEMANN

McFarland & Company, Inc., Publishers
Jefferson, North Carolina, and London

LIBRARY OF CONGRESS CATALOGUING-IN-PUBLICATION DATA

Lindemann, Richard H.F. (Richard Henry Ferdinand)
    The Dr. Seuss catalog : an annotated guide to works by Theodor
Geisel in all media, writings about him, and appearances of characters
and places in the books, stories and films / Richard H.F. Lindemann.
        p.   cm.
    Includes indexes.

    ISBN 0-7864-2223-8 (softcover : 50# alkaline paper)

    1. Seuss, Dr.— Bibliography.   2. Children's literature, American —
Bibliography.   3. Children's literature, American — Indexes.
4. Seuss, Dr.— Characters — Indexes.   I. Title.
Z8808.915.L56   2005
[PS3513.E2]
016.813'52 — dc22   2004029009

British Library cataloguing data are available

Manufactured in the United States of America

McFarland & Company, Inc., Publishers
  Box 611, Jefferson, North Carolina 28640
  www.mcfarlandpub.com

For N.S.v.N.
and M.F.P.,
in gratitude

ACKNOWLEDGMENTS

To the many people who lent their assistance, expertise and support during the compilation of this work, I am extremely grateful. In particular, I wish to thank Claudia Prescott of Dr. Seuss Enterprises, L.P., and Lynda Claassen, director of the Mandeville Special Collections Library (University of California, San Diego) for their unflagging cooperation and support, and Edward C. Lathem, who has offered valuable criticism and encouragement.

Special thanks for their kindness and cooperation likewise are due to Peggy Owens; to Barbara Krieger (Dartmouth College), Mike Teegarden and Susan Marston (Junior Library Guild), Cindy Stierle (Grolier Books), and Naomi Poulton (United Nations Environment Programme); to Elina Gertsman, David Goodblatt and Nobuko Smith for their linguistic assistance; and to the interlibrary loan unit of Geisel Library (University of California, San Diego).

I also gratefully acknowledge the Librarians Association of the University of California, which provided material support for my research. Finally, I wish to thank Kate and Harriet Lindemann for their encouragement and their patience.

Richard H. F. Lindemann
Fall 2004

TABLE OF CONTENTS

PREFACE

Theodor Seuss Geisel, publishing chiefly as the pseudonymous Dr. Seuss, created illustrations and composed stories for over seventy years. Although we remember him best as an illustrator and author of children's books, his career encompassed an unusually wide range of publishing interests. In the 1920s and 1930s, he frequently contributed both cartoons and humorous essays to popular magazines; as a commercial artist, his advertising campaigns were incredibly effective; the political cartoons that he drew for *PM* newspaper during the early 1940s were syndicated nationally; he won Academy Awards and Emmys for motion picture productions, animated shorts and features. As founder and president of Beginner Books, his influence on children's book publishing from the late 1950s onward was revolutionary, especially in establishing a different way of writing and designing elementary readers.

Despite these various accomplishments, Geisel remains above all a fabulist. His stories, frequently using outrageous creatures and scenes to act out some simple truth, engage the reader and teach him or her both about reading and about life. Geisel addresses fears and anxieties, respects childish amusement and nonsense, and validates the idiosyncracies of our individual imaginations, all without being preachy, condescending, or visually histrionic. Some stories are adventures, others are allegories. But regardless of the style, all of these works are playful, both visually and verbally: funny-sounding words and absurd creatures are the norm. Even when the characters are mean or scary (like The Grinch), there is foolishness to break the tension.

Geisel's prolific career, and his predilection for made-up words and creatures, suggest the usefulness of compiling jointly a bibliography and an iconography of his works. Geisel wrote or contributed illustrations for over seventy-five books, most of which have been reprinted repeatedly and translated into at least twenty-nine languages; worldwide volume sales of his works exceed 400 million copies. In addition, over 100 of his stories have appeared

1

in magazines, and nearly as many motion pictures, animated features and sound recordings have been released. The bibliographic listing of these, together with a corollary iconography of the nearly 900 made-up creatures, places and things that appear in Geisel's stories, provides a *vade mecum* for "Seussites" and an exhaustive record of his literary creations as well.

A Note About Pseudonyms

Theodor Seuss Geisel wrote and illustrated books for children under three different pseudonyms: Dr. Seuss, Theo. LeSieg and, once, Rosetta Stone. Early in his career, he also assumed other aliases for his magazine submissions, among them Anton Lang, Qincy Qilq, Xavier Ruppsknoff, Henry McSeuss Webster, Dr. Souss, Antoinette Seuss, Dr. Theophrastus Seuss, and Dr. Theodophilus Seuss (for further examples of rarely used pseudonyms, see byline names listed in section *C: Contributions to Magazines and Newspapers* [see especially C57]). He used his given name, Theodor (or Ted) Geisel, to indicate screenplay or production credits and for authorship of some of his work during U.S. Army Signal Corps service in World War II.

Dr. Seuss

While Geisel was a student at Dartmouth College, he edited, wrote and drew cartoons for the campus humor magazine *Jack o' Lantern*. It was in his senior year when he first used his mother's maiden name, Seuss, as a pseudonym to shield his identity from an irate dean. "Dr." was added in 1927 in recognition of the fact that he had abandoned working for his doctorate in English literature to become a cartoonist. Geisel hoped to reserve his given name for writing novels but never published any.

Theo. LeSieg

Geisel used the pseudonym "Theo. LeSieg" (Geisel spelled backwards) for works that he wrote but chose not to illustrate. In a letter to a scholar, Geisel wrote: "It is not that they [*i.e.* LeSieg stories] are, in my opinion, inferior. It is because I believe that Seuss is the wrong man to illustrate them. Most of them call for more realistic animals than he likes to do, or for human characters that he doesn't do very well at all" (*Gough*, 1986 —*see* F74). An earlier form of the pseudonym, "T. S. Lesieg," was in fact one of Geisel's first pen names, which he employed for the brief essay "A Pupil's Nightmare" in his high school newspaper, *The Central Recorder*, on January 21, 1920 [*see* C89]. A month earlier, he had signed a cartoon in the same newspaper "Pete, the Pessimist."

Rosetta Stone

Geisel and Michael Frith concocted this joint pseudonym in honor of Geisel's wife Audrey, whose maiden name was Stone, when they were collaborating on *Because a Little Bug Went Ka-CHOO!* The name proved unpopular; critics argued that it trivialized the authors' work, and the pseudonym never appeared again.

Manuscript Sources

Manuscript sources documenting Geisel's work, including rough drafts, original sketches and drawings, publication files, professional correspondence, scrapbooks, tear sheets from magazine and advertising campaigns, mementos, and photographs, are held principally by the Mandeville Special Collections Library, University of California, San Diego, in its Dr. Seuss Collection [MSS 230] (approximately 9,500 items, 1919–2003; electronically published finding aid on the World Wide Web). The bulk of that collection comprises working drafts and drawings for nearly all of his books, screenplays and other creative projects; personal papers are few but include documentation of his student life and military service.

The Rauner Special Collections Library, Dartmouth College, holds an annotated typescript draft for *The 500 Hats of Bartholomew Cubbins* (original drawings for that work are at UCSD), together with clippings files of magazine contributions, advertising artwork, alumnus files, and miscellaneous letters and interview transcripts. Despite assertions published variously that drafts or drawings for *And to Think That I Saw It on Mulberry Street* are held at Dartmouth College, the original drawings for that work were in private hands until recently, when they were acquired for Lloyd Cotsen; they are presently held by the Cotsen Children's Library, Princeton University. Special Collections, Butler Library, Columbia University, holds the papers of Geisel's publisher, Bennett Cerf, as well as the Vanguard Press and Random House archives, which together include approximately 750 items pertaining to Geisel as an author and as editor of Beginner Books. The Lyndon Baines Johnson Presidential Library holds the manuscript for *The Lorax*. Scattered materials reflecting Geisel's work in the U.S. Army Signal Corps are held variously by divisions of the Library of Congress and the National Archives and Records Administration.

The Catalog

This catalog begins with a bibliography of Geisel's published works, writings about Dr. Seuss, and compilations by others of his selected works. Part I lists Geisel's works and is arranged as follows:

Books and Book Illustrations: Major Works [nos. 1-65]
Books and Book Illustrations: Minor Works [nos. A1-A16]
Books and Book Illustrations: Anthologies, Collections and Selections [nos. B1-B30]
Contributions to Magazines and Newspapers [nos. C1-C133]
Screenplays, Film/Video, Multimedia and Theatrical/Musical Adaptations [nos. D1-D43]
Sound Recordings [nos. E1-E53]

Books by Dr. Seuss are arranged by date of first publication; readers seeking an entry by title are directed to the alphabetical title index, where citations to corresponding bibliographical entries may be found. Works appearing in other formats, including magazine submissions, motion pictures and sound recordings, are arranged alphabetically by title.

Dr. Seuss's first two books were published by Vanguard Press. Subsequently, Random House or Beginner Books, a division of Random House, published all of the trade books written by Geisel, regardless of pseudonym, in the United States and Canada. In addition, distribution and publication agreements with others have been numerous: Houghton Mifflin and E.M. Hale ("Cadmus Books"), as well as Scholastic, Inc., have entered into special contracts for publication and distribution in the educational market (mainly schools and libraries), while some early titles were issued simultaneously as Junior Literary Guild editions, typically in special library bindings with illustrated dust-jackets. Grolier Enterprises has distributed Dr. Seuss's books exclusively through mail order since 1965, chiefly through subscription book clubs. With a few early exceptions, Collins/ Harvill has enjoyed publication rights for works distributed in Great Britain and the Commonwealth countries outside Canada. Numerous translations worldwide, in twenty-nine languages, add to the list of publishers.

Editions of the works listed in Part I are recorded when they differ by date, publisher, or have a special edition statement. Most of these later "editions" are essentially reprints of the first edition, although more recent issues in board-book or flap-book format also reflect abridgement or modification of the original work. Less substantial variations, represented by different bindings or dust-jackets, are typically noted but not separately recorded. Among such variations, which appear within virtually every edition, are: binding variants (trade hardcover, library hardcover [often termed "Gibraltar" bindings], paperback, plain cloth hardcover with mounted illustration); presence or absence of dust-jackets (dust-jackets are presumed in the listings below unless their absence is noted); varying content in dust-jacket and back cover notes; presence or absence of illustrated paste-down endpapers and flyleaves; and imprint statements in later printings that reflect original cataloging data. Later printings of particular editions are not recorded. In some cases, the only reliable indicator of an earlier or a later printing is the price, which sometimes appears on the upper inner flap of the dust-jacket or as a price sticker on the upper cover. Where initial prices are known but were not printed on the piece, those amounts appear in brackets ([ ]).

Excluded from this listing are single cartoons and single-panel cartoon essays, filmstrips and advertising artwork, as well as brief fillers that Geisel submitted to student publications while he was in high school and college (a checklist of many of these cartoons appears in Philip Nel's *Dr. Seuss: American Icon* [*see* F143]). Likewise, the writing and cartooning that resulted from Geisel's service in the U.S. Army Signal Corps during World War II are excluded unless his involvement in that work was significant and identifiable. Collectibles, chiefly commercial spin-offs, toys, games, and promotional objects, are also excluded from the list. Pertinent World Wide Web sites are included when these are hosted by an institution.

Part II of the catalog (entries F1–F196) lists writings about Dr. Seuss, including biographical and critical works, interviews, and works by others that draw heavily from Dr. Seuss's writings and drawings. Academic theses and superficial news articles have not been included.

Part III is an Iconography that identifies the characters, places and terms of Dr. Seuss's works and the books, films and short stories in which each appears. Each reference to a work by Dr. Seuss is keyed to its entry number in Part I.

I. Works by Dr. Seuss

Books and Book Illustrations: Major Works

1937

1.0 *And to Think That I Saw It on Mulberry Street* / by Dr. Seuss. New York: Vanguard Press, 1937.

"Manufactured ... Duenewald Printing Corporation" appears at foot of t.p. *verso*.

Also distributed in soft-cover by Scholastic Magazines and by Grolier Enterprises as a "Book Club Edition"; some Grolier printings misspell Seuss as "Suess" in the copyright statement.

Reprinted in: *Six by Seuss; Your Favorite Seuss*.

1st issue: September, 1937; 15,000 copies; retail price $1.00. While subsequent printings have an ordinal printing statement on t.p. *verso*, the first printing carries no such statement. In verse, with most illustrations printed in five colors. This is the first published book written by Dr. Seuss, who initially gave it the title *The Story That No One Could Beat*. Twenty-seven publishers rejected the work before a college chum, Marshall McClintock, who had just been appointed children's editor at Vanguard Press, accidentally encountered Dr. Seuss on the street in New York and quickly agreed to a contract. Marco, the boy character in the book, is named after McClintock's son; the book is dedicated to McClintock's wife, Helene, "Mother of the One and Original Marco." Both Marco and Mulberry Street appear often in subsequent books and magazine stories written by Dr. Seuss. Mulberry Street exists in Geisel's home town, Springfield, Mass.

Subsequently, the work provided the basis for a musical composition by Deems Taylor entitled "Marco Takes a Walk: Variations for Orchestra, Op. 25" [unpublished; *see* D34.0], which was composed as accompaniment for Sterling Holloway's reading of the story on *The Family Hour* (CBS Radio, November 30, 1941) [*cf.* E2.0] and was performed by the New York Philharmonic at Carnegie Hall on November 15, 1942.

Printings and editions from late 1978 onward have revised text and, in some printings, altered illustration of the Chinese character in response to perceptions of racial stereotyping: "Chinaman" has become "Chinese man" (or "Chinese boy," as it appears in the Grolier Book Club edition), the character's face is lightened in tone, and his pigtail is shortened or eliminated.

1.1 *And to Think That I Saw It on Mulberry Street* / by Dr. Seuss. London: Country Life, 1939.

1.2 *And to Think That I Saw It on Mulberry Street* / by Dr. Seuss. Eau Claire, Wis.: E. M. Hale, [1947?], c1937.
"Special Edition."

1.3 *And to Think That I Saw It on Mulberry Street* / by Dr. Seuss. New York: Vanguard Press, 1964.

1.4 *And to Think That I Saw It on Mulberry Street* / by Dr. Seuss. New York: Scholastic Book Services, 1965.

1.5 *And to Think That I Saw It on Mulberry Street* / by Dr. Seuss. New York: Random House, 1965.
"A Vanguard Press Book."
Essentially, a later printing of 1.3, reflecting the acquisition of Vanguard Press by Random House. Eventually, the title was insinuated into the "Beginner Books" series.

1.6 *And to Think That I Saw It on Mulberry Street* / by Dr. Seuss. London: Collins, 1971.

1.7 *And to Think That I Saw It on Mulberry Street* / by Dr. Seuss. London: Fontana Picture Lions/Collins, 1979.

1.8 *And to Think That I Saw It on Mulberry Street* / by Dr. Seuss. New York: Random House, [1989].
"A Vanguard Press Book."
A reprint of 1.5; redistributed in 1997 with a cover label: "Special 60th Anniversary Edition" [*cf.* 1.10, which is a separate work].

1.9 *And to Think That I Saw It on Mulberry Street* / Geisel (Dr. Seuss). Louisville, Ky.: Amer. Printing House for the Blind, [199–], c1937. In braille.

1.10 *And to Think That I Saw It on Mulberry Street Coloring and Activity Book* / by Dr. Seuss. New York: Random House, 1997.
"Special 60th Anniversary Edition."
Includes the illustrated story, uncolored, for the reader to use as a coloring book, as well as additional puzzles and games for coloring [*cf.* 1.8, which describes a separate work].

1.11 *And to Think That I Saw It on Mulberry Street* / by Dr. Seuss. London: Collins, 2002.
"The Classic Collection."

1.12 *And to Think That I Saw It on Mulberry Street* / by Dr. Seuss. London: Collins, 2003.
"Green Back Books."

1.a And to Think That I Saw It on Mulberry Street [Afrikaans]
En dit nogal alles in Bosbessiestraat / Dr. Seuss; vertaal deur Lize Kampman. Cape Town: Anansi Uitgewers, 1991.

1.b And to Think That I Saw It on Mulberry Street [Danish]
Brumbassegade / tekst: Dr. Seuss; dansk bearbejdelse: Thomas Sigsgaard; tegninger: Thora Lund. [Copenhagen]: Munksgaard, [1964].

1.c And to Think That I Saw It on Mulberry Street [Hebrew]
Re'hov Tut: Sipur lo pashu't / me'et Doktor Sus; 'Ivrit: Le'ah Na'or. Jerusalem: Keter, 1990.

1.d And to Think That I Saw It on Mulberry Street [Japanese]
Maruberi dori no fushigi na dekigoto / saku Dokutā Sūsu; yaku Watanabe Shigeo. Tokyo: Nihon Paburisshingu, 1969.

1938

2.0 *The 500 Hats of Bartholomew Cubbins* / by Dr. Seuss, author of "And to Think That I Saw It on Mulberry Street." New York: Vanguard Press, 1938.
Also distributed in soft-cover by Scholastic Magazines and by Grolier Enterprises as a "Book Club Edition."
Also published in condensed version in *Children's Digest* [*see* C1].
Reprinted in: *Six by Seuss*; *Anthology of Children's Literature*, ed. E. Johnson and E. R. Sickles (N.Y.: Houghton Mifflin, 1948), pp. 465–470; and (with selected illustrations featuring golden highlighting), *Childcraft: The How and Why Library*, v. 2 (Chicago: Field Enterprises Educational Corp., 1964), pp. 150–165 [an abridged and simplified version of the story, adapted

by William S. Gray and May Hill Arbuthnot and illustrated anonymously by others, appears in the school reader: *More Streets and Roads* (Chicago: Scott, Foresman and Co., 1942), pp. 156–166 [*see* F75]].

1st issue: September, 1938; 10,000 copies, bound in black paper with illustrated covers and red cloth spine, upper and lower endpaper designs reversed, 31 cm. (later issues are bound in full paper, 28.7 cm.); dust-jacket lower inner flap has advertisement for *And to Think That I Saw It on Mulberry Street* with price at foot of ad; retail price $1.50. Earliest copies of the first printing show imprecise registration of the red ink, especially on the hat found on p. [6]; that registration is corrected in subsequent copies. Written in prose, with black-and-white illustrations highlighted in red. In drafting the text, Dr. Seuss eventually changed most of the characters' names (*e.g.*, King Derwin was initially "Hatalard" and Sir Snipps was "Cwerg"). The book is dedicated to "Chrysanthemum-Pearl," the Geisels' make-believe daughter.

2.1 *The 500 Hats of Bartholomew Cubbins* / by Dr. Seuss. London: Oxford University Press, 1940.
      1st issue: retail price 6/- net.

2.2 *The 500 Hats of Bartholomew Cubbins* / by Dr. Seuss. New York: New York Institute for the Education of the Blind, [1941].
      In braille.

2.3 *The 500 Hats of Bartholomew Cubbins* / by Dr. Seuss. Eau Claire, Wis.: E. M. Hale, [1947?], c1938.
      "Special Edition."

2.4 *The 500 Hats of Bartholomew Cubbins* / by Dr. Seuss. New York: Vanguard Press, 1965.

2.5 *The 500 Hats of Bartholomew Cubbins* / by Dr. Seuss. New York: Random House, 1965.
      "A Vanguard Press Book."
      Essentially, a later printing of 2.4, reflecting the acquisition of Vanguard Press by Random House.

2.6 *The 500 Hats of Bartholomew Cubbins* / by Dr. Seuss. New York: Scholastic Book Services, 1966.

2.7 *The 500 Hats of Bartholomew Cubbins* / by Dr. Seuss. London: Collins, 1966.

2.8 *The 500 Hats of Bartholomew Cubbins* / by Dr. Seuss. London: Fontana Picture Lions/Collins, 1979.

2.9 *The 500 Hats of Bartholomew Cubbins* / by Dr. Seuss. New York: Random House, 1989.
"A Vanguard Press Book."

2.a The 500 Hats of Bartholomew Cubbins [Afrikaans]
Die 500 Hoede van Sebastiaan Klippers / Dr. Seuss; [vertaal deur Lydia Snyman]. [Cape Town]: Anansi Uitgewers, 1989.

2.b The 500 Hats of Bartholomew Cubbins [German]
Die 500 Hüte des Barthel Löwenspross / von Dr. Seuss; [Übertragung aus dem Amerikanischen von Dr. Dichler-Appel]. Vienna: E. Mensa, 1951.

2.c The 500 Hats of Bartholomew Cubbins [Japanese]
Fushigi na gohyaku no bōshi = *The 500 Hats of Bartholomew Cubbins* / Shiesu Hakushi cho; Omori Takeo yaku. Tokyo: Toppan, 1949.
Cover title in Japanese and English; t.p. and text in Japanese; composed in vertical text to be opened from left-to-right.

2.d The 500 Hats of Bartholomew Cubbins [Japanese]
Fushigi na 500 no bōshi / Dokutā Sūsu saku e; Watanabe Shigeo yaku. Tokyo: Nihon Paburisshingu, 1969.
Composed in horizontal text to be opened from right-to-left.

2.e The 500 Hats of Bartholomew Cubbins [Japanese]
Fushigi na 500 no bōshi / Dokutā Sūsu saku e; Watanabe Shigeo yaku. Tokyo: Kaiseisha, 1981.

2.f The 500 Hats of Bartholomew Cubbins [Korean]
Basollomyu K'obinju ui moja 500-kae / Susu paksa kul, kurim; Kim Hye-ryong omgim. Soule: Sigongsa, 1994.

2.g The 500 Hats of Bartholomew Cubbins [Spanish]
Los 500 sombreros de Bartolomé Cubbins / Dr. Seuss; traducido por Eida de la Vega. New York: Lectorum, 1998.

1939

3.0 *The Seven Lady Godivas* / written and illustrated by Dr. Seuss. New York: Random House, 1939.
"First Printing" appears on t.p. *verso.*
1st issue: September, 1939; 7,500 copies in dust-jacket; retail price $1.75 (a few pre-publication copies were bound in wrappers). Written in prose for an adult audience, with black-and-white illustrations highlighted

in red and one drawing in blue-green ("a horse of another color"). Dr. Seuss's first book published by Random House, it was a commercial and critical failure due partly to the public's confusion about Dr. Seuss, by then an established children's writer, publishing a work with an adult theme. Three sets of "teaser" postcards illustrated by Dr. Seuss were distributed by the publisher to promote the book in 1939. The title went out of print without further printings, and the printing plates were regrained [*i.e.*, destroyed] in 1945; almost fifty years later, the work was reissued. Geisel was working on a stage adaptation of this work at the time of his death.

3.1 *The Seven Lady Godivas* / written and illustrated by Dr. Seuss. New York: Random House, 1987, c1967.

"Now reissued by multitudinous demand" appears on the dust-jacket; the book is described as a "commemorative edition" on the t.p. *verso*; bound with cloth spine and paper boards. Although copyright to this work was renewed in 1967, it remained out of print until this edition, which, because the original plates were destroyed, has illustrations printed in inferior quality compared to those in the 1939 edition.

300 copies of this "reissued edition" are specially bound in full tan cloth with a matching slip case, numbered and signed by the author.

4.0 *The King's Stilts* / written and illustrated by Dr. Seuss. New York: Random House, 1939.

Also distributed by Grolier Enterprises as a "Book Club Edition."

Reprinted in: *Dr. Seuss Storytime*.

1st issue: October, 1939; issued in yellow cloth boards with title on both covers printed in drop-out lettering on red panel, with b/w and red illustrated dust-jacket; "Printed ... by Duenewald Printing Corporation" appears on t.p. *verso*; 30.8 cm.; retail price $1.50. Subsequently issued in yellow or orange cloth boards with red lettering on upper cover and statement "Lithographed ... by Duenewald Printing Corporation" on t.p. *verso*. Later editions are bound in blue illustrated paper boards; 28.7 cm. Some printings during the 1940s have poor color registration. To promote the book, certificates illustrated by Dr. Seuss appointing the bearer "Assistant Keeper of the King's Patrol Cats" were printed. The book is dedicated to Alison Margaret and Deirdre Clodagh Budd (children of British friends) "... and all the Irish cats and seagulls on the shores of Inchydoney"; the quoted phrase is lacking in later issues.

Written in prose, with black-and-white illustrations highlighted in red. An abridged and simplified version of the story, revised by William S. Gray and May Hill Arbuthnot and illustrated anonymously by others, appears in the school reader: *Days and Deeds* (Chicago: Scott, Foresman and Co., 1943), pp. 196–214 [*see* F76].

4.1 *The King's Stilts* / written and illustrated by Dr. Seuss. London: Hamish Hamilton, 1942.

4.2 *The King's Stilts* / written and illustrated by Dr. Seuss. New York: Random House, 1967.

4.3 *The King's Stilts* / written and illustrated by Dr. Seuss. Louisville, Ky.: American Printing House for the Blind, [199–?], c1939.
     In braille.

4.a The King's Stilts [Hebrew]
     ha-Kabayim shel ha-melekh / me'et Doktor Sus; 'Ivrit: Le'ah Na'or. Jerusalem: Keter, 1979.

4.b The King's Stilts [Japanese]
     Osama no takeuma / Dokutā Sūsu saku; Mitsuyoshi Natsuya yaku; Tsukasa Osamu e. Tokyo: Gakushu Kenkyusha, 1968.

4.c The King's Stilts [Japanese]
     Osama no takeuma / Dokutā Sūsu saku e; Watanabe Shigeo yaku. Tokyo: Kaiseisha, 1983.

1940

5.0 *Horton Hatches the Egg* / by Dr. Seuss. New York: Random House, 1940.
Also distributed by Grolier Enterprises as a "Book Club Edition."
Also issued with an accompanying cassette sound recording in 1972.
Also published in condensed version in *Children's Digest* [*see* C46].
Reprinted in: *Dr. Seuss Storytime*; *Six by Seuss*.
"First Printing" appears on t.p. *verso*.
    1st issue: October, 1940; bound in plain full cloth in gray (with faux graining) [and later in brown or maroon], with title and author stamped in red on upper cover (later issues are bound in full color illustrated paper); "Author of 'Mulberry Street;' and 'King's Stilts'" appears below "Dr. Seuss" on upper dust-jacket, and "Testimonials! Testimonials!" appears at head of lower dust-jacket; retail price $1.50. The first issue was distributed in Canada by the Macmillan Co.; later issues show "Random House of Canada" as joint publisher on the t.p. Some copies printed between 1940

and 1946 show deteriorating lithography, with blues especially becoming greener and reds losing their original texture. The Grolier "Book Club Edition" was resized slightly larger [28.3 cm.] beginning in 1965, as were printings ©1968, causing negligible elongation of the illustrations; some of these later issues have green covers and illustrations with blue background coloring rather than the blue-green that appears in all other printings.

An incipient prose version of the story first appeared in *Judge* magazine (April, 1938), with the elephant being a female named Matilda [*see* C69]. While absurd creatures and playful rhymes were common to Dr. Seuss's magazine stories and cartooning, this book was a rash departure from the images and prose of his previous two works (*The King's Stilts* and *The Seven Lady Godivas*), and it established the style that typified his books from then on. Imposing an adult subtext within the story, in this instance welfare dependence, also became a frequent feature in later works.

5.1 *Horton Hatches the Egg* / by Dr. Seuss. Eau Claire, Wis.: E. M. Hale, c1940.
"Special Edition."
Issued in red cloth with illustrated upper cover showing Horton on his nested perch; "Cadmus Books" appears on spine.

5.2 *Horton Hatches the Egg* / by Dr. Seuss. London: Hamish Hamilton, [1942?].

5.3 *Horton Hatches the Egg* / by Dr. Seuss. London: Hamish Hamilton, 1942.
"Australian Edition."
Printed by Morris & Walker, Melbourne, for George Jaboor, Melbourne, Australasian representative of Hamish Hamilton Ltd., London.

5.4 *Horton Hatches the Egg* / by Dr. Seuss. London: Collins, 1962.

5.5 *Horton Hatches the Egg* / by Dr. Seuss. New York: Random House, 1968.
Also issued with an accompanying cassette sound recording in 1972, 1976, 1977, 1981, and 1991.
Also issued jointly as a media kit with *Horton Hears a Who!* in 1976.

5.6 *Horton Hatches the Egg* / by Dr. Seuss. [London]: Collins, 1979.
"Collins Colour Cubs" edition [15 cm.].

5.7 *Horton Hatches the Egg* / by Dr. Seuss. London: Collins, 1984.

5.8 *Horton Hatches the Egg* / by Dr. Seuss. Boston: National Braille Press, [1986?].
Reprinted in 1993.
In braille.

5.9 *Horton Hatches the Egg* / by Dr. Seuss. London: Collins, 1988.

5.10 *Horton Hatches the Egg* / by Dr. Seuss. London: Collins, 1992.

5.a Horton Hatches the Egg [Afrikaans]
Herrie broei die Eier uit / Dr. Seuss; vertaal deur Marié Heese. Cape Town: Anansi Uitgewers, 1990.

5.b Horton Hatches the Egg [Danish]
Horton ligger på aeg / Dr. Seuss; gendigtet på dansk af Jacob Andersen. Copenhagen: Høst, 1992.

5.c Horton Hatches the Egg [Dutch]
Slurfje past op het ei / Dr. Seuss; Nederlands van Katja en Kees Stip. Huizen: Goede Boek, [1975].

5.d Horton Hatches the Egg [German]
Der Elefant im Vogelnest / Dr. Seuss; deutsche Nachdichtung von Hans A. Halbey. Ravensburg: O. Maier, 1973.

5.e Horton Hatches the Egg [Italian]
L'uovo di Ortone / Dr. Seuss; [traduzione, Anna Sarfatti]. Florence: Giunti, c1994.
"GRU Under 7 [no.] 1."
Reprinted: Giunti junior, 2003.

5.f Horton Hatches the Egg [Japanese]
Zo no Hoton tamago o kaesu: Kono hiyoko wa dare no mono? / Dokutā Sūsu saku e; Shiraki Shigeru yaku. Tokyo: Kaiseisha, 1968.
Issued in an illustrated slip case.

5.g Horton Hatches the Egg [Japanese]
Zo no Hoton tamago o kaesu: Kono hiyoko wa dare no mono? / Dokutā Sūsu saku e; Shiraki Shigeru yaku. Tokyo: Kaiseisha, 1976.

5.h Horton Hatches the Egg [Polish]
Słoń który wysiedział jajko / Dr. Seuss; przeło˙zył Stanisław Barańczak. Poznań: Media Rodzina, 1995.
Reissued with an accompanying CD-ROM in 2003, with text in English and Polish.

5.i Horton Hatches the Egg [Portuguese]
    Tonho choca o ovo / por Dr. Seuss; tradução de Mônica Rodriques da
    Costa, Lavinia Fávero, Gisela Moreau. São Paulo: Editora Schwarcz,
    2001.
    "Edição bilingüe."

1947

6.0 *McElligot's Pool* / written and illustrated by Dr. Seuss. New York: Ran-
    dom House, 1947.
Also issued jointly with the Junior Literary Guild (so stated on t.p.) in
blue library binding with red lettering (no dust-jacket seen).
Also distributed by Grolier Enterprises as a "Book Club Edition."
Also published in condensed version in *Children's Digest* [*see* C70].
Reprinted in: *Dr. Seuss Storytime*; *Your Favorite Seuss*.
    1st issue: September, 1947; bound in green cloth with dark green
stamping and line illustration (fish's mouth open) on upper cover (at least
four binding states for the 1st edition are known, all in variant shades of
green–sequence undetermined); dust-jacket lower cover bears the statement: "This is the First Dr. Seuss Book Since 1940!"; retail price $2.50.
Issued simultaneously as a Junior Literary Guild Edition. Dr. Seuss was
working on the book as early as 1941. Approximately half of the illustrations are printed in full color, marking the first time that one of Dr. Seuss's
books utilized the technique. Some early printings appear on thin paper,
causing "see-through," and this shortcoming was remedied by early 1948.
Coloration varies widely among printings, and both gradation and inten-
sity of tints in later printings is generally inferior. The work, which earned
a Randolph Caldecott Honor Award from the American Library Association, is dedicated to Geisel's father (Theodor Robert Geisel).

6.1 *McElligot's Pool* / written and illustrated by Dr. Seuss. Eau Claire,
    Wis.: E. M. Hale, c1947.
    "Special Edition."

6.2 *McElligot's Pool* / written and illustrated by Dr. Seuss. Louisville, Ky.:
    American Printing House for the Blind, c1947.
    In braille.

6.3 *McElligot's Pool* / written and illustrated by Dr. Seuss. New York:
    Random House, 1974.

6.4 *McElligot's Pool* / written and illustrated by Dr. Seuss. Watertown,
    Mass.: Howe Press, Perkins School for the Blind, 1974.
    In braille.

6.5 *McElligot's Pool* / written and illustrated by Dr. Seuss. New York: Random House, 1975.

Also issued with an accompanying cassette sound recording in 1981.

Aside from different "Cataloging in Publication" and copyright statements, this issue is identical to, and probably a later printing of, 6.3.

6.51 *McElligot's Pool* / written and illustrated by Dr. Seuss. New York: Random House, 1975.

Identical to 6.5, but issued in paperback as a giveaway promotion for Crest toothpaste and Prell shampoo. "Free when you buy ..." appears in medallion on upper cover.

6.6 *McElligot's Pool* / written and illustrated by Dr. Seuss. London: Collins, 1975.

6.7 *McElligot's Pool* / written and illustrated by Dr. Seuss. [London]: Collins, 1990.

6.8 *McElligot's Pool* / written and illustrated by Dr. Seuss. [Boston]: National Braille Press, 1993.

In braille.

1948

7.0 ***Thidwick, the Big-Hearted Moose*** / written and illustrated by Dr. Seuss. New York: Random House, 1948.

Also issued jointly with the Junior Literary Guild in two binding states: blue library binding with maroon lettering; maroon library binding with white lettering (ill. dust-jacket).

Also distributed by Grolier Enterprises as a "Book Club Edition."

Also published in condensed version in *LIFE* [*see* C108] and *Children's Digest* [*see* C117].

Reprinted in: *Dr. Seuss Storytime*; *Dr. Seuss's Book of Bedtime Stories*.

1st issue: September, 1948; copyright statement (t.p. *verso*) includes "Oberly & Newell Lithograph Corp."; bound in red cloth boards with blue title and moose-head illustration on upper cover, and, subsequently, in blue cloth with black title/illustration; dust-jacket, with radiating blue stripes, lists five titles on lower cover (dust-jacket for later issues is solid blue); retail price $2.00. Later issues are bound in blue paper with illustrated cover. Published simultaneously as a "Junior Literary Guild Selection" bound in special unillustrated cloth in two states as described above. The book is dedicated to Helen [Palmer Geisel], Geisel's wife.

7.1 *Thidwick, the Big-Hearted Moose* / written and illustrated by Dr. Seuss.
Eau Claire, Wis.: E. M. Hale and Co., c1948.
"Special Edition."

7.2 *Thidwick, the Big-Hearted Moose* / written and illustrated by Dr. Seuss.
London: Collins, 1968.
1st issue: retail price 15*s.*/- net.

7.3 *Thidwick, the Big-Hearted Moose* / written and illustrated by Dr. Seuss.
New York: Random House, 1975.
Issued with an accompanying cassette sound recording.

7.4 *Thidwick, the Big-Hearted Moose* / written and illustrated by Dr. Seuss.
New York: Random House, 1976.
Also issued with an accompanying cassette sound recording in 1982
and 1993.
Also issued as "A Dr. Seuss Paperback Classic."

7.5 *Thidwick, the Big-Hearted Moose* / written and illustrated by Dr. Seuss.
London: Collins, 1990.

7.6 *Thidwick, the Big-Hearted Moose* / written and illustrated by Dr. Seuss.
Boston: National Braille Press, 1993.
In braille.

7.a Thidwick, the Big-Hearted Moose [Hebrew]
Tidvik ha-mus mitnaheg be-nimus / me'et Doktor Sus; 'Ivrit, Le'ah
Na'or. Jerusalem: Keter, 2001.

7.b Thidwick, the Big-Hearted Moose [Japanese]
Ohitoyoshi no ooshika / Dokutā Sūsu saku e; Watanabe Shigeo yaku.
Tokyo: Nihon Paburisshingu, 1969.

7.c Thidwick, the Big-Hearted Moose [Japanese]
Ohitoyoshi no ooshika / Dokutā Sūsu saku e; Watanabe Shigeo yaku.
Tokyo: Kaiseisha, 1985.

7.d Thidwick, the Big-Hearted Moose [Romanian]
Tidvic, cérbul inimă bună / written and illustrated by Dr. Seuss; tradus
și versificat din limba engleză: Nicolae Polverejan. Vârşęt [*i.e.*,
Vršac]: Ed. Libertatea, 1953.
Author statement appears on t.p. *verso.*

7.e Thidwick, the Big-Hearted Moose [Serbo-Croatian]
Tidvik: dobroćudni jelen / [translated by Viktor Dmitrijev]. Novi Sad:
Bratstvo-jedinstvo, 1952.

7.f Thidwick, the Big-Hearted Moose [Serbo-Croatian]
Tidvik: dobrodušni jelen' / [translated by Mikola M. Kočiš]. Ruski Kerestur: Ruske slovo, 1953.

1949

8.0 ***Bartholomew and the Oobleck*** / written and illustrated by Dr. Seuss. New York: Random House, 1949.
Also issued jointly with the Junior Literary Guild (so stated on t.p.) in blue library binding with white lettering; subsequently issued in pictorial cloth (ill. dust-jacket).
Also distributed by Grolier Enterprises as a "Book Club Edition."
Also issued with an accompanying cassette sound recording in 1972.
Reprinted in: *Dr. Seuss Storytime*; *A Hatful of Seuss*.
　　1st issue: October, 1949; bound in blue paper with illustrated covers, 31 cm.; code (60–90) at foot of upper dust-jacket flap; retail price $2.00. Subsequently bound in red paper with white backstrip, then [*ca.* 1960] in full red paper, 30.5 cm. (later issues bound in full red paper, 28.7 cm.). Written in prose (the last of Dr. Seuss's books in that genre) and printed with black-and-white illustrations highlighted in pale green. Some copies of the first printing are on inferior, thin paper with bleed-through evident. The book is dedicated to Kelvin C. Vanderlip, Jr., Geisel's godson. Dr. Seuss received a Randolph Caldecott Honor Award from the American Library Association for this work.

8.1 *Bartholomew and the Oobleck* / written and illustrated by Dr. Seuss. New York: Random House, 1976.

8.2 *Bartholomew and the Oobleck* / written and illustrated by Dr. Seuss. New York: Random House, 1977.
Also issued with an accompanying cassette sound recording in 1981.
Also issued as "A Dr. Seuss Paperback Classic."

8.3 *Bartholomew and the Oobleck* / Geisel (Dr. Seuss). Louisville, Ky.: American Printing House for the Blind, [199–], c1949.
In braille.

8.a Bartholomew and the Oobleck [Hebrew]
Gedalyahu veha-mistuck / me'et Doktor Sus; 'lvrit: Le'ah Na'or. Jerusalem: Keter, 1979.

8.b Bartholomew and the Oobleck [Japanese]
Fushigi na Ubetabeta / saku Dokutā Sūsu; yaku Watanabe Shigeo. Tokyo: Nihon Paburisshingu, 1969.

1950

9.0 *If I Ran the Zoo* / by Dr. Seuss. New York: Random House, 1950.

Also issued jointly with the Junior Literary Guild (so stated on t.p.), bound in red library binding with white lettering (no dust-jacket seen).

Also distributed by Grolier Enterprises as a "Book Club Edition."

Also issued with an accompanying cassette sound recording in 1972.

Reprinted in: *A Hatful of Seuss*; *Just What I'd Do*; *Your Favorite Seuss*.

Also published in condensed version in *Redbook* [*see* C55] and *Children's Digest* [*see* C56].

1st issue: October, 1950; lower cover lists seven Dr. Seuss titles; 31 cm.; retail price $2.00. Later issues, from *ca.* 1960 onward, are slightly smaller: 28.7 cm. This work earned a Randolph Caldecott Honor Award from the American Library Association. The story came from an idea that his mother had given Geisel in 1927, when she herself was experimenting with writing. Many of the creatures that appear in this work were adapted for use in the animated feature *The Hoober-Bloob Highway* [*see* D25.0]. The book is dedicated to Toni and Michael Gordon Tackaberry Thompson, Geisel's godchildren.

In 1959, a set of snap-assembly models based on creatures in this work was sold by Revelle, in conjunction with Random House, under the name *Dr. Seuss Zoo.* Each model was also sold separately: "Norval the Bashful Blinket"; "Gowdy the Dowdy Grackle"; "Tingo the Noodle Topped Stroodle"; and "Roscoe the Many Footed Lion."

9.1 *If I Ran the Zoo* / by Dr. Seuss. Eau Claire, Wis.: E. M. Hale, c1950. "Special Edition."

9.2 *If I Ran the Zoo* / by Dr. Seuss. New York: Random House, 1977. Also issued with an accompanying cassette sound recording.

9.3 *If I Ran the Zoo* / by Dr. Seuss. New York: Random House, 1978. Also issued as "A Dr. Seuss Paperback Classic."

9.4 *If I Ran the Zoo* / by Dr. Seuss. New York: Random House, 1980. Also issued with an accompanying cassette sound recording.

9.5 *If I Ran the Zoo* / by Dr. Seuss. Louisville, Ky.: American Printing House for the Blind, [199–?], c1950.
In braille.

9.6 *If I Ran the Zoo* / by Dr. Seuss. London: CollinsChildren's, 2000.

9.7 *If I Ran the Zoo* / by Dr. Seuss. London: Collins, 2002.

9.8 *If I Ran the Zoo* / by Dr. Seuss. London: Collins, 2003.
   "Yellow Back Book."

9.a If I Ran the Zoo [Russian]
   Esli bi Ya Bil Direktorom Zooparka. [In *Doctor Siuss* / v perevodakh
      Vladimira Gandelsmana; khudozhnik Mikhail Belomlinski. New
      York: Slovo / Word, 1998. Pp. 7ff.] [*see* B16.0]

1952

Gerald McBoing Boing [see: D19.0]

1953

10.0 Scrambled Eggs Super! / by Dr. Seuss. New York: Random House,
      1953.
   Also distributed by Grolier Enterprises as a "Book Club Edition."
   Also published in abridged version in *Children's Digest* [*see* C98].
   Also issued with an accompanying cassette sound recording in 1982.
   Also issued as "A Dr. Seuss Paperback Classic."
   Reprinted in: *Dr. Seuss Storybook*; *Dr. Seuss Storytime*.
      1st issue: 31 cm., with illustrated lower cover listing eight titles; retail
   price $2.50. Subsequently [*ca.* 1984] issued slightly smaller (28.7 cm.)
   with reduced lower margin. The book is dedicated to the Childs family,
   who had befriended Geisel while he was participating in the 2nd Writers' Conference at the University of Utah (July 1949). Other workshop
   participants included Vladimir Nabokov, Wallace Stegner, William Carlos Williams, and John Crowe Ransom.

10.1 *Scrambled Eggs Super!* / by Dr. Seuss. [Boston]: National Braille Press,
      1993.
         In braille.

10.2 *Scrambled Eggs Super!* / by Dr. Seuss. London: Collins, 2001.

10.3 *Scrambled Eggs Super!* / by Dr. Seuss. London: Collins, 2003.
      "Yellow Back Book."

10.a Scrambled Eggs Super! [Hebrew]
      Yofi shel chavita mikashkeshet! / Doktor Sus; 'lvrit: Le'ah Na'or. Jeru-
         salem: Keter, 1999.

10.b Scrambled Eggs Super! [Japanese]
      Obake tamago no iri tamago / saku Dokutā Sūsu; yaku Watanabe Shi-
         geo. Tokyo: Nihon Paburisshingu, 1971.

1954

11.0 *Horton Hears a Who!* / by Dr. Seuss. New York: Random House, 1954.
Also issued jointly with the Junior Literary Guild (so stated on t.p.), in red library binding with white lettering (ill. dust-jacket).
Also distributed by Grolier Enterprises as a "Book Club Edition."
Also issued with an accompanying cassette sound recording in 1976 and 1981.
Also issued jointly as a media kit with *Horton Hatches the Egg* in 1976.
Reprinted in: *Dr. Seuss Storytime*; *A Hatful of Seuss*; *Dr. Seuss's Book of Bedtime Stories*; *Your Favorite Seuss*.

    1st issue: lower cover illustration comprises "small persons" family across head and depicts Horton's ears fully drawn (in later issues, the left ear outline drops off into text on lower cover); retail price $2.50. An allegory on the value and the importance of the individual ("A person's a person. No matter how small ..."), the theme of this story developed as a result of Geisel's visiting schools in post-war Japan during the early 1950s while working on a project for *LIFE* magazine [*see* C59]. The book is dedicated to Mitsugi Nakamura, a professor at Kyoto, Japan.

11.1 *Horton Hears a Who!* / by Dr. Seuss. Louisville, Ky.: American Printing House for the Blind, c1954.
    In braille.

11.2 *Horton Hears a Who!* / by Dr. Seuss. Eau Claire, Wis.: E. M. Hale, c1954.
    "Special Edition."

11.3 *Horton Hears a Who!* / by Dr. Seuss. London: Collins, 1976.

11.4 *Horton Hears a Who!* / by Dr. Seuss. New York: Random House, 1982.
    Also issued with an accompanying cassette sound recording in 1982 and 1990.

11.5 *Horton Hears a Who!* / by Dr. Seuss. London: Collins, 1990.

11.6 *Horton Hears a Who!* / by Dr. Seuss. London: Collins, 1992.

11.7 *Horton Hears a Who!* / by Dr. Seuss. Boston: National Braille Press, 1993.
    In braille.

11.8 *Horton Hears a Who! Coloring and Activity Book* / by Dr. Seuss. New York: Random House, 1998.
    "Special Collectors Edition."

Includes the illustrated story, uncolored, for the reader to use as a coloring book, as well as additional puzzles and games for coloring.

11.a Horton Hears a Who! [German]
 Horton hört ein Staubkorn reden / Dr. Seuss; deutsche Nachdichtung von Hans A. Halbey. Ravensburg: O. Maier, 1974.

11.b Horton Hears a Who! [German]
 Horton hört ein Hu! / von Dr. Seuss; Deutsch von Eike Schönfeld. Hamburg: Rogner und Bernhard, 2003.

11.c Horton Hears a Who! [Italian]
 Ortone e i piccoli chi! / by Dr. Seuss; traduzione de Anna Sarfatti. Florence: Giunti junior, 2002.

11.d Horton Hears a Who! [Japanese]
 Zo no Hoton hitodasuke / saku Dokutā Sūsu; yaku Watanabe Shigeo. Tokyo: Nihon Paburisshingu, 1970.

11.e Horton Hears a Who! [Japanese]
 Zo no Hoton hitodasuke / saku Dokutā Sūsu; yaku Watanabe Shigeo. Tokyo: Kaisheisha, 1985.

11.f Horton Hears a Who! [Spanish]
 Horton escucha a Quién! / Dr. Seuss; traducido por Yanitzia Canetti. New York: Lectorum Publications, 2003.

1955

12.0 *On Beyond Zebra* / by Dr. Seuss. New York: Random House, 1955.
Also issued jointly with the Junior Literary Guild, in red library binding with white lettering (ill. dust-jacket).
Also distributed by Grolier Enterprises as a "Book Club Edition."
Also issued with an accompanying cassette sound recording in 1982.

 1st issue: lower cover with publisher's advertisement listing ten titles; retail price $2.50. Conrad Cornelius o'Donald o'Dell having learned all of his ABC's, Dr. Seuss introduces him to an alphabet that "… starts where *your* alphabet ends." The result is nineteen new letters that resemble runic symbols, each with its own special verse, and a final baroque design that encourages the reader to further inventions. The book is dedicated to Helen [Palmer Geisel], Geisel's wife.

12.1 *On Beyond Zebra* / by Dr. Seuss. Eau Claire, Wis.: E. M. Hale, 1955. "Special Edition."

12.2 *On Beyond Zebra* / by Dr. Seuss. New York: Random House, 1983. Also issued as "A Dr. Seuss Paperback Classic."

12.3 *On Beyond Zebra* / by Dr. Seuss. London: Collins, 1999.

1956

13.0 *If I Ran the Circus* / by Dr. Seuss. New York: Random House, 1956.
Also issued jointly with the Junior Literary Guild, in red library binding with white lettering (ill. dust-jacket with twin curtains).
Also distributed by Grolier Enterprises as a "Book Club Edition."
Also issued with an accompanying cassette sound recording in 1981.
Reprinted in: *Dr. Seuss Storytime*; *Just What I'd Do*.

1st issue: upper cover with twin pink curtains, pink lower cover listing twelve Dr. Seuss titles; retail price $2.50. The cover design later was changed to incorporate a single billowing red curtain on the upper cover. This work was written following the formula established earlier in *If I Ran the Zoo* and is dedicated to Geisel's father (Theodor Robert Geisel). A poem preliminary to this book, with completely different text and illustrations, appeared in *Children's Activities* (June, 1955) [*see* C54].

13.1 *If I Ran the Circus* / by Dr. Seuss. London: Collins, 1969.

13.2 *If I Ran the Circus* / by Dr. Seuss. Watertown, Mass.: Howe Press, 1974.
In braille.

13.3 *If I Ran the Circus* / by Dr. Seuss. New York: Random House, 1984. Also issued as "A Dr. Seuss Paperback Classic."

13.4 *If I Ran the Circus* / by Dr. Seuss. Boston: Reprinted for Howe Press, Perkins School for the Blind by National Braille Press, 1984.
In braille.

13.5 *If I Ran the Circus* / by Dr. Seuss. London: Collins, 2002. "Yellow Back Book."

13.6 *If I Ran the Circus* / by Dr. Seuss. London: Collins, 2003.

13.a If I Ran the Circus [Hebrew]
Im hayah li kirkas / Doktor Sus; 'lvrit: Le'ah Na'or. Jerusalem: Keter, 1991.

13.b If I Ran the Circus [Japanese]
Boku ga sakasu yattanara / saku Dokutā Sūsu; yaku Watanabe Shigeo. Tokyo: Nihon Paburisshingu, 1970.

1957

14.0 ***The Cat in the Hat*** / by Dr. Seuss. New York: Random House, 1957. "Beginner Book B-1" [first trade issue lacks this designation].

Also issued with an accompanying cassette sound recording in 1974, 1976 and 1982.

Also distributed by Grolier Enterprises as a "Book Club Edition."

Reprinted in: *The Dr. Seuss Read Along Library*; *Dr. Seuss's Beginner Book Classics*; *Read and Learn with Dr. Seuss*; *The Complete Cat in the Hat*; *The Dr. Seuss Miniature Collection*; *Your Favorite Seuss*.

Also adapted in book form (2003) from the motion picture adaptation [*see* D4.5].

1st trade issue: "For Beginning Readers" logo appears on upper dull-finish cover and on upper dust-jacket; dust-jacket has blackboard illustration on lower cover; subsequently bound in slick-finish paper; retail price [$1.95 — pricing is absent from dust-jacket]. Later trade issues show the more familiar "Cat in the Hat" Beginner Books logo, either on the cover or the head of the spine; eventually, the editor's note describing the work, which appears as text within a "Cat in the Hat" outline on p. [62], was eliminated.

Published simultaneously as a textbook (Houghton Mifflin; *see* 14.1 below) and a trade book (Random House), *The Cat in the Hat* served as a prototype for and became the first title in the Beginner Books series that followed. The story contains a limited vocabulary (223 different simple words drawn from a word list provided by Houghton Mifflin), an icono-clastic plot and stimulating associative illustrations, all characteristics that pundits in the "Why Johnny can't read" movement had proposed as alter-natives to the simplistic "Dick and Jane" basal readers then in use. Although the book sold poorly to schools, it was an immediate success in the public market, selling over 200,000 copies in the first year alone.

A perversion of this work entitled *The Cat Not in the Hat!* by Dr. Juice (as told to Alan Katz and illustrated by Chris Wrinn), parodying the murder trial of O. J. Simpson, was published by Dove Books (Beverley Hills, Calif.) in 1996, but distribution was blocked and the work has never been released [*see* F101].

14.1 *The Cat in the Hat* / by Dr. Seuss. Boston: Houghton Mifflin (The Riverside Press), 1957.

"Educational edition"; without the series logo on cover or spine title that appear in the trade edition; originally priced at [$1.60].

14.2 *The Cat in the Hat* / by Dr. Seuss. Buffalo, N.Y.: Braille Group Sis-terhood of Temple Beth Am., [19 —], c1957.

In braille.

14.3 *The Cat in the Hat* / by Dr. Seuss. Glasgow: Williams Collins, 1958.

14.4 *The Cat in the Hat* / by Dr. Seuss. London: Hutchinson, [1958].

14.5 *The Cat in the Hat* / by Dr. Seuss. New York: Random House, sponsored by the National Braille Press, c1958.
    "Children's Braille Book Club."

14.6 *The Cat in the Hat* / by Dr. Seuss. [*S.l.*: *s.n.*, 1960?].
    Unbound, in large print for the visually impaired; printed without illustrations.

14.7 *The Cat in the Hat* / by Dr. Seuss. London: Collins, 1961.
    "New Edition."

14.8 *The Cat in the Hat* / by Dr. Seuss. Watertown, Mass.: Howe Press, c1975.
    In braille.

14.9 *The Cat in the Hat* / by Dr. Seuss. Louisville, Ky.: American Printing House for the Blind, 1979.
    In braille.

14.10 *The Cat in the Hat* / by Dr. Seuss. London: Collins, 1980.

14.11 *The Cat in the Hat* / by Dr. Seuss. Boston: Reprinted for Howe Press, Perkins School for the Blind, by National Braille Press, 1982.
    In braille.

14.12 *The Cat in the Hat* / by Dr. Seuss. Boston: Reprinted for Howe Press, Perkins School for the Blind, by National Braille Press, 1984.
    In braille.

14.13 *The Cat in the Hat* / by Dr. Seuss. New York: Random House, 1985.
    Also issued with an accompanying cassette sound recording in 1987, 1988, and 1992.
    Some issues bound in facsimile cover and dust-jacket of the 1st printing [*q.v.*, 14.0], with archaic Beginner Books logo. Subsequently issued in deluxe binding for special issues [*see* 14.20; B9.0].

14.14 *The Cat in the Hat* / by Dr. Seuss. London: Collins, 1992.

14.15 *The Cat in the Hat* / by Dr. Seuss. [Boston]: National Braille Press, 1992.
    In braille.

14.16 *The Cat in the Hat* / by Dr. Seuss. Livonia, Mich.: Seedlings, 1992. In braille.

14.17 *The Cat in the Hat* / by Dr. Seuss. New York: Random House, 1994. "Reduced-Size Edition." [17 cm.]
Also issued with a stuffed doll with box title: *The Cat in the Hat: With a Cuddly Doll and a Collectible Book.*

14.18 *The Cat in the Hat* / by Dr. Seuss. London: HarperCollins, 1995. Issued with an accompanying cassette sound recording.

14.19 *The Cat in the Hat* / by Dr. Seuss. London: Collins, 1996. "Ted Smart Publication 1996." (T.p. *verso*)

14.20 *The Cat in the Hat* / by Dr. Seuss. New York: Random House, 1997. "Special Deluxe Edition."
Bound in full blue cloth with a matching slip case; binding identical to the volume appearing in the set *Dr. Seuss's Beginner Book Classics* [1992] [*see* B9.0].

14.21 *The Cat in the Hat* / by Dr. Seuss. New York: Random House; Distr. by Grolier Enterprises, 1997.
"Special Edition."
"Celebrating the 40th Birthday of the Cat in the Hat"; includes extra-illustrated material.

14.22 *The Cat in the Hat* / by Dr. Seuss. London: HarperCollins, 1997. "Special Edition."
"Celebrating the 40th Birthday of the Cat in the Hat"; includes extra-illustrated material. Essentially a reprint of 14.21 for British distribution.

14.23 *The Cat in the Hat* / by Dr. Seuss. New York: Random House, [1997] c1985.
"This is a very special edition ..." [lower cover]. [91 mm.]
Distributed by Macy's department stores, issued with a stuffed Cat-in-the-Hat doll, to which the book is attached at the head of the spine with a red elastic cord.

14.24 *The Cat in the Hat* / by Dr. Seuss. London: CollinsChildren's, 2001.

14.25 *The Cat in the Hat* / by Dr. Seuss. Cincinnati, Ohio: Clovernook Printing House for the Blind, 2001.
In braille.

14.26 *The Cat in the Hat* / by Dr. Seuss. London: Collins, 2003.
Issued with an accompanying cassette sound recording (a reissue of
14.18).

14.27 *The Cat in the Hat* / by Dr. Seuss. London: Collins, 2004.
Issued with an accompanying sound recording (a reissue of 14.18).

14.28 *The Cat in the Hat* / by Dr. Seuss. New York: Random House, 2004.
Issued with an accompanying sound recording (a reissue of 14.18).

14.a The Cat in the Hat [Chinese]
Dai mao zi di mao / wen tu Susi bo shi; yi Zhan Hongzhi = *The Cat
the Hat* / by Dr. Seuss. Taipei: Yuan-Liu, 1992.
Text in Chinese and English.

14.b The Cat in the Hat [Danish]
Katten med hatten / af Dr. Seuss; dansk tekst, Karl Nielsen. Copen-
hagen: Carlsen, 1979.
"Katten med hatten bøger 1."

14.c The Cat in the Hat [Dutch]
De kat met de hoed / door Dr. Seuss; vertaling, Katja en Kees Stip.
Huizen, N.H. [Netherlands]: Goede Boek, [1975].
"Beginnersboeken 1."

14.d The Cat in the Hat [French]
Le Chat au chapeau / par le Dr. Seuss; traduit de l'anglais par Jean
Vallier. New York: Random House, 1967.
Cover title: *The Cat in the Hat: In English and French.*
"A Beginner Book in French FB-1."
Text in French and English.

14.e The Cat in the Hat [French]
Le Chat chapeauté / Dr. Seuss; traduit de l'américain par Anne-Laure
Fournier Le Ray. Paris: Pocket jeunesse, 2004.
"Kid pocket."

14.f The Cat in the Hat [German]
Der Katz mit dem Latz / von Dr. Seuss; aus dem Amerikanischen von
Hans A. Halbey. Reinbek bei Hamburg: Carlsen Verlag, 1979.
"CarlsenTaschenBücher 1."

14.g The Cat in the Hat (with *There's a Wocket in My Pocket!*) [German]
Der Kater mit Hut. [And] *In meiner Tasche ist eine Zasche* / Dr. Seuss;
aus dem Amerikanischen von Eike Schönfeld und Sven Böttcher.
Frankfurt am Main: Rogner und Bernhard, 1999.

Reprinted: Affoltern a. A.: Buch, 2000.
Der Kater mit Hut reissued singly in reduced size paperback: Munich: Piper, 2004.

14.h The Cat in the Hat [Greek]
'Enas gatos me kapélo / by Seuss. Athens: Libanēs, 2003.

14.i The Cat in the Hat [Hebrew]
Hatul ta'alul / me'et Doktor Sus; 'Ivrit: Le'ah Na'or. Jerusalem: Keter, 1971.

14.j The Cat in the Hat [Hebrew]
Hatul ta'alul / me'et Doktor Sus; 'Ivrit: Le'ah Na'or. Jerusalem: Keter, 1990.

14.k The Cat in the Hat [Italian]
Il gatto col cappello / Dr. Seuss; traduzione dall'inglese di Anna Sarfatti; illustrazioni dell'autore. Florence: Giunti, 1996.
"GRU Under 7 [no.] 22."

14.l The Cat in the Hat [Italian]
Il gatto e il cappello matto / by Dr. Seuss. Florence: Giunti junior, 2004.
Possibly a reprint of 14.k employing the title of the motion picture adaptation as released in Italy; not seen.

14.m The Cat in the Hat [Latin]
Cattus Petasatus: The Cat in the Hat in Latin / qui libellus est a Doctore Seuss, primo Anglice compositus, at nunc (quod vix credas) in sermonem Latinum a Guenevera Tunberg et Terentio Tunberg conversus! Wauconda, Ill.: Bolchazy-Carducci, 2000.
Includes Latin-English glossary.

14.n The Cat in the Hat [Maori]
The Cat in the Hat = Te poti mau potae / by Dr. Seuss; translated by Hirini Melbourne. Aukland: Collins, 1983.
Text in Maori and English."

14.o The Cat in the Hat [Polish]
Kot Prot / Dr. Seuss; przeło˙zył Stanisław Barańczak. Poznań: Media Rodzina, 1996.
Reissued with an accompanying CD-ROM in 2003, with text in English and Polish.

14.p The Cat in the Hat [Portuguese]
O gato de cartola / Dr. Seuss; orientação Eliane M. Rozenblum; adap-

tação brasileira Jorge Alexandre Faure Pontual. Rio de Janeiro: Editora de Orientação Cultural, 1972.

14.q The Cat in the Hat [Portuguese]
O gatola da cartola / Dr. Seuss; tradução de Mônica Rodriques da Costa, Lavinia Fávero, Gisela Moreau. São Paulo: Editora Schwarcz, 2000.
"Edição bilingüe."

14.r The Cat in the Hat [Spanish]
El gato ensombrerado / escrito por Dr. Seuss; traducido por Carlos Rivera. New York: Beginner Books, 1967.
Cover title: *The Cat in the Hat: In English and Spanish.*
"SB-1."
   Text in Spanish and English.

14.s The Cat in the Hat [Spanish]
El gato ensombrerado / escrito por Dr. Seuss; traducido por Carlos Rivera. New York: Beginner Books, 1985.
   Text in Spanish and English.

14.t The Cat in the Hat [Spanish]
El gato ensombrerado / escrito por Dr. Seuss; traducido por Carlos Rivera. New York: Random House, 1993.
Issued with an accompanying cassette sound recording.
   Text in Spanish and English.

14.u The Cat in the Hat [Spanish]
El gato ensombrerado / escrito por Dr. Seuss; traducido por Carlos Rivera. New York: Beginner Books, 1995.
   Text in Spanish and English.

14.v The Cat in the Hat [Spanish]
El gato garabato / Dr. Seuss; [traducción y adaptación, P. Rozarena]. Madrid: Altea, 2003.

14.w The Cat in the Hat [Swedish]
Katten i hatten / Dr. Seuss; svensk text: Lennart Hellsing. Stockholm: Carlsen, 1978.

14.x The Cat in the Hat [Yiddish]
Di Kats der Payats = *The Cat in the Hat* / fun Dr. Sus; Yidish: Sholem Berger. New York: Twenty-Fourth Street Books, 2003.
   Text in Yiddish and romanized Yiddish.

15.0 *How the Grinch Stole Christmas* / by Dr. Seuss. New York: Random House, 1957.

Also issued jointly with the Junior Literary Guild, in green library binding with white lettering (ill. dust-jacket).

Also distributed by Grolier Enterprises as a "Book Club Edition."

Also issued with an accompanying cassette sound recording in 1975, 1976, 1981, and 2000.

Also published in condensed version in *Redbook* [*see* C51].

Also distributed for Sunday newspaper comics publication [*see* C51.1].

Reprinted in: *Dr. Seuss Storytime*; *Six by Seuss*; *The Dr. Seuss Miniature Collection*; *Your Favorite Seuss*.

Also adapted in book form (2000) from the motion picture [*see* D29.6].

1st issue: full panel advertisement for *The Cat in the Hat* on lower cover and lower dust-jacket; 14 titles listed on lower dust-jacket flap; retail price $2.50. An abridged version of the story appeared first in *Redbook* and gained in popularity chiefly through the animated motion picture adaptation that was broadcast on television [*see* D29.0]. The book was written during the spring of 1957 at the suggestion of the publisher, who thought it inappropriate that Dr. Seuss had written nothing about Christmas. The Grinch proved to be Geisel's favorite among all of Dr. Seuss's characters; a less sinister prototype had been introduced a few years earlier in "Hoobub and the Grinch" (*Redbook* magazine, May 1955) [*see* C43]. The book is dedicated to Teddy Owens, Geisel's namesake and the infant son of his niece Peggy.

15.1 *How the Grinch Stole Christmas* / by Dr. Seuss. Louisville, Ky.: American Printing House for the Blind, c1957.
In braille.

15.2 *How the Grinch Stole Christmas* / by Dr. Seuss. London: Collins, 1973.

15.3 *How the Grinch Stole Christmas* / by Dr. Seuss. New York: Random House, 1985.
Also issued with an accompanying cassette sound recording in 1988.
Redistributed in 1997 with a cover label: "Special 60th Anniversary Edition" [*cf.* 15.6, which is a separate work].

15.4 *How the Grinch Stole Christmas* / by Dr. Seuss. Boston, Mass.: National Braille Press, [1988?].
In braille.

15.5 *How the Grinch Stole Christmas* / by Dr. Seuss. London: Collins, 1990.

15.6 *How the Grinch Stole Christmas Coloring Book* / by Dr. Seuss. New York: Random House, 1997.
"Special 40th Anniversary Edition."
Includes the illustrated story, uncolored, for the reader to use as a coloring book [*cf.* 15.3, which describes a separate work].

15.7 *How the Grinch Stole Christmas* / by Dr. Seuss. New York: Random House, [1998] c1985.
"... reduced size ..." [lower cover]. [91 mm.]
Distributed by Macy's department stores, issued with a stuffed Grinch doll, to which the book is attached at the head of the spine with an elastic cord.

15.8 *How the Grinch Stole Christmas* / by Dr. Seuss. London: Collins, 2000.

15.9 *The Grinch Pops Up!* / by Dr. Seuss. New York: Random House, 2002.
How the Grinch Stole Christmas pop-up book.

15.10 *How the Grinch Stole Christmas* / Dr. Seuss. London: Collins, 2002.

15.11 *How the Grinch Stole Christmas* / by Dr. Seuss. London: Collins, 2003.
"Yellow Back Book."

15.a How the Grinch Stole Christmas [French]
Comment le Grinch a volé Noël / Dr. Seuss; traduit de l'américain par Anne-Laure Fournier Le Ray. [Paris]: Pocket jeunesse, 2000.

15.b How the Grinch Stole Christmas [German]
Wie der Grinch Weihnachten gestohlen hat / Dr. Seuss; aus dem Amerikanischen von Eike Schönfeld. Frankfurt am Main: Rogner und Bernhard, 2000.
Reissued in reduced paperback size: Munich: Piper, 2002.

15.c How the Grinch Stole Christmas [Hungarian]
Hogyan lopta el a Görcs a karácsonyt / Dr. Seuss; ford. Tandori Dezső. Budapest: Arktisz, 2000.

15.d How the Grinch Stole Christmas [Icelandic]
Þegar Trölli stal jólunum / eftir Dr. Seuss; Þorsteinn Valdimarsson ísl. [Reykjavik]: Örn og Örlygur, 1974.
Printed by Collins, Glasgow; reissued: Mál og menning, 2001.

15.e How the Grinch Stole Christmas [Italian]
Il Grinch / Dr. Seuss; traduzione di Fiamma Izzo e Ilva Tron; illustrazioni dell'autore. Milan: Mondadori, 2000.

15.f How the Grinch Stole Christmas [Japanese]
Ijiwaru Gurinchi no Kurisumasu / Dokutā Sūsu saku e; Watanabe Shigeo yaku. Tokyo: Nihon Paburisshingu, 1971.

15.g How the Grinch Stole Christmas [Japanese]
Gurinchi / Dokutā Sūsu saku e; Itsuji Akemi yaku. Tokyo: Ātisuto Hausu, 2000.

15.h How the Grinch Stole Christmas [Latin]
Quomodo Invidiosulus Nomine Grinchus Christi Natalem Abrogaverit / by Dr. Seuss; qui libellus est a Doctore Seuss, primo Anglice compositus; at nunc (quod vix credas) in sermonem Latinum a Guenevera Tunberg (iuvante Terentio Tunberg) conversus! Wauconda, Ill.: Bolchazy-Carducci Publishers, 1998.
Published as a Latin language reader, identical in appearance to English language editions, but with Latin text and an appended glossary.

15.i How the Grinch Stole Christmas [Portuguese]
Como o Grinch roubou o Natal / Dr. Seuss; tradução de Mônica Rodriques da Costa, Lavinia Fávero, Gisela Moreau. São Paulo: Comp. Des Letrinhas, 2000.

15.j How the Grinch Stole Christmas [Spanish]
Cómo el Grinch róbo la Navidad! / Dr. Seuss; traducido por Yanitzia Canetti. New York: Lectorum Publications, 2000.

1958

16.0 ***The Cat in the Hat Comes Back!*** / by Dr. Seuss. New York: Beginner Books; Distr. by Random House, 1958.
"Beginner Books B-2" [first issue lacks this designation].
Also distributed by Grolier Enterprises as a "Book Club Edition."
Also issued with an accompanying cassette sound recording in 1977.
Also issued with an interactive CD-ROM in 1997.
Reprinted in: *The Dr. Seuss Read Along Library*, set 2; *Read and Learn with Dr. Seuss*; *The Complete Cat in the Hat.*
"First Printing" appears on t.p. *verso.*
    1st issue: "For Beginning Readers" logo appears on upper glazed paperboard cover; cover title in blue shadowed lettering; advertisement for "Beginner Books," featuring a blackboard, appears on dust-jacket lower cover; retail price [$1.95 — pricing is absent from dust-jacket]. Later issues have cover title lettering in white and, eventually, show the more familiar

"Cat in the Hat" Beginner Books logo on the upper cover. Published simultaneously as a textbook (Houghton Mifflin; *see* 16.1 below) and a trade book (Random House), this sequel to *The Cat in the Hat* initially had the working title *The Cat Comes Back*; the first printing comprised 100,000 copies.

16.1   *The Cat in the Hat Comes Back!* / by Dr. Seuss. Boston: Houghton Mifflin, 1958.

    1st issue has editor's note describing the work, which appears as text within a "Cat in the Hat" outline following the final page of the story; that note is not present in the Random House edition; retail price [$1.60].

16.2   *The Cat in the Hat Comes Back!* / by Dr. Seuss. Louisville, Ky.: American Printing House for the Blind, 1960, c1958.

    In braille.

16.3   *The Cat in the Hat Comes Back!* / by Dr. Seuss. [*S.l.: s.n., ca.* 1960?].

    Unbound, in large print for the visually impaired; printed without illustrations.

16.4   *The Cat in the Hat Comes Back!* / by Dr. Seuss. London: Collins, 1961.

16.5   *The Cat in the Hat Comes Back!* / by Dr. Seuss. [London]: Collins, 1980.

16.6   *The Cat in the Hat Comes Back!* / by Dr. Seuss. New York: Beginner Books, 1986.

Also issued with an accompanying cassette sound recording.

16.7   *The Cat in the Hat Comes Back!* / by Dr. Seuss. Livonia, Mich.: Seedlings Braille Books for Children, 1992, c1958.

    In braille.

16.8   *The Cat in the Hat Comes Back!* / by Dr. Seuss. London: Collins, 1992.

16.9   *The Cat in the Hat Comes Back!* / by Dr. Seuss. London: HarperCollins, 1995.

Issued with an accompanying cassette sound recording.

16.10   *The Cat in the Hat Comes Back!* / by Dr. Seuss. Cincinnati, Ohio: Clovernook Printing House for the Blind, 2001.

    In braille.

16.11   *The Cat in the Hat Comes Back!* / by Dr. Seuss. London: Collins, 2003.

Issued with an accompanying cassette sound recording (a reissue of 16.9); also issued by Collins Picture Lions.

16.a The Cat in the Hat Comes Back! [Afrikaans]
Die kat kom weer / deur Dr. Seuss; in Afrikaans berym deur Leon Rousseau. Cape Town: Human & Rousseau, 1972.

16.b The Cat in the Hat Comes Back! [Chinese]
Dai mao zi di mao hui lai le! / wen tu Susi bo shi; yi Zhan Hongzhi = *The Cat in the Hat Comes Back!* / by Dr. Seuss. Taipei: Yuan-Liu, 1992.
Text in Chinese and English.

16.c The Cat in the Hat Comes Back! [Dutch]
De kat met de hoed komt terug / Dr. Seuss; vertaling, Katja en Kees Stip. Huizen, N.H. [Netherlands]: Goede Boek, [1975]. "Beginnersboeken 4."

16.d The Cat in the Hat Comes Back! [Hebrew]
Hatul ta'alul hozer! / me'et Doktor Sus; 'lvrit: Le'ah Na'or. Jerusalem: Keter, 1979.

16.e The Cat in the Hat Comes Back! [Spanish]
El gato con sombrero viene de nuevo / Dr. Seuss; traducido por Yanitzia Canetti. New York: Lectorum, 2004.

17.0 *Yertle the Turtle and Other Stories* / by Dr. Seuss. New York: Random House, 1958.

Includes: *Yertle the Turtle*; *Gertrude McFuzz*; *The Big Brag*. Some of these stories were subsequently also published as separate books [see below].

Also distributed by Grolier Enterprises as a "Book Club Edition."

Also issued with accompanying cassette sound recording in 1972.

Reprinted in: *Six by Seuss*; *Ten Tall Tales by Dr. Seuss*; *Your Favorite Seuss*. *Yertle the Turtle* and *Gertrude McFuzz* were also reprinted in: *Dr. Seuss Storytime*.

The stories were previously published, with slight variations, in *Redbook*: "The Big Brag" (December, 1950); "Yertle the Turtle" (April, 1951); "Gertrude McFuzz" (July, 1951) [*see* C8, C132, and C32 respectively].

1st issue: "Other books by Dr. Seuss" list at end begins with *How the Grinch Stole Christmas*; blank green lower cover; dust-jacket upper flap begins: "By Popular Request ..."; retail price $2.95. In the fable "Yertle the Turtle," King Yertle represents Adolph Hitler; some early rough drawings of the character even reveal a mustache. The rabbit and the bear in "The Big Brag" are the same as the characters in "The Rabbit, the Bear and the Zinniga-Zanniga" [*see* C92]. The book is dedicated to the families of college classmates: Joseph Sagmaster, an Oxford classmate who introduced Geisel to fellow student Helen Palmer (whom Geisel married soon after); and Donald Bartlett, a fellow Dartmouth graduate who was also an Oxford classmate and remained a life-long friend.

17.1 *Yertle the Turtle and Other Stories* / by Dr. Seuss. Boston: Houghton Mifflin, 1958.
    Published jointly with Random House for the educational market.

17.2 *Yertle the Turtle and Other Stories* / by Dr. Seuss. Louisville, Ky.: American Printing House for the Blind, c1958.
    In braille.

17.3 *Yertle the Turtle and Other Stories* / by Dr. Seuss. London: Collins, 1963.

17.4 *Yertle the Turtle and Other Stories* / by Dr. Seuss. New York: Random House, 1979.
    Also issued with an accompanying cassette sound recording in 1981.

17.5 *Yertle the Turtle and Other Stories* / by Dr. Seuss. New York: Random House, 1986.
    Also issued, in paperback, with an accompanying cassette sound recording in 1992.

17.6 *Yertle the Turtle and Other Stories* / by Dr. Seuss. London: Collins, 1992.

17.7 [Yertle the Turtle and Other Stories: Yertle the Turtle; Gertrude McFuzz]
    Yertle the Turtle, and Gertrude McFuzz / by Dr. Seuss. [London]: Collins, 1979.
    "Collins Colour Cubs" edition [15 cm.].

17.8 [Yertle the Turtle and Other Stories: The Big Brag]
    The Big Brag / by Dr. Seuss. New York: Random House, 1998.
    "A Little Dipper Book" [15 cm.].

17.a Yertle the Turtle and Other Stories [Dutch]
    Xildbad de Schildpad en andere verhalen / Dr. Seuss; Nederlands van Katja en Kees Stip. Huizen, N.H. [Netherlands]: Goede Boek, [1973].
    Includes: *Xildbad de Schildpad* [Yertle the Turtle]; *Floesje Prat* [Gertrude McFuzz]; *Het grote gebluf* [The Big Brag].

17.b Yertle the Turtle and Other Stories [Hebrew]
    ha-Melekh Tsav-Tsav: 've-sipurim a'herim / [transl. by Le'ah Goldberg]. [Tel Aviv]: Sifriyat Po'alim, 1981.

17.c Yertle the Turtle and Other Stories: The Big Brag [Danish] *Pralhansene* / Dr. Seuss; på dansk ved Christopher Maaløe. [Copenhagen]: Gyldendal, [1972].

17.d Yertle the Turtle and Other Stories: The Big Brag [French] *Le Plus vantard* / Dr. Seuss; adapté de l'américain par Christian Poslaniec. Paris: L'École des loisirs, 1986.

17.e Yertle the Turtle and Other Stories: The Big Brag [Norwegian] *Storskryterne* / til norsk ved Inger Hagerup. Oslo: Gyldenhal, 1972.

17.f Yertle the Turtle and Other Stories: The Big Brag [Swedish] *Storskrytarna* / Dr. Seuss; svensk text, Britt G. Hallqvist. Stockholm: A. Bonniers, 1972.

17.g Yertle the Turtle and Other Stories: Yertle the Turtle [Afrikaans] *Willie die Skillie* / Dr. Seuss; vertaal deur Marié Heese. [Cape Town]: Anansi Uitgewers, 1989.

17.h Yertle the Turtle and Other Stories: Yertle the Turtle [Danish] *Palle Padde* / Dr. Seuss; på dansk ved Christopher Maaløe. [Copenhagen]: Gyldendal, [1972]

17.i Yertle the Turtle and Other Stories: Yertle the Turtle [French] *Yaourtu la tortue* / Dr Seuss; adapté de l'américain par Christian Poslaniec. Paris: L'École des loisirs, 1986.

17.j Yertle the Turtle and Other Stories: Yertle the Turtle [Norwegian] *Padda Sifadda* / til norsk ved Inger Hagerup. Oslo: Gyldenhal, 1972.

17.k Yertle the Turtle and Other Stories: Yertle the Turtle [Russian] *Cherepashiy Korol.* [In *Doctor Siuss* / v perevodakh Vladimira Gandelsmana; khudozhnik Mikhail Belomlinski. New York: Slovo / Word, 1998. Pp. 47ff.] [*see* B16.0]

17.l Yertle the Turtle and Other Stories: Yertle the Turtle [Swedish] *Adda Sköldpadda* / Dr. Seuss; svensk text, Britt G. Hallqvist. Stockholm: A. Bonniers, 1972.

1959

18.0 *Happy Birthday to You!* / by Dr. Seuss. New York: Random House, 1959.

Also issued jointly with the Junior Literary Guild, in blue library binding with white lettering (ill. dust-jacket).

Also distributed by Grolier Enterprises as a "Book Club Edition."
Reprinted in: *Your Favorite Seuss*.

1st issue: photo of Geisel and "The Dr. Seuss Zoo" Revelle toy models on lower cover; retail price $2.95. The dust-jacket (foot of upper flap) notes: "This is the first Dr. Seuss book entirely in full color." Previously, *McElligot's Pool* had also had full-color printing, but for only about half of the illustrations. *Happy Birthday to You!* thus marks the beginning of a consistent effort to publish books in vibrant colors — most previous works have sparse splashes of coloring (mainly reds, blues and yellows) to highlight illustrations that are chiefly line drawings.

18.1 *Happy Birthday to You!* / by Dr. Seuss. New York: Random House, 1987.

18.2 *Happy Birthday to You!* / by Dr. Seuss. [Boston]: National Braille Press, 1993.
    In braille.

18.3 *Happy Birthday to You!: A Pop-Up Book* / by Dr. Seuss. New York: Random House, 2003.

18.a Happy Birthday to You! [German]
    Heut' hast du Geburtstag! / von Dr. Seuss. Frankfurt am Main: Rogner und Bernhard, 2002.

18.a Happy Birthday to You! [Hebrew]
    Yom huledet 'samea'h / me'et Doktor Sus; 'Ivrit: Le'ah Na'or. Jerusalem: Keter, 1987.
    Reissued in 1994.

18.c Happy Birthday to You! [Japanese]
    Otanjobi omedeto / saku Dokutā Sūsu; yaku Watanabe Shigeo. Tokyo: Nihon Paburisshingu, 1971.

1960

19.0 *Green Eggs and Ham* / by Dr. Seuss. New York: Beginner Books, 1960.
"Beginner Books B-16."
Also distributed jointly with P. D. Eastman's *Go, Dog, Go* by Grolier Enterprises as a "Book Club Edition."
Also issued with an accompanying sound cassette recording in 1972 and 1977.
Reprinted in: *The Dr. Seuss Read Along Library*, set 2; *Dr. Seuss's Beginner Book Classics*; *The Dr. Seuss Miniature Collection*; *Your Favorite Seuss*.

Also adapted for musical performance [*see* D15.0].

1st issue: upper cover lacks both "Beginner Books" logo and boxed statement: "50 Word Vocabulary" (although those features do appear on the dust-jacket); "Beginner Books" logo at head of spine lacks "R" registered trademark symbol; sewing for first gathering appears in gutter at p. 3 (most subsequent early issues show logo on cover and sewing at p. 9); retail price $1.95. This work represents the first Dr. Seuss title in the Beginning Beginner Books series, launched by Random House to publish pre-primers based on a 144-word list. Dr. Seuss wrote the book on a bet with his publisher, Bennett Cerf, that he couldn't write a book using only fifty different words. In winning the wager, Dr. Seuss wrote a book that has sold more copies than any of his other works and is the best selling of all children's books anywhere.

19.1 *Green Eggs and Ham* / by Dr. Seuss. Louisville, Ky.: American Printing House for the Blind, c1960.
In braille.

19.2 *Green Eggs and Ham* / by Dr. Seuss. Newark, N.J.: Meyer Center, New Jersey Commission for the Blind, c1960.
In braille.

19.3 *Green Eggs and Ham* / by Dr. Seuss. West Hartford, Conn.: Connecticut Braille Assoc., Large Type Division, c1960.
Text in large type.

19.4 *Green Eggs and Ham* / by Dr. Seuss. [London]: Collins, 1962.

19.5 *Green Eggs and Ham* / by Dr. Seuss. London: Collins, 1980.

19.6 *Green Eggs and Ham* / by Dr. Seuss. New York: Beginner Books, 1988.

19.7 *Green Eggs and Ham* / by Dr. Seuss. Boston: National Braille Press, [1988?].
In braille.

19.8 *Green Eggs and Ham* / by Dr. Seuss. London: Collins, 1992.
Issued with an accompanying cassette sound recording.

19.9 *Green Eggs and Ham* / by Dr. Seuss. [Boston]: National Braille Press, 1993.
In braille.

19.10 *Green Eggs and Ham* / by Dr. Seuss. London: HarperCollins, 1995.
Issued with an accompanying cassette sound recording.

Reissued jointly with the book and sound recording of *Fox in Socks* ("Gift Pack 22") in 1996.

19.11   *Green Eggs and Ham* / by Dr. Seuss. [London]: HarperCollins, 1997. "The Classic Collection."

19.12   *Green Eggs and Ham* / by Dr. Seuss. New York: Beginner Books, 1998.
"Special Deluxe Edition."
Bound in full orange cloth with a matching slip case; binding identical to the volume appearing in the set *Dr. Seuss's Beginner Book Classics* [1992] [*see* B9.0].

19.13   *Green Eggs and Ham* / by Dr. Seuss. London: Collins, 1999.
"40th Anniversary Edition." Issued with an accompanying cassette sound recording.

19.14   *Green Eggs and Ham* / Dr. Seuss; adapted by Aristides Ruiz. New York: Random House, 2001.
"1st Nifty Lift-and-Look Books Ed."
The story, modified and augmented with flaps and peel-off stickers.

19.15   *Green Eggs and Ham* / by Dr. Seuss. Livonia, Mich.: Seedlings Braille Books, 2002.
In braille.

19.16   *Green Eggs and Ham* / by Dr. Seuss. London: Collins, 2002.

19.17   *Green Eggs and Ham* / by Dr. Seuss. London: Collins, 2003.
Issued with an accompanying cassette sound recording (a reissue of 19.10); also issued by Collins Picture Lions.

19.a Green Eggs and Ham [Chinese]
Huo tui chia lü tan / wen tu Susi bo shi; yi Hao Guangcai = *Green Eggs and Ham* / by Dr. Seuss. Taipei: Yuan-Liu, 1992.
Text in Chinese and English.

19.b Green Eggs and Ham [Dutch]
Groene eieren met ham / door Dr. Seuss; vertaling, Katja en Kees Stip. Huizen, N.H. [Netherlands]: Goede Boek, [1975].
"Beginnersboeken 3."

19.c Green Eggs and Ham [Hebrew]
Lo ra' ev ve-lo ohev / me'et Doktor Sus; 'Ivrit: Le'ah Na'or. Jerusalem: Keter, 1982.

19.d Green Eggs and Ham [Italian]
Prosciutto e uova verdi / by Dr. Seuss; traduzione di Anna Sarfatti. Florence: Giunti junior, 2002.

19.e Green Eggs and Ham [Latin]
Green Eggs and Ham in Latin = Virent Ova! Viret Perna!! / a Doctore Seuss; in sermonem Latinum a Guenevera Tunberg et Terentio Tunberg conversus. Wauconda, Ill.: Bolchazy-Carducci Press, 2003. With Latin-to-English glossary.

19.f Green Eggs and Ham [Spanish]
Huevos verdes con jamón / por Dr. Seuss; traducción de Aída E. Marcuse. New York: Lectorum Publications, 1992.

20.0 *One Fish, Two Fish, Red Fish, Blue Fish* / by Dr. Seuss. New York: Beginner Books, 1960.
"Beginner Books B-13."
Also distributed by Grolier Enterprises as a "Book Club Edition."
Also issued with an accompanying cassette sound recording in 1977, 1980 (by Fisher-Price Toys) and 1987.
Reprinted in: *The Dr. Seuss Read Along Library*, set 2; *Dr. Seuss's Beginner Book Classics.*

1st issue: page facing t.p. is blank; no printer's code; blank lower cover; dust-jacket lower cover lists ten titles, all priced at $1.95; retail price $1.95. Dr. Seuss's increased interest in phonics is evident throughout this book.

20.1 *One Fish, Two Fish, Red Fish, Blue Fish* / by Dr. Seuss. Louisville, Ky.: American Printing House for the Blind, c1960.
In braille.

20.2 *One Fish, Two Fish, Red Fish, Blue Fish* / by Dr. Seuss. Hartford, Conn.: Connecticut Braille Assoc., Large Type Division, c1960.
Text in large type.

20.3 *One Fish, Two Fish, Red Fish, Blue Fish* / by Dr. Seuss. London: Collins, 1962.

20.4 *One Fish, Two Fish, Red Fish, Blue Fish* / by Dr. Seuss. New York: Beginner Books, 1988.

20.5 *One Fish, Two Fish, Red Fish, Blue Fish* / by Dr. Seuss. London: Collins, 1984.

20.6 *One Fish, Two Fish, Red Fish, Blue Fish* / by Dr. Seuss. London: Collins, 1990.

20.7 *One Fish, Two Fish, Red Fish, Blue Fish* / by Dr. Seuss. [Boston]: National Braille Press, 1994.
   In braille.

20.8 *One Fish, Two Fish, Red Fish, Blue Fish* / Dr. Seuss. New York: Random House, 2001.
   "Bright and Early Bath Book Ed."

20.9 *One Fish, Two Fish, Red Fish, Blue Fish: Dr. Seuss's Book of Funny Things.* London: Collins Picture Lions, 2003.
   "Dr. Seuss Board Book." Also issued by Collins with and without audio cassette recording.

20.a One Fish, Two Fish, Red Fish, Blue Fish [Chinese]
   Yi tiao yu, liang tiao yu, hong di yu, lan di yu! / wen tu Susi bo shi; yi Hao Guangcai = *One Fish, Two Fish, Red Fish, Blue Fish* / by Dr. Seuss. Taipei: Yuan-Liu, 1992.
   Text in Chinese and English.

20.b One Fish, Two Fish, Red Fish, Blue Fish [Dutch]
   Visje één, visje twee, visje visje in de zee / door Dr. Seuss; vertaling: Katja en Kees Stip. Huizen, N.H. [Netherlands]: Goede Boek, [1975].
   "Beginnersboeken 2."

20.c One Fish, Two Fish, Red Fish, Blue Fish [Hebrew]
   D'varim muzarim korim basfarim / me'et Doktor Sus; 'Ivrit: Le'ah Na'or. Jerusalem: Keter, 1980.

20.d One Fish, Two Fish, Red Fish, Blue Fish [Spanish]
   Un pez, dos peces, pez rojo, pez azul /Dr. Seuss; [traducción y adaptación, P. Rozarena]. Madrid: Altea, 2003.

1961

21.0 *The Sneetches and Other Stories* / written and illustrated by Dr. Seuss. New York: Random House, 1961.

Includes: *The Sneetches; The Zax; Too Many Daves; What Was I Scared Of?* Some of these stories were subsequently also published as separate books [see below].

Also distributed by Grolier Enterprises as a "Book Club Edition."

Also issued with an accompanying cassette sound recording in 1972 and 1981.

Reprinted in: *Dr. Seuss Storytime*; *A Hatful of Seuss*; *Ten Tall Tales by Dr. Seuss*; *Your Favorite Seuss*.

Also adapted as a work book stressing concepts: *Sneetches are Sneetches: Learn About Same and Different* / adapted by Linda Hayward and Cathy Goldsmith [*see* F86].

1st issue: blank page facing t.p. and blank blue lower cover; twenty books listed on lower dust-jacket flap; retail price $2.95. An earlier version of *The Sneetches* appeared in *Redbook* (July, 1953) [*see* C106]; an earlier version of *The Zax* appeared under the title "The Zaks" in *Redbook* (March, 1954) [*see* C133].

21.1 *The Sneetches and Other Stories* / written and illustrated by Dr. Seuss. London: Collins, 1965.

21.2 *The Sneetches and Other Stories* / written and illustrated by Dr. Seuss. London: Collins, 1984.

21.3 *The Sneetches and Other Stories* / written and illustrated by Dr. Seuss. London: Collins, 1988.

21.4 *The Sneetches and Other Stories* / written and illustrated by Dr. Seuss. New York: Random House, 1989.

21.5 *The Sneetches and Other Stories* / Dr. Seuss. London: Collins, 2003.

21.6 [The Sneetches and Other Stories: The Sneetches; What Was I Scared Of?]
The Sneetches, and What Was I Scared Of? / by Dr. Seuss. [London]: Collins, 1979.
"Collins Colour Cubs" edition [15 cm.].

21.7 [The Sneetches and Other Stories: What Was I Scared Of?]
What Was I Scared Of? / by Dr. Seuss. New York: Random House, 1997.
"1st Random House Little Dipper Ed." [15 cm.].

21.8 [The Sneetches and Other Stories: What Was I Scared Of?]
What Was I Scared Of? / by Dr. Seuss. New York: Scholastic Inc., 1997.
A reprint of 21.7 for the educational market.

21.a The Sneetches and Other Stories [Dutch]
De Fnuiken en andere verhalen / tekst en tekeningen van Dr. Seuss; Nederlands van Katja en Kees Stip. Huizen, N.H. [Netherlands]: Goede Boek, [1973], c1961.
Includes: *De Fnuiken* [The Sneetches]; *De Zippen* [The Zax]; *Te veel*

Pukken [Too Many Daves]; *Ik ben niet bang!* [What Was I Scared Of?].

21.b The Sneetches and Other Stories [German]
Die Schnipfen und andere Geschichten / Dr. Seuss; deutsche Nachdichtung von Hans A. Halbey. Ravensburg: O. Maier, 1973.

21.c The Sneetches and Other Stories [Hebrew]
ha-Snits'im ve-sipurim aherim / Doktor Sus; 'lvrit: Le'ah Na'or. Jerusalem: Keter, 2002.

21.d The Sneetches and Other Stories [Italian]
Gli Snicci e altre storie / by Dr. Seuss; traduzione di Anna Sarfatti. Florence: Giunti junior, 2002.

22.0 *Ten Apples Up on Top!* / by Theo. LeSieg; illustrated by Roy McKie. New York: Beginner Books, 1961.
"Beginner Books B-19."
"75 Word Vocabulary" and Beginner Books logo appear on the dust-jacket but are absent from the upper cover.
Also distributed by Grolier Enterprises as a "Book Club Edition."
Also issued with accompanying cassette sound recording and P. D. Eastman's *Go, Dog, Go!* in 1974.
1st issue: foot of t.p. *verso* has © statement only (without printer's code); dust-jacket lower cover (at foot) includes Beginner Books address in drop-out lettering within olive frame; Beginner Books logo on spine and on dust-jacket spine lack © symbol; retail price $1.95. A counting book.

22.1 *Ten Apples Up on Top!* / by Theo. LeSieg; illustrated by Roy McKie. London: Collins, 1963.

22.2 *Ten Apples Up on Top!* / by Theo. LeSieg; illustrated by Roy McKie. New York: Beginner Books, 1989.

22.3 *Ten Apples Up on Top!* / by Dr. Seuss writing as Theo. LeSieg; illustrated by Roy McKie. New York: Random House, 1998.
"Bright and Early Board Books."
Printed in small format on thick paper boards rather than paper.

22.4 *Ten Apples Up on Top!* / by Dr. Seuss writing as Theo. LeSieg; illustrated by Roy McKie. London: Collins, [199–?].

22.5 *Ten Apples Up on Top!* / Dr. Seuss; illustrated by Roy McKie. London: Collins, 2003.
"Green Back Books."

22.6 *Ten Apples Up on Top!* / by Dr. Seuss writing as Theo. LeSieg; illustrated by Roy McKie. New York: Random House, 2004.

22.a Ten Apples Up on Top! [German]
   Mit Äpfeln zählen lernen: Mit nur 165 verschiedenen Wörten / Theo LeSieg; deutsche Bearbeitung, Ilse May; Illustrationen, Roy McKie. Munich: F. Schneider Verlag, 1971.

22.b Ten Apples Up on Top! [Japanese]
   Minna no atama ni ringo ga jukko / saku Seo Resuīgu; e Roi Makkī; bun Sakanishi Shiho. Tokyo: Nihon Paburissingu, [1968?].

1962

23.0 *Dr. Seuss's Sleep Book*. New York: Random House, 1962.
   Also distributed by Grolier Enterprises as a "Book Club Edition."
   Also issued with an accompanying cassette sound recording in 1972.
   Reprinted in: *Dr. Seuss Storytime*; *A Hatful of Seuss*; *Dr. Seuss's Book of Bedtime Stories*; *Your Favorite Seuss*.
      1st issue: September, 1962; blank white lower cover; retail price $2.95. The blue-green color on some covers printed *ca.* 1988 has slipped in value towards pale green; coloration was corrected in subsequent bindings. Dr. Seuss completed the final draft in April, 1962, and the book was marketed as celebrating the twenty-fifth anniversary of Dr. Seuss's first book, *And to Think That I Saw It on Mulberry Street*. The book is dedicated to Marie and Bert Hupp, La Jolla, Calif., neighbors of the Geisels.

23.1 *Dr. Seuss's Sleep Book*. Louisville, Ky.: American Printing House for the Blind, c1962.
      In braille.

23.2 *Dr. Seuss's Sleep Book*. London: Collins, 1964.
      1st printing: bound in blue cloth with blank covers; list price: 12s/6d net.

23.3 *Dr. Seuss's Sleep Book*. London: Collins, 1984.

23.4 *Dr. Seuss's Sleep Book*. London: Collins, 1988.

23.5 *Dr. Seuss's Sleep Book*. New York: Random House, 1990.

23.6 *Dr. Seuss's Sleep Book*. London: Collins, 2001.

23.7 *Dr. Seuss's Sleep Book*. London: Collins, 2003.
      "Yellow Back Book."

23.a   Dr. Seuss's Sleep Book [Dutch]
Dr. Seuss' slaap boek / Nederlands van Katja en Kees Stip. Huizen: Goede Boek, [1974].

23.b   Dr. Seuss's Sleep Book [Hebrew]
Lailah 'tov / me'et Doktor Sus; 'lvrit: Le'ah Na'or. Jerusalem: Keter, 1994.

23.c   Dr. Seuss's Sleep Book [Japanese]
Dokutā Sūsu no nemutai hon / saku Dokutā Sūsu; yaku Watanabe Shigeo. Tokyo: Nihon Paburisshingu, 1971.

23.d   Dr. Seuss's Sleep Book [Norwegian]
Dr. Seuss' sovebok: en surrete søvnbok for deg som skal sove. Stavanger: Sandvik, 2002.

23.e   Dr. Seuss's Sleep Book [Russian]
Sonnoe Tsarstvo. [In *Doctor Siuss* / v perevodakh Vladimira Gandelsmana; khudozhnik Mikhail Belomlinski. New York: Slovo / Word, 1998. Pp. 29ff.] [*see* B16.0]

1963

24.0   *Dr. Seuss's ABC*. New York: Beginner Books, 1963.
"Beginner Books B-30."
Also distributed by Grolier Enterprises as a "Book Club Edition."
Also issued with an accompanying cassette sound recording in 1977 and 1989.
Also issued with an interactive CD-ROM in 1995.
Reprinted in: *The Dr. Seuss Read Along Library*, set 2; *Dr. Seuss's Beginner Book Classics*; *Dr. Seuss's Bright and Early Board Books*; *Read and Learn with Dr. Seuss*.

     1st issue: blank t.p. *verso*; © statement appears alone on t.p., without cataloging-in-publication data; blank blue lower cover; retail price $1.95. Dr. Seuss had attempted an illustrated "ABC" book earlier in his career, composed partly during a European tour in the early 1930s, but he was unable to find a publisher.

24.1   *Dr. Seuss's ABC* / Dr. Seuss. London: Collins, 1964.

24.2   *Dr. Seuss's ABC*. Watertown, Mass.: Howe Press, Perkins School for the Blind, 1974, c1963.
Reprinted in 1984.
In braille.

24.3 *Dr. Seuss['s] ABC* / Dr. Seuss. [London]: Collins, 1980.

24.4 *Dr. Seuss's ABC.* Boston, Mass.: National Braille Press, Inc., 1982.
Reprinted in 1993.
In braille.

24.5 *Dr. Seuss's ABC.* St. Paul, Minn.: Communication Center, State Services for the Blind, [199–?].
In braille.

24.6 *Dr. Seuss's ABC.* New York: Beginner Books, 1991.
Also issued with an accompanying cassette sound recording in 1991 and 1992, and with a CD-ROM in 1995.

24.7 *Dr. Seuss's ABC.* London: Collins, 1993.

24.8 *Dr. Seuss's ABC: An Amazing Alphabet Book!* New York: Random House, 1996.
"A Bright and Early Board Book."
Printed in small format on thick paper boards rather than paper.

24.9 *Dr. Seuss's A.B.C.* London: HarperCollins, 1997.
"A Bright and Early Board Book."
Printed in small format on thick paper boards rather than paper.

24.10 *Dr. Seuss'[s] ABC.* London: Collins, 2003.
Issued with an accompanying cassette sound recording (a reissue of 24.6); also issued by Collins Picture Lions.

24.11 *Dr. Seuss's ABC: An Amazing Alphabet Book!* New York: Random House, 2003.
"A Bright and Early Board Book."
Special oversized ed. (32 cm.).

24.a Dr. Seuss's ABC [Chinese]
Susi bo shi ABC jiao shi = *Dr. Seuss's ABC* / wen tu Susi bo shi; yi Hao Guangcai.
Taipei: Yuan-Liu, 1992.
Text in Chinese and English.

25.0 *Hop on Pop* / by Dr. Seuss. New York: Beginner Books, 1963.
"Beginner Books B-29."
Also distributed by Grolier Enterprises as a "Book Club Edition."
Reprinted in: *The Dr. Seuss Read Along Library*; *Reading Is Fun with Dr. Seuss.*

Reprinted, abridged, in: *Ready, Set, Read!: The Beginning Reader's Treasury* / compiled by Joanna Cole and Stephanie Calmenson (New York: Doubleday, 1990).

Adapted as a pop-up book (with *Oh Say Can You Say?*) [*see* B28.0].

Also adapted as a rhyming work book: *I Am Not Going to Read Any Words Today!: Learn About Rhyming Words* / adapted by Linda Hayward and Cathy Goldsmith [*see* F82].

1st issue: page facing t.p. is blank; retail price $1.95. On upper cover: "The Simplest Seuss for Youngest Use."

25.1 *Hop on Pop* / by Dr. Seuss. Louisville, Ky.: American Printing House for the Blind, c1963.
In braille.

25.2 *Hop on Pop* / by Dr. Seuss. London: Collins, 1964.
1st issue: retail price 8/6 net.

25.3 *Hop on Pop* / by Dr. Seuss. Watertown, Mass: Howe Press, 1973.
Reprinted in 1984.
In braille.

25.4 *Hop on Pop* / by Dr. Seuss. London: Collins, 1980.

25.5 *Hop on Pop* / by Dr. Seuss. New York: Beginner Books, 1991.

25.6 *Hop on Pop* / by Dr. Seuss. Boston: National Braille Press, 1992.
In braille.

25.7 *Hop on Pop* / by Dr. Seuss. London: Collins, 1993.

25.8 *Hop on Pop* / by Dr. Seuss. London: Collins Picture Lions, 2003.

25.9 *Hop on Pop* / by Dr. Seuss. New York: Random House, 2004.
"Bright and Early Board Books."
Printed in small format on thick paper boards rather than paper.

25.a Hop on Pop [Chinese]
Lao ba shen shang tiao / wen tu Susi bo shi; yi Hao Guangcai = *Hop on Pop* / by Dr. Seuss. Taipei: Yuan-Liu, 1992.
Text in Chinese and English.

25.b Hop on Pop [Dutch]
Stap op pap / Dr. Seuss; vertaling, Katja en Kees Stip. Huizen, N.H. [Netherlands]: Goede Boek, [1973].
"Beginnersboek 5."

1964

26.0 ***The Cat in the Hat Beginner Book Dictionary*** / by the Cat himself
and P. D. Eastman. New York: Beginner Books, 1964.
Later noted as one of the "Big Beginner Books."
Sometimes misnamed *The Cat in the Hat Dictionary*.
Also distributed by Grolier Enterprises as a "Book Club Edition."

    1st issue: only the © statement appears on the t.p. *verso*, without cat-
aloging-in-publication data; lower dust-jacket has three increasingly large
white blocks of text; retail price $2.95. Prose introduction by Dr. Seuss.
Most of the work, including all of the illustration, is by P. D. Eastman.
Dr. Seuss was an early collaborator while the project was being consid-
ered as *The Dr. Seuss Dictionary*, but he subsequently distanced himself
from the work and never included it in his *résumé*. The dictionary was
published in a larger size (8 × 11 inches) than typical Beginner Books in
order to compete more effectively in the marketplace; the work was subsequently adapted for translation into Chinese, French and Spanish [*see*
26.a-d.*].

26.1 *The Cat in the Hat Beginner Book Dictionary* / by the Cat himself and
    P. D. Eastman. London: Collins, 1965.

26.2 *The Cat in the Hat Beginner Book Dictionary* / by the Cat himself
    and P. D. Eastman. [London]: Collins, 1987.

26.3 *The Cat in the Hat Beginner Book Dictionary* / Dr. Seuss; illustrated
    by P. D. Eastman. London: Collins, 2002.
    "Revised edition."

26.a The Cat in the Hat Beginner Book Dictionary [Chinese]
    Susi bo shi er tong Ying yu zi dian = The Cat in the Hat Beginner Book
    Dictionary / zhu Susi bo shi; yi Luo Zhuqian. Taipei: Yuan-Liu,
    1992.
      Text in Chinese and English.

26.b The Cat in the Hat Beginner Book Dictionary [French]
    The Cat in the Hat Beginner Book Dictionary in French. New York:
    Beginner Books, 1965.
    Adaptation and translation by Odette Filloux.
    Also published in condensed version in *McCall's* [*see* C14].
      Text in French and English.

26.c The Cat in the Hat Beginner Book Dictionary [French]
    The Cat in the Hat Beginner Book Dictionary in French, based on the

original Beginner Book Dictionary / by P. D. Eastman; adapted into beginner's French by Odette Filloux. [London]: Collins, 1967.
Text in French and English.

26.d The Cat in the Hat Beginner Book Dictionary [Spanish]
The Cat in the Hat Beginner Book Dictionary in Spanish. New York: Beginner Books, 1966.
Adaptation and translation by Robert R. Nardelli.
Text in Spanish and English.

1965

27.0 *Fox in Socks* / by Dr. Seuss. New York: Beginner Books, 1965.
"Beginner Books B-38."
Also distributed by Grolier Enterprises as a "Book Club Edition."
Also issued with an accompanying cassette sound recording in 1965, 1972, 1976, 1986, 1988, and 1995.
Also published in condensed version in: *Ladies' Home Journal* [*see* C30].
Reprinted in: *The Dr. Seuss Read Along Library*; *Dr. Seuss's Beginner Book Classics*; *Rhymes, Riddles and Nonsense*; *The Dr. Seuss Miniature Collection.*
    1st issue: cover has statement "A Tongue Twister for Super Children" (later issues replace this cover statement with a lengthier one that begins: "This is a book you READ ALOUD ..."); plain lower cover; lower dust-jacket with three progressively larger white panels containing book titles; retail price $1.95. Couched as a set of tongue-twisters, this work attempts to demonstrate peculiarities in spoken English and to promote proper enunciation for children. As such, it differs from other Dr. Seuss books in addressing precise speaking rather than reading skills. The book is dedicated to La Jollans Mitzi Long and Audrey Dimond of the fictitious "Mt. Soledad Lingual Laboratories"; Geisel would marry Audrey in 1968.

27.1 *Fox in Socks* / by Dr. Seuss. [London]: Collins, 1966.
"BB24."
    1st issue: retail price 8/6 net.

27.2 *Fox in Socks* / by Dr. Seuss. London: Collins, 1980.

27.3 *Fox in Socks* / by Dr. Seuss. New York: Random House, sponsored by the National Braille Press, c1986.
"Children's Braille Book Club."
Issued with an accompanying cassette sound recording.
    In braille.

27.4 *Fox in Socks* / by Dr. Seuss. London: Collins, 1992. "Mini Edition." [15 cm.]

27.5 *Fox in Socks* / by Dr. Seuss. New York: Beginner Books, 1993.

27.6 *Fox in Socks* / by Dr. Seuss. Boston: National Braille Press, 1993. In braille.

27.7 *Fox in Socks* / by Dr. Seuss. London: HarperCollins, 1995.
Issued with an accompanying cassette sound recording.
Reissued jointly with the book and sound recording of *Green Eggs and Ham* ("Gift Pack 22") in 1996.

27.8 *Fox in Socks* / by Dr. Seuss. London: Collins, 2003.
Issued with an accompanying cassette sound recording (a reissue of 27.7); also issued by Collins Picture Lions.

27.a Fox in Socks [Chinese]
Hu li chuan wa zi / wen tu Susi bo chi; yi Hao Kuang-ts'ai = *Fox in Socks* / by Dr. Seuss. Taipei: Yuan-Liu, 1992.
Text in Chinese and English.

27.b Fox in Socks [Dutch]
Fokke op sokken / Dr. Seuss; vertaling: Katja en Kees Stip. Huizen, N.H. [Netherlands]: Goede Boek, [1973].
"Beginnerboeken 6."

27.c Fox in Socks [Hebrew]
Ba 'im garbayim / me'et Doktor Sus; 'Ivrit: Le'ah Na'or. Jerusalem: Keter, 1980.

28.0 ***I Had Trouble in Getting to Solla Sollew*** / by Dr. Seuss. New York: Random House, 1965.
Also distributed by Grolier Enterprises as a "Book Club Edition."
Also issued with an accompanying cassette sound recording in 1982.
Reprinted in: *Dr. Seuss Storytime*; *Dr. Seuss's Fabulous Fables*.

1st issue: blank lower cover; dust-jacket lower cover has publisher's advertisement listing twenty-five Dr. Seuss titles; retail price $2.95. The "Poozer" drawings in this allegory on perseverence are strikingly similar in composition to those in the story "I Can Lick 30 Tigers Today!," published four years later. The book is dedicated to Geisel's niece, Margaretha "Peggy" Dahmen Owens.

28.1 *I Had Trouble in Getting to Solla Sollew* / by Dr. Seuss. London: Collins, 1967.
1st issue: blank pale blue lower cover; retail price 15/- net.

28.2 *I Had Trouble in Getting to Solla Sollew* / by Dr. Seuss. New York: Random House, [1988?].
Also issued with an accompanying cassette sound recording.
Also issued as "A Dr. Seuss Paperback Classic."

28.3 *I Had Trouble in Getting to Solla Sollew* / by Dr. Seuss. London: Collins, 1990.

28.4 *I Had Trouble in Getting to Solla Sollew* / by Dr. Seuss. New York: Random House, 1993.

28.5 *I Had Trouble in Getting to Solla Sollew* / by Dr. Seuss. Boston: National Braille Press, 1993.
In braille.

28.a I Had Trouble in Getting to Solla Sollew [Dutch]
Je bent nog niet in Niemandsverdriet / Dr. Seuss; [vertaling: Katja en Kees Stip]. Huizen, N.H. [Netherlands]: Goede Boek, [1976].

28.b I Had Trouble in Getting to Solla Sollew [Hebrew]
Yesh li tsarot aval lo ka-eleh / me'et Doktor Sus; 'Ivrit: Le'ah Na'or. Jerusalem: Keter, 1986.

29.0 *I Wish That I Had Duck Feet* / by Theo. LeSieg; illustrated by B. Tobey. New York: Random House, 1965.
"Beginner Books B-40."
Also distributed by Grolier Enterprises as a "Book Club Edition."
Also issued with an accompanying cassette sound recording in 1975.
Reprinted in: *The Big Green Book of Beginner Books*.
    1st issue: retail price $1.95.

29.1 *I Wish That I Had Duck Feet* / by Theo. LeSieg; illustrated by B. Tobey. London: Collins, 1967.
"B-27."

29.2 *I Wish That I Had Duck Feet* / by Theo. LeSieg; illustrated by B. Tobey. New York: Random House, 1993.

29.3 *I Wish That I Had Duck Feet* / by Dr. Seuss writing as Theo. LeSieg; illustrated by B. Tobey. London: Collins, 1999.

29.4 *I Wish That I Had Duck Feet* / Dr. Seuss; illustrated by B. Tobey. London: Collins, 2004.

29.a I Wish That I Had Duck Feet [German]
Ich wünsche mir ...: Mit 295 verschiedenen Wörtern / Theo LeSieg;

deutsche Bearbeitung, Ilse May; Illustrationen, B. Tobey. Munich and Vienna: F. Schneider, 1971.

1966

30.0 *Come Over to My House* / by Theo. LeSieg; illustrated by Richard Erdoes. New York: Beginner Books, 1966.
"Beginner Books BE-44."
Also distributed by Grolier Enterprises as a "Book Club Edition."
1st issue: retail price $1.95.

30.1 *Come Over to My House* / by Theo. LeSieg; illustrated by Richard Erdoes. London: Collins, 1967.

30.a Come Over to My House [Afrikaans]
Maak jou tuis in my huis / deur Theo. Le Sieg; Afrikaanse beryming deur Leon Rousseau; met volkleur-illustrasies deur Richard Erdoes. Cape Town: Human & Rousseau, 1974.

30.b Come Over to My House [Swedish]
Kom hem till mig / av Theo Le Sieg; illustrationer av Richard Erdoes; översättning och bearbetning av Ingrid Klera och Barbro Hilmersson. Stockholm: Tidens, 1968.

1967

31.0 *The Cat in the Hat Song Book* / by Dr. Seuss; piano score and guitar chords by Eugene Poddany. New York: Random House, 1967.
"19 Seuss-Songs for Beginning Singers."
Also issued with an accompanying cassette sound recording in 1967 and 1972.
Selected songs also issued as a recording in 2003.
Includes: "Let Us All Sing"; "The Super-Supper March"; "My Uncle Terwilliger Waltzes with Bears"; "In My Bureau Drawer"; "The No Laugh Race"; "Plinker Plunker"; "Hurry Hurry Hurry!"; "Cry a Pint"; "Ah-A-A-A-A-A-H...Choo"; "I Can Figure Figures"; "Somebody Stole My Hoo-to Foo-to Boo-to Bah"; "Rainy Day in Utica, N.Y."; "Lullaby for Mr. Benjamin B. Bickelbaum"; "Happy Birthday to Little Sally Spingel Spungel Sporn"; "My Uncle Terwilliger Likes to Pat"; "Yawn Song"; "The Left-Sock Thievers"; "Drummers Drumming (A Round)"; "Party Parting."
1st issue: without dust-jacket; retail price [$2.95]. Although Dr.

Seuss insisted that children could sing these songs, their melodies in particular proved daunting and the work was not a success. Besides *The Lady Godivas*, it is the only Dr. Seuss title ever to go out of print. The book is dedicated to "Lark and Lea of Ludington Lane," the daughters of Audrey Stone and Grey Dimond and Geisel's soon-to-be stepdaughters.

31.1 *The Cat in the Hat Song Book* / by Dr. Seuss; piano score and guitar chords by Eugene Poddany. London: Collins, 1968.

31.2 *The Cat in the Hat Song Book* / by Dr. Seuss; piano score and guitar chords by Eugene Poddany. New York: Random House, 2002.

1968

32.0 ***The Eye Book*** / by Theo. LeSieg; illustrated by Roy McKie. New York: Random House, 1968.
"Bright & Early Books BE 2."
Also distributed by Grolier Enterprises as a "Book Club Edition."
Also issued as a sound recording in 1974.
    1st issue: "Bright & Early Books" appears at head of spine without illustrated logo; printing history numeric code absent from t.p. *verso*; retail price $1.95.

32.1 *The Eye Book* / by Theo. LeSieg; illustrated by Roy McKie. London: Collins, 1969.
"BE 1."

32.2 *The Eye Book* / by Dr. Seuss, writing as Theo. LeSieg; illustrated by Joe Mathieu. New York: Random House, 2001.

32.3 *The Eye Book* / by Dr. Seuss, writing as Theo. LeSieg; illustrated by Joe Mathieu. London: Collins, 2001.

32.a The Eye Book [Hebrew]
Sefer ha-'ayin / me-et Dr. Sus be-shem ha-'et Ti'o Lesig; iyurim, G'o Matyu; 'lvrit, Le'ah Na'or. Jerusalem: Keter, 2002.

33.0 ***The Foot Book*** / by Dr. Seuss. New York: Random House, 1968.
"Bright & Early Books BE 1."
Also distributed by Grolier Enterprises as a "Book Club Edition."
Also issued with an accompanying cassette sound recording in 1976 and, jointly with *Mr. Brown Can Moo, Can You?*, in 1989.

Reprinted in: *The Dr. Seuss Read Along Library*; *Dr. Seuss's Bright and Early Board Books*.

Also adapted as a work book stressing concepts: *Wet Foot, Dry Foot, Low Foot, High Foot: Learn About Opposites and Differences* / adapted by Linda Hayward and Cathy Goldsmith [*see* F87].

1st issue: "Bright & Early Books" appears at head of spine without illustrated logo; dust-jacket lower panel has publisher's advertisement for first four Bright & Early Books; retail price $1.95. *The Foot Book* was written in response to a call for books for a younger audience than previous "Beginner Books" had addressed, and the work became the first title in the "Bright & Early Books" series.

33.1 *The Foot Book* / by Dr. Seuss. London: Collins, 1969.
   "Bright & Early Books BE 2."

33.2 *The Foot Book* / by Dr. Seuss. London: Collins, 1982.

33.3 *The Foot Book* / by Dr. Seuss. St. Paul, Minn.: Communication Center, State Services for the Blind, [199–?], c1968.
   In braille.

33.4 *The Foot Book* / by Dr. Seuss. Boston: National Braille Press, 1993, c1968.
   In braille.

33.5 *The Foot Book: Dr. Seuss's Wacky Book of Opposites*. New York: Random House, 1996.
   "A Bright and Early Board Book."
   Printed in small format on thick paper boards rather than paper.

33.6 *The Foot Book: Dr. Seuss's Wacky Book of Opposites*. London: HarperCollins, 1997.
   "A Bright and Early Board Book."
   Printed in small format on thick paper boards rather than paper.

33.7 *The Foot Book* / Dr. Seuss. New York: Random House, 2002.
   "1st Nifty Lift-and-Look Books Edition."
   "With Fabulous Flaps and Peel-Off Stickers."

33.8 *The Foot Book: Dr. Seuss's Wacky Book of Opposites*. New York: Random House, 2003.
   "A Bright and Early Board Book."
   Special oversized ed. (32 cm.).

33.9 *The Foot Book: Dr. Seuss's Wacky Book of Opposites.* New York: Random House; Livonia, Mich.: Seedlings Braille Books, [2003?].
In braille.

33.10 *The Foot Book: Dr. Seuss's Wacky Book of Opposites.* London: Collins, 2004.

33.a The Foot Book [Chinese]
Guai jiao bao dian / wen tu Susi bo shi; yi Hao Guangcai = *The Foot Book* / by Dr. Seuss. Taipei: Yuan-Liu, 1992.
Text in Chinese and English.

33.b The Foot Book [Dutch]
Het voetenboek / Nederlands van Katja en Kees Stip. Huizen: Goede Boek, [1974].
Subsequently issued under the title: *Dr. Seuss' voeten boek.*

33.c The Foot Book [Hebrew]
Seferegel / me'et Doktor Sus; 'Ivrit: Le'ah Na'or. Jerusalem: Keter, 1982.

1969

34.0 *I Can Lick 30 Tigers Today! and Other Stories* / by Dr. Seuss. New York: Random House, 1969.
Also distributed by Grolier Enterprises as a "Book Club Edition."
Includes: *I Can Lick 30 Tigers Today!*; *King Looie Katz*; *The Glunk That Got Thunk.*
I Can Lick 30 Tigers Today! and *King Looie Katz* were reprinted in: *Dr. Seuss Storytime.*
Also issued with an accompanying cassette sound recording in 1982.
Reprinted in: *Ten Tall Tales by Dr. Seuss.*
1st issue: lower cover has publisher's advertisement listing twenty-nine Dr. Seuss titles; issued without dust-jacket; retail price [$2.95].
These three stories are about the Cat in the Hat's daughter, son and "great great great great grandpa," who are identified on the upper illustrated endpapers (which are lacking in some later issues, including paperback versions and Grolier "Book Club Edition" copies). Each story stands alone and has its own simple theme. *The Glunk That Got Thunk* was first published in *Woman's Day* (July, 1969) [*see* C33]. The book is dedicated to Audrey [Stone Geisel], whom Geisel had married a year earlier.

34.1 *I Can Lick 30 Tigers Today! and Other Stories* / by Dr. Seuss. London: Collins, 1970.

34.2 *I Can Lick 30 Tigers Today! and Other Stories* / by Dr. Seuss. New York: Random House, [1988?].
Also issued as "A Dr. Seuss Paperback Classic."
   Lacks illustrated endpapers that, in prior issues, introduce the characters in the stories.

34.3 *I Can Lick 30 Tigers Today! and Other Stories* / by Dr. Seuss. London: Collins, 1990.

34.a I Can Lick 30 Tigers Today! and Other Stories: I Can Lick 30 Tigers Today!; King Looie Katz [Russian]
Segodnya Izobyn 30 Tigrov; *Korol Lui Kotoriy.* [In *Doctor Siuss* / v perevodakh Vladimira Gandelsmana; khudozhnik Mikhail Belomlinski. New York: Slovo / Word, 1998. Pp. 43ff and 23ff.] [*see* B16.0]

35.0 *My Book About Me, By Me Myself: I Wrote It! I Drew It!* / with a little help from my friends Dr. Seuss and Roy McKie. New York: Beginner Books, 1969.
["Big Beginner Books."]
   1st issue: blank yellow lower cover; without dust-jacket; retail price [$2.95]. Illustrations by Roy McKie. An activity book that also teaches general concepts and is meant to be used more than read.

35.1 *My Book About Me, By Me Myself: I Wrote It! I Drew It!* / with a little help from my friends Dr. Seuss and Roy McKie. London: Collins, 1973.

35.2 *My Book About Me, By Me Myself: I Wrote It! I Drew It!* / with a little help from my friends Dr. Seuss and Roy McKie. London: Collins, 1997.

35.a My Book About Me, By Me Myself: I Wrote It! I Drew It! [Chinese]
Wo ti shu / [Wen tu Susi bo shi chi Lo-i Mai-k'a; yi Zeng Yangqing] = *My Book About Me, By Me Myself* / Dr. Seuss and Roy McKie. Taipei: Yuan-Liu, 1992.
   Text in Chinese and English.

35.b My Book About Me, By Me Myself: I Wrote It! I Drew It! [Hebrew]
ha-Sefer sheli 'al 'atsmi / Doktor Sus; ve-Roi Meki; uve-'lvrit: Le'ah Na'or. Jerusalem: Keter, 1984.

1970

36.0 *I Can Draw It Myself: By Me, Myself* / with a little help from my friend Dr. Seuss. New York: Random House, 1970.

["Big Beginner Books."]

1st issue: spiral bound (later issues are saddle-stapled); lower cover blank; publisher statement inside upper cover; retail price [$2.95]. Dr. Seuss published this book as a more imaginative alternative to coloring books, which he deemed uncreative for children.

36.1 *I Can Draw It Myself: By Me, Myself* / with a little help from my friend Dr. Seuss. London: Collins, 1971.

Cited in Richardson (*see* F160); neither seen nor verified.

37.0 *Mr. Brown Can Moo! Can You?* / by Dr. Seuss. New York: Random House, 1970.

"Bright & Early Books BE 7."

On cover: "Dr. Seuss's Book of Wonderful Noises."

Also distributed by Grolier Enterprises as a "Book Club Edition."

Also issued with an accompanying cassette sound recording in 1976 and, jointly with *The Foot Book*, in 1989.

Also published in condensed version in *McCall's* [*see* C72].

Reprinted in: *The Dr. Seuss Read Along Library*; *Dr. Seuss's Bright and Early Board Books*.

Also adapted as a phonics work book: *Boom Boom Boom!: Learn About the Sound of B and Other Stuff* / adapted by Linda Hayward and Cathy Goldsmith [*see* F80].

1st issue: "Bright & Early Books" appears at head of spine without illustrated logo; dust-jacket lower cover shows three b&w photos; retail price $1.95.

37.1 *Mr. Brown Can Moo! Can You?* / by Dr. Seuss. London: Collins, 1971. "BB 7."

37.2 *Mr. Brown Can Moo! Can You?* / by Dr. Seuss. London: Collins, 1981.

37.3 *Mr. Brown Can Moo! Can You?* / by Dr. Seuss. Detroit, Mich.: Seedlings Braille Books for Children, [1987?].
In braille.

37.4 *Mr. Brown Can Moo! Can You?* / by Dr. Seuss. St. Paul, Minn.: Communication Center, State Services for the Blind, [199–?].
In braille.

37.5 *Mr. Brown Can Moo! Can You?: Dr. Seuss's Book of Wonderful Noises*. New York: Random House, 1996.
"A Bright and Early Board Book."
Printed in small format on thick paper boards rather than paper.

37.6 *Mr. Brown Can Moo! Can You?* / by Dr. Seuss. London: Harper-Collins, 1998.
"A Bright and Early Board Book."

37.7 *Mr. Brown Can Moo! Can You?* / by Dr. Seuss. Topeka, Kan.: Econo-Clad Books, 2000.

37.8 *Mr. Brown Can Moo! Can You?: Dr. Seuss's Book of Wonderful Noises.* London: Collins Picture Lions, 2003.
"Adapted Ed.; Dr. Seuss Board Books."
Also issued as a "Blue Back Book."

37.9 *Mr. Brown Can Moo! Can You?: Dr. Seuss's Book of Wonderful Noises.* New York: Random House, 2003.
"A Bright and Early Board Book."
Special oversized ed. (32 cm.).

37.a Mr. Brown Can Moo! Can You? [Chinese]
Bulang xian sheng xue niu jiao / wen tu Susi bo shi; yi Zeng Yangqing = *Mr. Brown Can Moo! Can You?* / by Dr. Seuss. Taipei: Yuan-Liu, 1992.
Text in Chinese and English.

37.b Mr. Brown Can Moo! Can You? [Dutch]
Meneer de Bruin doet Boe! en hoe! / Nederlands van Katja en Kees Stip. Huizen, N.H. [Netherlands]: Goede Boek, [1974].

37.c Mr. Brown Can Moo! Can You? [Hebrew]
Adon Bu 'oseh mu / Doktor Sus; 'Ivrit: Le'ah Na'or. Jerusalem: Keter, 1991.

1971

38.0 *I Can Write! A Book by Me, Myself* / with a little help from Theo. LeSieg and Roy McKie. New York: Beginner Books, 1971.
"Bright & Early Books."
Also distributed by Grolier Enterprises as a "Book Club Edition."
1st issue: "Bright & Early Books" appears at head of spine without illustrated logo; without dust-jacket or printer's code; retail price [$2.95].
A counting book, with ruled sections for copying numbers and words.

39.0 *The Lorax* / by Dr. Seuss. New York: Random House, 1971.
Also distributed by Grolier Enterprises as a "Book Club Edition."
Also issued with an accompanying cassette sound recording in 1981 and 1992.

Also published in condensed version in *Woman's Day* [*see* C66].

Reprinted in: *Dr. Seuss Storytime*; *Six by Seuss*; *Dr. Seuss's Fabulous Fables*; *Your Favorite Seuss*.

1st issue: without dust-jacket; foot of t.p. *verso* has © statement but is without cataloging-in-publication data or printer's code; lower cover lists thirty-two Dr. Seuss titles.

Geisel's own favorite among all of Dr. Seuss's works and translated into the most different languages, *The Lorax* is an ecological fable about exploitation and pollution of natural resources by big business. Local logging interests in northern California attempted but failed to ban the title from a second grade school required reading list in 1989. UNEP [United Nations Environment Programme] distributed translations in cheap wrapper format, mainly in non–Western languages, from the mid-1980s onward as a part of its educational publications program. The book is dedicated to Geisel's wife Audrey and her daughters, Lark and Lea Dimond.

39.1 *The Lorax* / by Dr. Seuss. London: Collins, 1972.

39.2 *The Lorax* / by Dr. Seuss. London: Collins, 1988.

39.3 *The Lorax: Miniature Book and Hand Puppet* / Dr. Seuss. New York: Random House, 1998.

Issued as a "Book and Puppet Package" (28 × 17 × 10 cm.) comprising a miniature printing of the book (12 cm.), a hand puppet of the Lorax, and a brochure entitled "Be a Lorax Helper — Help Build the Dr. Seuss Lorax Forest." The packaged kit promotes the Dr. Seuss Lorax Forest, a part of the Global ReLeaf 2000 reforestation program sponsored by American Forests. Simultaneously, the miniature book was distributed separately [*see* 39.31].

39.31 *The Lorax* / Dr. Seuss. New York: Random House, [1998] c1971.

A miniature printing (12 cm.) of the 1971 edition, distributed separately and as a kit with a hand puppet of the Lorax [*see* 39.3].

39.4 *The Lorax* / by Dr. Seuss. London: Collins, 2004.

Also issued with a cassette sound recording.

39.a The Lorax [Afrikaans]

Die Loraks / deur Dr. Seuss; Afrikaanse beryming deur Leon Rousseau. Cape Town: Human & Rousseau, 1973.

39.b The Lorax [Afrikaans]

Die Loraks / Dr. Seuss; beryming deur Philip De Vos. Johannesburg: Hodder & Stoughton, 1993.

Published in wrapper format under the auspices of the United
Nations Environment Programme [UNEP].

39.c The Lorax [Arabic]
   [*The Loraks* / Dr. Seuss. Tunisia: Published by the Government, 198–?].
   Title and imprint uncertain. Published in wrapper format under
   the auspices of the United Nations Environment Programme [UNEP].

39.d The Lorax [Arabic]
   [*The Loraks* / Dr. Seuss. Bahrain: Published by the Government, 1987?].
   Title and imprint uncertain. Published in wrapper format under
   the auspices of the United Nations Environment Programme [UNEP].

39.e The Lorax [Bengali]
   [*The Lorax* / Dr. Seuss. India?, 198–?].
   Title and imprint uncertain. Published in wrapper format under
   the auspices of the United Nations Environment Programme [UNEP].

39.f The Lorax [Chinese]
   Laoleisi di gu shi / Susi bo shih = *The Lorax* / Dr. Seuss. Beijing:
   Zhongguo huan jing chu ban she, 1986.
   Published in wrapper format under the auspices of the United
   Nations Environment Programme [UNEP].

39.g The Lorax [Dutch]
   De Lorax / Dr. Seuss; [vertaling: Katja en Kees Stip]. Huizen, N.H.
   [Netherlands]: Goede Boek, [1975].

39.h The Lorax [German]
   Der Lorax / Dr. Seuss; deutsche Nachdichtung von Hans A. Halbey.
   Ravensburg: O. Maier, 1974.

39.i The Lorax (with *Oh, the Places You'll Go!*) [German]
   Wie schön, soviel wirst du sehn! [And] *Der Lorax* / Dr. Seuss; aus dem
   Amerikanischen von Eike Schönfeld und Uda Strätling. Frankfurt
   am Main: Rogner und Bernhard, 2000.

39.j The Lorax [Hebrew]
   ha-Lore'ks / Doktor Sus; 'Ivrit, Le'ah Na'or. Jerusalem: Keter, 1971.
   Reissued in 1996.

39.k The Lorax [Italian]
   Lorax: Storia di un nano che parlo invano / Dr. Seuss; traduzione di
   Carla Martinolli. Milano: A. Mondadori Editore, 1974.

39.l The Lorax [Portuguese]

O Lorax / Dr. Seuss; tradução de Claudio R. P. Fornari. [Brazil: Dept. Of Education, 1985?].

Place and date of publication uncertain. 20,000 copies printed and distributed throughout the school system; published in wrapper format under the auspices of the United Nations Environment Programme [UNEP].

39.m The Lorax [Spanish]

El Lorax / Dr. Seuss; traducido por Aída E. Marcuse. New York: Lectorum, 1993.

39.n The Lorax [Swahili]

Lorax / Dr. Seuss. Nairobi: UNEP, [1988?].

Original publication date uncertain; reissued in 1992. Published in wrapper format under the auspices of the United Nations Environment Programme [UNEP].

39.o The Lorax [Thai]

L ̦ōk læk: Plæchāk nangsū The Lorax / kh ̦ōng Dr. Seuss. [Bangkok]: Kromwikhākān Krasūangsuksāthikān, 1985.

Published in wrapper format under the auspices of the United Nations Environment Programme [UNEP].

39.p The Lorax [Urdu]

[*The Lorax* / Dr. Seuss. Pakistan?, 198–?].

Title and imprint uncertain. Published in wrapper format under the auspices of the United Nations Environment Programme [UNEP].

1972

40.0 *In a People House* / by Theo. LeSieg; illustrated by Roy McKie. New York: Random House, 1972.

"Bright & Early Books BE12."

Also distributed by Grolier Enterprises as a "Book Club Edition."

1st issue: "Bright & Early Books" appears at head of spine without illustrated logo; t.p. *verso* has © statement and cataloging-in-publication data in card format; retail price $2.50.

40.1 *In a People House* / by Theo. LeSieg; illustrated by Roy McKie. St. Paul, Minn.: Communication Center, State Services for the Blind, c1972.

In braille.

40.2 *In a People House* / by Theo. LeSieg; illustrated by Roy McKie. London: Collins, 1973.

41.0 *Marvin K. Mooney, Will You Please Go Now!* / by Dr. Seuss. New York: Random House, 1972.
"Bright & Early Books BE 13."
Also distributed by Grolier Enterprises as a "Book Club Edition."
Also issued with a cassette sound recording in 1977.
Reissued in: *The Dr. Seuss Read Along Library*, set 2; *Bright and Early Read Along Library*; *Reading Is Fun with Dr. Seuss*.
Also reissued in a kit , including an accompanying sound recording (1977, 1989), with: *There's a Wocket in My Pocket!*

1st issue: "Bright & Early Books" appears at head of spine without illustrated logo; cataloging-in-publication data appear in card format below © statement; retail price $2.50.

Dr. Seuss later adapted the text of this work in response to political developments surrounding "Watergate," replacing each instance of Marvin K. Mooney's name with Richard M. Nixon's. Art Buchwald published the adaptation in his newspaper column under the title: "OK, RMN, Get Out the Old Zike Bike!" [*see* C79].

41.1 *Marvin K. Mooney, Will You Please Go Now!* / by Dr. Seuss. London: Collins, 1973.

41.2 *Marvin K. Mooney, Will You Please Go Now!* / by Dr. Seuss. New York: Random House, [1977].
Issued jointly, as a kit, with *There's a Wocket in My Pocket!* and a cassette sound recording.

41.3 *Marvin K. Mooney, Will You Please Go Now!* / by Dr. Seuss. New York: Random House, 1989.
Issued jointly, as a kit, with *There's a Wocket in My Pocket!* and a cassette sound recording [a reissue of 41.2].

41.4 *Marvin K. Mooney, Will You Please Go Now!* / by Dr. Seuss. London: Collins, 2003.
"Blue Back Book." Also issued by Collins Picture Lions.

41.a Marvin K. Mooney, Will You Please Go Now! [Chinese]
Si ma bu lü bai tuo ni juai zou! / wen tu Susi bo shi; yi Hao Guangcai = *Marvin K. Mooney, Will You Please Go Now!* / by Dr. Seuss. Taipei: Yuan-Liu, 1992.
Text in Chinese and English.

41.b Marvin K. Mooney, Will You Please Go Now! [Hebrew]
    Beni ben Buni, matai kevar telekh? / me'et Doktor Sus; 'Ivrit: Le'ah
    Na'or. Jerusalem: Keter, 1980.

1973

42.0 *Did I Ever Tell You How Lucky You Are?* / by Dr. Seuss. New York:
    Random House, 1973.
Also distributed by Grolier Enterprises as a "Book Club Edition."
Also issued with an accompanying cassette sound recording in 1993.
Reprinted in: *Dr. Seuss Storytime*; *Dr. Seuss's Fabulous Fables*.

    1st issue: without dust-jacket or printer's code; © and cataloging-in-
publication data appear on otherwise blank t.p. *verso*; lower cover with
publisher's advertisement for "36 world-famous" Dr. Seuss books; retail
price [$3.50]. Using absurdity, this book encourages the reader by show-
ing how much worse life could be. Many of the scenes were adapted for
use in the animated television feature *Halloween Is Grinch Night* [*see*
D23.0]. The book is dedicated to "Phyllis the Jackson," Geisel's agent.

42.01 *Did I Ever Tell You How Lucky You Are?* / by Dr. Seuss. New York:
    Random House, 1973.
        Identical to 42.0, but issued in paperback as a giveaway promo-
    tion for Crest toothpaste and Prell shampoo. "Free when you buy
    …" appears in medallion on upper cover.

42.1 *Did I Ever Tell You How Lucky You Are?* / by Dr. Seuss. London:
    Collins, 1974.

42.2 *Did I Ever Tell You How Lucky You Are?* / by Dr. Seuss. [London]:
    Collins, 1979.
"Collins Colour Cubs" edition [15 cm.].

42.3 *Did I Ever Tell You How Lucky You Are?* / by Dr. Seuss. London:
    Collins, 1990.

42.4 *Did I Ever Tell You How Lucky You Are?* / Dr. Seuss. London: Collins,
    2002.

42.5 *Did I Ever Tell You How Lucky You Are?* / Dr. Seuss. London: Collins,
    2004.

43.0 *The Many Mice of Mr. Brice* / by Theo. LeSieg; illustrated by Roy
    McKie. New York: Beginner Books, 1973.
"Pop-Up" appears on spine.

"Bright & Early Books BE 15."

Also published with different cover but identical contents as: *The Pop-Up Mice of Mr. Brice* (Random House) [*see* 43.2-4].

1st issue: "Bright & Early Books" appears at head of spine without illustrated logo; without dust-jacket; retail price [$2.50]. Paper engineering, by Ib Penick, includes two pop-up constructions and numerous moveable paper features designed to be manipulated by the reader.

43.1 *The Many Mice of Mr. Brice* / by Theo. LeSieg; illustrated by Roy McKie. London: Collins, 1974.

43.2 *The Pop-Up Mice of Mr. Brice* / by Theo. LeSieg; illustrated by Roy McKie. New York: Random House, 1989.

43.3 *The Pop-Up Mice of Mr. Brice* / by Theo. LeSieg; illustrated by Roy McKie. London: Collins, 1989.

43.4 *The Pop-Up Mice of Mr. Brice* / by Theo. LeSieg; illustrated by Roy McKie. London: Collins, 1991.
     "New Edition."

44.0 *The Shape of Me and Other Stuff* / by Dr. Seuss. New York: Beginner Books, 1973.
     "Bright & Early Books BE 16."
     Also distributed by Grolier Enterprises as a "Book Club Edition."
     Also issued with an accompanying cassette sound recording in 1978.
     Reissued in: *Bright and Early Read Along Library*, set 2.

1st issue: "Bright & Early Books" appears at head of spine without illustrated logo; unadorned Bright & Early Books logo centered on lower cover; retail price $2.50. This book about simple concepts is illustrated exclusively with silhouettes.

44.1 *The Shape of Me and Other Stuff* / by Dr. Seuss. London: Collins, 1974.

44.2 *The Shape of Me and Other Stuff* / by Dr. Seuss. London: Collins, 1982.

44.3 *The Shape of Me and Other Stuff: Dr. Seuss's Surprising Word Book.* New York: Random House, 1997.
     "A Bright and Early Board Book."
        Printed in small format on thick paper boards rather than paper.

44.a The Shape of Me and Other Stuff [Chinese]
     Xing zhuang da wang guo / wen tu Susi bo shi; yi Zeng Yangqing =

The Shape of Me and Other Stuff / by Dr. Seuss. Taipei: Yuan-Liu, 1992.
    Text in Chinese and English.

44.b The Shape of Me and Other Stuff [Hebrew]
    Tsurot tserurot / Doktor Sus; 'lvrit: Le'ah Na'or. Jerusalem: Keter, 1991.

1974

Dr. Seuss Storybook [see: B3.1]

Dr. Seuss Storytime [see: B3.0]

45.0 *Great Day for Up!* / by Dr. Seuss; pictures by Quentin Blake. New York: Beginner Books, 1974.
"Bright & Early Books BE 19."
Also distributed by Grolier Enterprises as a "Book Club Edition."
Also issued with an accompanying cassette sound recording in 1975.
Reissued in: *Bright and Early Read Along Library; The Big Green Book of Beginner Books.*
    1st issue: "Bright & Early Books" appears at head of spine without illustrated logo; without dust-jacket; printer's code: 1 2 3 ... 0; retail price [$2.50]. Generally, when Geisel collaborated as the author with another illustrator, he used the pseudonym Theo. LeSieg; his publishing this work under the name Dr. Seuss is an oddity.

45.1 *Great Day for Up!* / by Dr. Seuss; pictures by Quentin Blake. London: Collins, 1975.

45.2 *Great Day for Up!* / by Dr. Seuss; pictures by Quentin Blake. London: Collins, 1982.

45.3 *Great Day for Up!* / by Dr. Seuss; pictures by Quentin Blake. Boston: National Braille Press, 1993.
    In braille.

45.4 *Great Day for Up!* / by Dr. Seuss; pictures by Quentin Blake. London: HarperCollins, 1997.

45.a Great Day for Up! [Chinese]
    Tiao yue di yi tian / wen Susi bo shi; tu Kunte Bulaike; yi Zeng Yangqing = *Great Day for Up!* / by Dr. Seuss; pictures by Quentin Blake. Taipei: Yuan-Liu, 1992.
    Text in Chinese and English.

46.0 *There's a Wocket in My Pocket!* / by Dr. Seuss. New York: Beginner
Books, 1974.
"Bright & Early Books BE 18."
Also distributed by Grolier Enterprises as a "Book Club Edition."
Also issued with an accompanying cassette sound recording in 1976.
Reissued in a kit, including an accompanying sound recording (1977,
1989), with: *Marvin K. Mooney, Will You Please Go Now!*
Reissued in: *The Dr. Seuss Read Along Library* [set 1]; *Bright and Early Read
Along Library* [set 1]; *Dr. Seuss's Bright and Early Board Books.*
Also adapted as an arithmetic work book: *I Can Add Upside Down!* /
adapted by Linda Hayward and Cathy Goldsmith [*see* F83].
    1st issue: "Bright & Early Books" appears at head of spine without
illustrated logo; without dust-jacket; printer's code: 1 2 3 ... 0; retail price
[$2.50].

46.1 *There's a Wocket in My Pocket!* / by Dr. Seuss. St. Paul, Minn.: Communication Center, State Services for the Blind, c1974.
    In braille.

46.2 *There's a Wocket in My Pocket!* / by Dr. Seuss. London: Collins, 1975.

46.3 *There's a Wocket in My Pocket!* / by Dr. Seuss. London: Collins, 1981.

46.4 *There's a Wocket in My Pocket!* / by Dr. Seuss. Livonia, Mich.: Seedlings Braille Books for Children, 1990.
    In braille.

46.5 *There's a Wocket in My Pocket!: Dr. Seuss's Book of Ridiculous Rhymes*
/ Dr. Seuss. New York: Random House, 1996.
"A Bright and Early Board Book."
    Printed in small format on thick paper boards rather than paper.

46.6 *There's a Wocket in My Pocket!* / by Dr. Seuss. London: Collins, 1997.
"A Bright and Early Board Book."

46.7 *There's a Wocket in My Pocket!* / by Dr. Seuss. London: Collins, 2003.
"Blue Back Book."

46.a There's a Wocket in My Pocket! [Chinese]
Yi zhi mao guai zai wo di kou dai / wen tu Susi bo shi; yi Hao Guang-
cai = *There's a Wocket in My Pocket!* / by Dr. Seuss. Taipei: Yuan-
Liu, 1992.
    Text in Chinese and English.

46.b There's a Wocket in My Pocket! [Dutch]
Ik heb een Gak in mijn Zak! / Dr. Seuss; vertaling, Katja en Kees Stip. Huizen, N.H. [Netherlands]: Goede Boek, 1976. "Benjaminboeken BE3."

46.c There's a Wocket in My Pocket! (with *The Cat in the Hat*) [German]
Der Kater mit Hut. [And] *In meiner Tasche ist eine Zasche* / Dr. Seuss; aus dem Amerikanischen von Eike Schönfeld und Sven Böttcher. Frankfurt am Main: Rogner und Bernhard, 1999.
Reprinted: Affoltern a. A.: Buch, 2000.

46.d There's a Wocket in My Pocket! [Hebrew]
Yesh li g'is ba-kis / me'et Doktor Sus; 'Ivrit: Le'ah Na'or. Jerusalem: Keter, 1980.

46.e There's a Wocket in My Pocket! [Italian]
Il mostrino nel taschina / Dr. Seuss; illustrazioni dell'autore; [traduzione, Anna Sarfatti]. Florence: Giunti, 1995.
"GRU Under 7 [no.] 18."

46.f There's a Wocket in My Pocket! [Italian]
C'e un mostrino nel taschino / by Dr. Seuss; traduzione di Anna Sarfatti. Florence: Giunti junior, 2003.

47.0 *Wacky Wednesday* / by Theo. LeSieg; illustrated by George Booth. New York: Beginner Books, 1974.
"Beginner Books B59."
Also distributed by Grolier Enterprises as a "Book Club Edition."
Reissued in: *The Big Green Book of Beginner Books.*
　1st issue: without dust-jacket; printer's code: 1 2 3 ... 0; retail price [$2.50]. This "what's-wrong-with-this-picture" counting book has the Beginner Book logo purposely printed upside down on the cover. Dr. Seuss toyed with yet another pseudonym in preliminary sketches for the cover: "Hjalmar Bonstable, Jr."

47.1 *Wacky Wednesday* / by Theo. LeSieg; illustrated by George Booth. London: Collins, 1975.

47.2 *Wacky Wednesday* / by Dr. Seuss writing as Theo. LeSieg; illustrated by George Booth. London: Collins, 1999.

47.a Wacky Wednesday [Danish]
Skørtorsdag / af Theo. LeSieg; tegninger af George Booth; dansk tekst, Christopher Maaløe. Copenhagen: Carlsen, 1979.

"Carlsen Pocket-Bøger 5."
"George Washington" is replaced with "General Kamp."

47.b Wacky Wednesday [German]
Was für ein verrückter Freitag / von Theo. LeSieg; illustriert von George Booth; [aus dem Amerikanischen von Marion von der Kammer]. Reinbek bei Hamburg: Carlsen Verlag, c1979.
"CarlsenTaschenBücher 5."
"George Washington" is replaced with "Frederick the Great."

47.c Wacky Wednesday [Swedish]
Underliga onsdan / text: Theo. LeSieg; bild: George Booth; svensk text: Karin Darje. Stockholm: Carlsen, 1978.
"Carlsen Pocket 5."
"George Washington" is replaced with "General Strid."

1975

48.0 *Because a Little Bug Went Ka-CHOO!* / by Rosetta Stone; illustrated by Michael Frith. New York: Beginner Books, 1975.
"Beginner Books B-61."
Also distributed by Grolier Enterprises as a "Book Club Edition."
Also issued with an accompanying cassette sound recording in 1978.

1st issue: without dust-jacket; printer's code: 1 2 3 ... 0; retail price [$2.50]. "Rosetta Stone" is a joint pseudonym for Geisel and Michael Frith, who collaborated on the text; Geisel never employed that pen name again.

48.1 *Because a Little Bug Went Ka-CHOO!* / by Rosetta Stone; illustrated by Michael Frith. London: Collins, 1976.

49.0 *Oh, the Thinks You Can Think!* / by Dr. Seuss. New York: Beginner Books, 1975.
"Beginner Books B-62."
Also issued with an accompanying cassette sound recording in 1977 and 1986.
Reissued in: *The Dr. Seuss Read Along Library*, set 2, and *Reading Is Fun with Dr. Seuss*.

1st issue: without dust-jacket; printer's code: 1 2 3 ... 0; retail price [$2.95].

49.1 *Oh, the Thinks You Can Think!* / by Dr. Seuss. London: Collins, 1976.

49.2 *Oh, the Thinks You Can Think!* / by Dr. Seuss. London: Collins, 1984.

49.3   *Oh, the Thinks You Can Think!* / by Dr. Seuss. London: Collins, 2000.

49.4   *Oh, the Thinks You Can Think!* / by Dr. Seuss. London: Collins, 2004.

49.a   Oh, the Thinks You Can Think! [Chinese]
> *Hsiang tsen me hsiang chiu tsen me hsiang!* / wen tu Susi bo shi; yi
> Hao Guangcai = *Oh, the Thinks You Can Think!* / by Dr. Seuss.
> Taipei: Yuan-Liu, 1992.
>   Text in Chinese and English.

49.b   Oh, the Thinks You Can Think! [Dutch]
> *Denk er maar eens lekker op los!* / Dr. Seuss; vertaling, Katja en Kees
> Stip. Huizen, N.H. [Netherlands]: Goede Boek, 1976.
> "Beginnersboeken 12."

49.c   Oh, the Thinks You Can Think! [Hebrew]
> *Kamah tov la-heshov* / me'et Doktor Sus; 'lvrit: Le'ah Na'or. Jerusalem:
> Keter, 1982.

49.d   Oh, the Thinks You Can Think! [Spanish]
> *La de cosas que puedes pensar!* / Dr. Seuss.; [adaptación y traducción,
> P. Rozarena] Madrid: Altea, 2003.

50.0   ***Would You Rather Be a Bullfrog?*** / by Theo. LeSieg; illustrated by
Roy McKie. New York: Beginner Books, 1975.
"Bright & Early Books BE 21."
Also distributed by Grolier Enterprises as a "Book Club Edition."
Reissued in: *The Big Green Book of Beginner Books.*
Also issued with an accompanying sound cassette recording in: *Bright and
Early Read Along Library*, set 2.
>   1st issue: without dust-jacket; printer's code: 1 2 3 ... 0; retail price
[$2.95].

50.1   *Would You Rather Be a Bullfrog?* / by Theo. LeSieg; illustrated by
> Roy McKie. London: Collins, 1976.
> "BB 90."

1976

51.0   ***The Cat's Quizzer*** / by Dr. Seuss. New York: Beginner Books, 1976.
Also distributed by Grolier Enterprises as a "Book Club Edition."
> "Big Beginner Books."
> Reprinted in: *Rhymes, Riddles and Nonsense.*
> 1st issue: without dust-jacket; with printer's code: 1 2 3 ... 0; retail

price [$3.95]. This book, which is overtly didactic compared to most of Dr. Seuss's other works, tests basic knowledge and problem-solving skills.

51.1 *The Cat's Quizzer* / by Dr. Seuss. London: Collins, 1977.

51.2 *The Cat's Quizzer* / by Dr. Seuss. [London]: Collins, 1990.

51.3 *The Cat's Quizzer: Are You Smarter Than the Cat in the Hat?* / by Dr. Seuss. New York: Beginner Books, 1993.

51.a The Cat's Quizzer [Chinese]
Mao mi da cai mi / wen tu Susi bo shi; yi Zhan Hongzhi = *The Cat's Quizzer* / by Dr. Seuss. Taipei: Yuan-Liu, 1992.
Text in Chinese and English.

51.b The Cat's Quizzer [Hebrew]
Hatul sha'alul / katav ve-tsiyer Doktor Sus; 'Ivrit: Le'ah Na'or. Jerusalem: Keter, 1990.

The Dr. Seuss Read Along Library [see: B4.0]

52.0 *Hooper Humperdink–? Not Him!* / by Theo. LeSieg; illustrated by Charles E. Martin. New York: Beginner Books, 1976.
"Bright & Early Books BE 25."
Also distributed by Grolier Enterprises as a "Book Club Edition."
Also issued with an accompanying sound cassette recording in: *Bright and Early Read Along Library*, set 2.
Subsequently published under the name Dr. Seuss, with illustrations by James Stevenson [*see* 52.2].
1st issue: without dust-jacket; printer's code: 1 2 3 ... 0; retail price [$2.95]. An alphabet book centered on first names.

52.1 *Hooper Humperdink–? Not Him!* / by Theo. LeSieg; illustrated by Charles E. Martin. Glasgow: Collins, 1977.
"BB 20."

52.2 *Hooper Humperdink–? Not Him!* / by Dr. Seuss; illustrated by James Stevenson. New York: Beginner Books, 1997.
Distribution delayed; not released to date.

1977

The Dr. Seuss Read Along Library [see: B4.1]

53.0 *Please Try to Remember the First of Octember!* / by Theo. LeSieg; illustrated by Arthur Cumings. New York: Beginner Books, 1977.

"Beginner Books B-63."

Also distributed by Grolier Enterprises as a "Book Club Edition."

Also issued with an accompanying cassette sound recording in 1988.

      1st issue: without dust-jacket; printer's code: 1 2 3 ... 0; retail price [$2.95].

53.1 *Please Try to Remember the First of Octember!* / by Theo. LeSieg; illustrated by Arthur Cumings. London: Collins, 1978.

53.2 *Please Try to Remember the First of Octember!* / by Dr. Seuss writing as Theo. LeSieg; illustrated by Arthur Cumings. London: Collins, 1999.

1978

Bright and Early Read Along Library [see: B5.0]

54.0 *I Can Read with My Eyes Shut!* / by Dr. Seuss. New York: Beginner Books, 1978.

"Beginner Books B-64."

Also distributed by Grolier Enterprises as a "Book Club Edition."

Also issued with an accompanying cassette sound recording.

Reprinted in: *Reading Is Fun with Dr. Seuss.*

      1st issue: printer's code: 1 2 3 ... 0; issued without dust-jacket; retail price [$3.50].

      Geisel suffered from cataracts and came close to losing his eyesight in the mid-1970s, making this work quasi-autobiographical. The book is dedicated to Geisel's ophthalmologist, "David Worthen, E.G. [Eye Guy]."

54.1 *I Can Read with My Eyes Shut!* / by Dr. Seuss. [London]: Collins, 1979.

54.2 *I Can Read with My Eyes Shut!* / by Dr. Seuss. London: Collins, 1986.

54.3 *I Can Read with My Eyes Shut!* / by Dr. Seuss. London: Collins, 2003. "Yellow Back Book." Also issued by Collins Picture Lions.

54.a I Can Read with My Eyes Shut! [Chinese]
    Bi zhuo yan jing ye neng du! / wen tu Susi bo shi; yi Hao Guangcai = *I Can Read with My Eyes Shut!* / by Dr. Seuss. Taipei: Yuan-Liu, 1992. Text in Chinese and English.

54.b I Can Read with My Eyes Shut! [Hebrew]
    Li-kero be-enayim atsumot / me'et Doktor Sus; 'Ivrit: Le'ah Na'or. Jerusalem: Keter, 1982.
      Reissued in 1990.

1979

55.0 *Oh Say Can You Say?* / by Dr. Seuss. New York: Beginner Books, 1979.
"Beginner Books B-65."
On cover: "Oh my brothers! Oh my sisters! These are Terrible Tongue
Twisters!"
Also distributed by Grolier Enterprises as a "Book Club Edition."
Also issued with an accompanying cassette sound recording in 1987.
Adapted as a pop-up book (with *Hop on Pop*) [*see* B28.0].
Reprinted in: *Rhymes, Riddles and Nonsense.*

    1st issue: without dust-jacket or printer's code (later printings carry
coding). The book is dedicated to "Lee Groo the Enunciator" (*i.e.*, Lea
Grey Dimond, Geisel's younger stepdaughter).

55.1 *Oh Say Can You Say?* / by Dr. Seuss. London: Collins, 1980.

55.2 *Oh Say Can You Say?* / by Dr. Seuss. London: Collins, 1986.

55.3 *Oh Say Can You Say?* / by Dr. Seuss. London: Collins, 1999.

55.a Oh Say Can You Say? [Chinese]
    Shuo hua rao kou ling / wen tu Susi bo shi; yi Zeng Yangqing = *Oh
    Say Can You Say?* / by Dr. Seuss. Taipei: Yuan-Liu, 1992.
        Text in Chinese and English.

55.b Oh Say Can You Say? [Spanish]
    Trabalenguas de mareo / Dr. Seuss; [traducción y adaptación, Atalaire].
    Madrid: Altea, 2003.

1980

56.0 *Maybe You Should Fly a Jet! Maybe You Should Be a Vet!* / by Theo.
    LeSieg; illustrated by Michael J. Smollin. New York: Beginner Books,
    1980.
"Beginner Books B-67."
Also distributed by Grolier Enterprises as a "Book Club Edition."
Reissued in: *The Big Green Book of Beginner Books.*

    1st issue: without dust-jacket; printer's code: 1 2 3 ... 0; retail price
[$3.95].

56.1 *Maybe You Should Fly a Jet! Maybe You Should Be a Vet!* / by Theo.
    LeSieg; illustrated by Michael J. Smollin. Hempstead, N.Y.: Helen
    Keller Braille Library, c1980.
        In braille.

56.2 *Maybe You Should Fly a Jet! Maybe You Should Be a Vet!* / by Theo. LeSieg; illustrated by Michael J. Smollin. London: Collins, 1981.

1981

57.0 ***The Tooth Book*** / by Theo. LeSieg; illustrated by Roy McKie. New York: Beginner Books, 1981
"Bright & Early Books BE 25."
Also distributed by Grolier Enterprises as a "Book Club Edition."
Subsequently published under the name Dr. Seuss, with illustrations by Joe Mathieu [*see* 57.3].
     1st issue: without dust-jacket; printer's code: 1 2 3 ... 0; retail price [$3.95].

57.1 *The Tooth Book* / by Theo. LeSieg; illustrated by Roy McKie. Newark, N.J.: Meyer Center, New Jersey Commission for the Blind, c1981. In braille.

57.2 *The Tooth Book* / by Theo. LeSieg; illustrated by Roy McKie. Glasgow: Collins, 1982.

57.3 *The Tooth Book* / by Dr. Seuss writing as Theo. LeSieg; illustrated by Joe Mathieu. New York: Random House, 2003.
"Bright and Early Board Books."
     Printed in small format on thick paper boards rather than paper.

57.a The Tooth Book [Hebrew]
Sefer ha-shen / me-et Dr. Sus be-shem ha-'et Ti'o Lesig; iyurim, Roi Mekki; 'Ivrit, Nimah Karaso. Moshav Ben-Shemen: Modan, 2002.

1982

58.0 ***Hunches in Bunches*** / by Dr. Seuss. New York: Random House, 1982.
Also distributed by Grolier Enterprises as a "Book Club Edition."
Also issued with an accompanying cassette sound recording.
     1st issue: without dust-jacket; printer's code: 1 2 3 ... 0; retail price [$5.95].
     A heart attack interrupted Geisel's work on this book, which conveys a general mood of frustration and the potential for disruption by our own imaginings.

58.1 *Hunches in Bunches* / by Dr. Seuss. London: Collins, 1983.
     Cited in Richardson (*see* F160); neither seen nor verified.

1984

59.0 *The Butter Battle Book* / by Dr. Seuss. New York: Random House, 1984.

Also distributed by Grolier Enterprises as a "Book Club Edition."

Also issued with an accompanying sound cassette recording.

1st issue: blank lower cover except for universal price code, issued without dust-jacket; printer's code: 1 2 3 ... 0; retail price [$6.95]. 500 deluxe copies of the first printing are numbered and signed by the author and issued specially bound in full blue cloth with a matching blue cloth slip case.

This allegory on war, the arms race and nuclear proliferation, with its doubtful outcome, brought criticism to Dr. Seuss by those who thought that the book's tone was too dark and threatening. The work, which Geisel dedicated to his wife Audrey, was first released on his 80th birthday and was awarded the PEN Los Angeles Center Award for children's literature in 1985.

59.1 *The Butter Battle Book* / by Dr. Seuss. London: Collins, 1984.

59.2 *The Butter Battle Book* / by Dr. Seuss; transcribed by Phyllis Hultz. Detroit: Seedlings Braille Books for Children, 1986.
   In braille.

59.a The Butter Battle Book [Hebrew]
   ha-Milhamah ha-ayumah al ha-hemah / me'et Doktor Sus; 'Ivrit, Le'ah Na'or. Jerusalem: Keter, 1984.
   Reissued in 1986.

59.b The Butter Battle Book [Italian]
   La battaglia del burro / by Dr. Seuss; traduzione di Anna Sarfatti. Florence: Giunti junior, 2002.

59.c The Butter Battle Book [Portuguese]
   Abaixo o lado de baixo / do Dr. Seuss; na tradução e adaptação de Cora Rónai. Rio de Janeiro: Editora Record, [1987?], c1984.

1986

60.0 *You're Only Old Once!* / by Dr. Seuss. New York: Random House, 1986.

1st issue: March, 1986; 250,000 copies; printer's code: 1 2 3 ... 0; retail price $9.95; a special deluxe edition of 500 copies was issued in full teal cloth with a matching slip case. Later printings have the printer's mark "B9" on the title page *verso*.

Dr. Seuss wrote this "Book for Obsolete Children" at the age of 81, and it was released on his birthday, March 2. It is one of the only two books that he wrote for adults (the other one is *The Seven Lady Godivas*). Inspiration and material for the work came from his whiling away hours as a patient in physicians' waiting rooms by sketching what he observed and experienced. The book is dedicated to Geisel's Dartmouth College graduating class of 1925.

60.1 *You're Only Old Once!* / by Dr. Seuss. London: Fontana/Collins, 1986.

1987

61.0 *I Am NOT Going to Get Up Today!* / by Dr. Seuss; illustrated by James Stevenson. New York: Beginner Books, 1987.
"Beginner Books B-74."
Also distributed by Grolier Enterprises as a "Book Club Edition."
Also issued with an accompanying cassette sound recording in 1988 and 1990.
Reissued in: *The Big Green Book of Beginner Books*.
1st printing: printer's code: 1 2 3 ... 0; issued without dust-jacket; retail price [$5.95].
As with *Great Day for Up!*, authoring this work as Dr. Seuss in collaboration with another illustrator is an oddity; usually, Geisel evoked "Theo. LeSieg" for such collaborations.

61.1 *I Am NOT Going to Get Up Today!* / by Dr. Seuss; illustrated by James Stevenson. [London]: Collins, 1988.

61.2 *I Am NOT Going to Get Up Today!* / by Dr. Seuss; illustrated by James Stevenson. Boston, Mass.: National Braille Press, [1991?].
In braille.

1990

62.0 *Oh, the Places You'll Go!* / by Dr. Seuss. New York: Random House, 1990.
Also distributed by Grolier Enterprises as a "Book Club Edition."
Reprinted in: *Your Favorite Seuss*.
Also adapted loosely, and drawing also from most of Dr. Seuss's other books, as: *Oh, Baby, the Places You'll Go! A Book to Be Read in Utero* / adapted by Tish Rabe from the works of Dr. Seuss [*see* F155].

1st issue: printer's code: 1 2 3 ... 0; retail price $12.95. Written in 1989 while Geisel was in poor health, this was the last Dr. Seuss book published before Geisel's death in 1990; he was adapting the work as an animated feature at the time.

62.1 *Oh, the Places You'll Go!* / by Dr. Seuss. London: Collins, 1990.

62.2 *Oh, the Places You'll Go!* / by Dr. Seuss. New York: Random House, 1993.
"Special Deluxe Edition."
Bound in full teal cloth with a matching slip case.

62.3 *Oh, the Places You'll Go!* / by Dr. Seuss. Stuart, Fla.: Braille International, [1997?].
In braille.

62.4 *Oh, the Places You'll Go!* / by Dr. Seuss. Topeka, Kan.: Econo-Clad Books, 2000.

62.5 *Oh, the Places You'll Go!* / by Dr. Seuss. London: Collins Picture Lions, 2003.

62.6 *Oh, the Places You'll Pop Up!: A Pop-Up Book* / Dr. Seuss. New York: Random House, 2003.
Mini-pop-up adaptation.

62.a Oh, the Places You'll Go! (with *The Lorax*) [German]
Wie schön, soviel wirst du sehn! [And] *Der Lorax* / Dr. Seuss; aus dem Amerikanischen von Eike Schönfeld und Uda Strätling. Frankfurt am Main: Rogner und Bernhard, 2000.

62.b Oh, the Places You'll Go! [Hebrew]
Im yots'im magi'im li-mekomot nifla'im / Doktor Sus; 'Ivrit Le'ah Na'or. Jerusalem: Keter, 1992.

62.c Oh, the Places You'll Go! [Latin]
Dr. Seuss O, Loca Tu Ibis (Oh, the Places You'll Go): A Beginning Latin Reader and Activity Text / by Theodor S. Geisel; translated by Leone Roselle; illustrated by Scott W. Earle. Portland, Maine: J. Weston Walch, 1994.
None of Dr. Seuss's illustrations is reproduced. Text is followed by student exercises and a Latin-English glossary. Issued with an accompanying teacher's guide.

62.d Oh, the Places You'll Go! [Portuguese]
Ah, os lugares aonde voce ira! / Dr. Seuss; tradução de Mônica Rod-

riques da Costa, Lavinia Fávero, Gisela Moreau. São Paulo: Companhia das Letrinhas, 2002.
In Portuguese and English.

62.e Oh, the Places You'll Go! [Spanish]
Oh, cuán lejos llegarás! / Dr. Seuss; traducido por Aída E. Marcuse. New York: Lectorum Publications, 1993.

62.f Oh, the Places You'll Go! [Swedish]
Hela världen är din! / Dr. Seuss; svensk text av Margareta Stormstedt. Stockholm: Rabén & Sjögren, 1992.

1991

Six by Seuss [see: B8.0]

1992

Dr. Seuss's Beginner Book Classics [see: B9.0]

1994

63.0 *Daisy-Head Mayzie* / by Dr. Seuss. New York: Random House, 1994.
Also distributed by Grolier Enterprises as a "Book Club Edition."
Also recorded for distribution to the blind (Louisville, Ky.: American Printing House for the Blind, 1996); also issued in braille in a collection of children's stories in: *Expectations,* vol. 49 (1997).

1st issue: retail price $15.00. Originally written as a live-action screenplay in the 1960s, but ultimately produced posthumously as an animated feature [*see* D6.0] that was then adapted in book format. Although the book was based on the animated feature, book distribution preceded the film's premier.

63.1 *Daisy-Head Mayzie* / by Dr. Seuss. Livonia, Mich.: Seedlings, Braille Books for Children, [1995].
In braille.

63.2 *Daisy-Head Mayzie* / by Dr. Seuss. London: HarperCollins, 1995.

63.3 *Daisy-Head Mayzie* / by Dr. Seuss. London: Picture Lions, 1995.

63.4 *Daisy-Head Mayzie* / by Dr. Seuss. London: Collins, 1996.

1996

A Hatful of Seuss [see: B11.0]

64.0 *My Many Colored Days* / by Dr. Seuss; paintings by Steve Johnson and Lou Fancher. New York: Knopf; distr. by Random House, 1996. "First edition."
A Junior Library Guild Selection.
   Published posthumously and without Geisel's editorial participation; issued with paper cutout dust-jacket. Dr. Seuss wrote the text in 1973 with the preliminary title *My Different-Colored Days,* and he prepared preliminary sketches with the intention that some other artist would provide the finished illustrations. His hope at the time was to develop Beginner Books with different concepts and styles than those published previously, and his vision for this work was based on beautiful illustrations and sensational colors. The work as published comprises full-page reproductions of canvas paintings with text overprint.

64.1 *My Many Colored Days* / by Dr. Seuss. New York: Knopf [National Braille Press], 1997.
   In braille.

64.2 *My Many Colored Days* / by Dr. Seuss; illustrated by Steve Johnson with Lou Fancher. New York: Scholastic, [1997], c1996.
   A reprint edition for the educational market.

64.3 *My Many Coloured Days* / by Dr. Seuss; paintings by Steve Johnson and Lou Fancher. London: Hutchinson, 1998.

64.4 *My Many Colored Days* / by Dr. Seuss; paintings by Steve Johnson and Lou Fancher. New York: Knopf; distr. by Random House, 1998. "First Board Book Edition."
   Cover with square cutouts.

64.5 *My Many Coloured Days* / by Dr. Seuss; paintings by Steve Johnson and Lou Fancher. London: Red Fox, 2001.

64.a My Many Colored Days [French]
   Ma vie en rose: enfantaisie / par Dr. Seuss; illustrations par Steve Johnson et Lou Fancher [trad. de l'américain par Catherine de La Clergerie]. Paris: Albums Circonflexe, 1997.

64.b My Many Colored Days [German]
   Jeder Tag hat eine Farbe / von Dr. Seuss; illustriert von Steve Johnson und Lou Fancher; ins Deutschen übertragen von Uli Blume. Munich: Bertelsmann, 1997.

64.c My Many Colored Days [Hebrew]
> *ha-Yamim ha-tsiv'onim sheli* / me-et Dr. Sus; tirgum, Beni Hendel, tsiyurim Stiv G'onso ve-Lu Pants'er. Tel Aviv: Modan, 1997.

64.d My Many Colored Days [Korean]
> *Haru haru tarun saekkal* / kul Dakt'ŏ Susu; kurim Suts'ibu Chon-sun, Lu P' angsyo; omgim Kim Hyon-jin. Seoul: Sams ŏng Ch'ulp'ansa, 2002.
>
> Reissued in 2003.

Read and Learn with Dr. Seuss [see: B12.0]

1997

The Big Green Book of Beginner Books [see: B13.0]

Dr. Seuss's Bright and Early Board Books [see: B14.0]

1998

Dr. Seuss's Book of Bedtime Stories [see: B17.0]

65.0 ***Hooray for Diffendoofer Day!*** / Dr. Seuss; with some help from Jack Prelutsky & Lane Smith. New York: Alfred A. Knopf; distr. by Random House, 1998.

A main selection of Children's Book-of-the-Month Club; a Junior Library Guild Selection.

"First edition."

Loosely adapted posthumously from an unfinished manuscript entitled "Miss Bonkers" that Dr. Seuss had begun *ca.* 1988, the facsimile of which, with commentary by Geisel's publisher Janet Schulman, appears at the end of this book. While the concept is by Dr. Seuss, the verse is by Prelutsky and the drawings by Smith. Smith's drawings incorporate some of Dr. Seuss's sketches in collage style. For a discussion of Smith's illustrating, see F27.

65.1 *Hooray for Diffendoofer Day!* / Dr. Seuss; with some help from Jack Prelutsky & Lane Smith; design by Molly Leach. New York: Scholastic, 1998.

> A reprint edition for the educational market.

65.a Hooray for Diffendoofer Day! [Hebrew]
> *Hedad le-Yom Shonshoni meyuhad!* / [Dr. Seuss; with some help from Jack Prelutsky & Lane Smith; translated by Nimah Karaso]. Moshav, Ben-Shemen: Modan, 2001.

Just What I'd Do [see: B18.0]

1999

Reading Is Fun with Dr. Seuss [see: B20.0]

Ten Tall Tales by Dr. Seuss [see: B22.0]

2001

Rhymes, Riddles and Nonsense [see: B25.0]

2002

The Complete Cat in the Hat [see: B26.0]

Dr. Seuss's Fabulous Fables [see: B27.0]

Hop on Pop-Up!: How to Raise a Happy Father with a Little Help from the Good Doctor! [see: B28.0]

2003

The Best of Dr. Seuss [see: B12.1]

Rhymes, Riddles and Nonsense [see: B25.0]

2004

Your Favorite Seuss [see: B30.0]

Books and Book Illustrations: Minor Works

1930

A1.0 *Program of the Twentieth Annual Winter Carnival of the Dartmouth Outing Club* / [illustrations by Dr. Seuss]. Hanover, N.H.: Dartmouth Outing Club, 1930.
    Eight-page program with cover title: *Carnival, 1930*; heavily illustrated with unsigned cartoons by Dr. Seuss.

1931

A2.0 *Boners: Being a Collection of Schoolboy Wisdom, or Knowledge as It Is Sometimes Written* / compiled from classrooms and examination papers by Alexander Abingdon [pseud.], and illustrated by Dr. Seuss. New York: Viking Press, 1931.

Published February, 1931 (two printings "before publication" [so stated on t.p. *verso*] are also recorded); bound in red cloth with black lettering and illustrated dust-jacket; retail price $1.00. *Boners* is the first book that Dr. Seuss illustrated. Sequels included: *More Boners*, which Dr. Seuss also illustrated [*see* A2.1]; *Still More Boners*; and *Prize Boners for 1932* (the first editions of the latter two works were illustrated by Virginia Huget). Dr. Seuss's illustrations were reprinted in subsequent compilations that included *Boners* [i.e., *The Omnibus Boners*] (New York: Blue Ribbon Books, 1931) [*see* A2.2] and *The Pocket Book of Boners: An Omnibus of Schoolboy Howlers and Unconscious Humor* [*see* A2.3–.33].

A2.01 [Boners.]
Herrings Go About the Sea in Shawls: ... and Other Classic Howlers from Classrooms and Examination Papers [originally titled Boners*]* / compiled by Alexander Abingdon and illustrated by Dr. Seuss. New York: Viking, 1997.
A reprint of *Boners* [A2.0].

A2.1 *More Boners* / compiled from classrooms and examination papers by Alexander Abingdon; illustrated by Dr. Seuss. New York: The Viking Press, 1931.

1st printing: April, 1931; bound in green cloth with illustrated dust-jacket; retail price $1.00. The sequel to *Boners* [*see* A2.0], it was published in numerous printings during the same year, and again in the series compilations: *The Omnibus Boners* and *The Pocket Book of Boners* [*see* A2.2–.33].

A2.2 [Omnibus Boners.]
Boners: Being a Collection of Schoolboy Wisdom, or Knowledge as It is Sometimes Written / compiled from classrooms and examination papers by Alexander Abingdon, and illustrated by Dr. Seuss [and Virginia Huget]. New York: Blue Ribbon Books, [1931].
Cover title: *The Omnibus Boners*.
The work was also issued with spine title *The Omnibus Boners* but with blank covers. It reprints as a collected work, with each section having its own title page and separate pagination: *Boners*; *More Boners*; and, *Still More Boners*. Dr. Seuss illustrated the first two parts and Virginia Huget illustrated the final part.

A2.21 *The Boners Omnibus: Boners — More Boners — Still More Boners …* / by Alexander Abingdon, and illustrated by Dr. Seuss & Virginia Huget. New York: Sun Dial Press, 1942.
"Center Books Edition."
A reprint of A2.2.

A2.3 *The Pocket Book of Boners: An Omnibus of Schoolboy Howlers and Unconscious Humor* / illustrated by Dr. Seuss. New York: Readers' League of America, 1932.
"Armed Services Edition."
A compilation of text and illustrations appearing in: *Boners*; *More Boners*; *Still More Boners*; and *Prize Boners for 1932*.

A2.31 *The Pocket Book of Boners: An Omnibus of Schoolboy Howlers and Unconscious Humor* / illustrated by Dr. Seuss. New York: Pocket Books, Inc., 1934.
1st printing: February 1934; 2nd printing: October 1935; 3rd printing: November 1936.

A2.32 *The Pocket Book of Boners: An Omnibus of Schoolboy Howlers and Unconscious Humor* / illustrated by Dr. Seuss. New York: Pocket Books, Inc., 1941.
Issued in numerous printings, including "Wartime Book" reprint [1944] on thin paper.

A2.33 *The Pocket Book of Boners: An Omnibus of Schoolboy Howlers and Unconscious Humor* / illustrated by Dr. Seuss. New York: Pocket Books, 1961.
"Pocket Book Edition."

A3.0 ***Program of the Twenty-First Annual Winter Carnival of the Dartmouth Outing Club*** / [illustrations by Dr. Seuss]. Hanover, N.H.: Dartmouth Outing Club, 1931.
Eight-page program with cover title: *Carnival, 1931*; heavily illustrated with cartoons, some signed "Dr. Seuss" or "Dr. S."

1932

A4.0 ***Program of the Twenty-Second Annual Winter Carnival of the Dartmouth Outing Club*** / [illustrations by Dr. Seuss]. Hanover, N.H.: Dartmouth Outing Club, 1932.
Program with a center-fold illustration by Dr. Seuss; cover title: *Carnival, 1932*.

1933

A5.0 *Are You a Genius?* **Second series** / by Robert A. Streeter and Robert G. Hoehn; with six illustrations by Dr. Seuss. New York: Frederick A. Stokes Co., 1933.

Issued in full green cloth with illustrated upper cover. The first series, with illustrations by Otto Soglow, was published in 1932; both series were subsequently published together in a collected work [*see* A5.1–2].

A5.1 *Are You a Genius?* First and second series / by Robert A. Streeter and Robert G. Hoehn; with illustrations by O. Soglow and Dr. Seuss. New York: Blue Ribbon Books, 1933.

A5.2 *Are You a Genius?* First and second series / by Robert A. Streeter and Robert G. Hoehn; with illustrations by O. Soglow and Dr. Seuss. New York: Blue Ribbon Books, 1936.

A6.0 *In One Ear ...* / by Frank Sullivan. New York: Viking Press, 1933. Frontispiece and dust-jacket illustrations by Dr. Seuss.

A7.0 *Secrets of the Deep, or, The Perfect Yachtsman* / by Old Captain Taylor; [illustrations by Dr. Seuss]. 2 vols. [*S.l.*]: Essomarine, 1934–1936. Cover title.

Vol. 1 reprinted in 1935.

Pamphlets (34 p. each; 23 cm.), comprising text and cartoons (in blue and red) but sparse advertising, that provide boating tips in a humorous vein; authorship is unknown but has been attributed to Geisel. "Aquatints by Dr. Seuss" appears on vol. 2 cover only. Followed by the sequel *The Log of the Good Ship* [*see* A14.0].

As a commercial artist for Standard Oil, Dr. Seuss enjoyed great success, first with his "Quick, Henry — the Flit!" insecticide cartoon advertisements [*see* B1.0] and, later, with his "Seuss Navy" campaign for Essomarine, with which this work, its sequel, and various print ads, brochures, and materials printed for distribution at trade shows (such as a program for the skit *Little Dramas of the Deep*, presented at the Motor Boat & Sportsmen's Show in New York, 1938, and a humorous newspaper published in several issues during January, 1941, edited by Dr. Seuss and entitled *The Sea Lawyer's Gazette*) are associated.

1935

A8.0 *The Bedroom Companion, or, A Cold Night's Entertainment: Being a Cure for Man's Neuroses, a Sop to His Frustrations, a Nightcap of Forbidden Ballads, Discerning Pictures, Scurrilous Essays, in Fine a Steam-*

ing Bracer for the Forgotten Male. New York: Farrar & Rinehart, 1935. Includes two illustrations by Dr. Seuss, on pp. 27 and 122.

1937

A9.0 *Mystery Puzzles: More "Minute Mysteries"* / by Austin Ripley ... with seven full page illustrations by Dr. Seuss and other decorations by Lloyd Coe. New York: Frederick A. Stokes Co., 1937.

A collection of mystery stories with accompanying illustrations by Dr. Seuss.

A10.0 *Spelling Bees: The Oldest and the Newest Rage* / by Albert Deane; illustrated by Dr. Seuss. New York: Frederick A. Stokes Co., 1937.

Issued in a dust-jacket; retail price $1.00. A preparatory book for spelling bee contestants, written in humorous style, with cartoons and cover art by Dr. Seuss.

1938

A11.0 *How's Tricks?: 125 Tricks and Stunts to Amaze Your Friends* / by Gerald Lynton Kaufman. New York: Frederick A Stokes Co., 1938.

Frontispiece and dust-jacket illustration by Dr. Seuss; all other illustrations are by Kaufman.

1940

A12.0 *An Ode in Commemoration of Bennet Cerf's Thirty-Ninth Birthday* / written and delivered by Doctor Seuss. Philadelphia: [Privately printed for Bennet Cerf], 1940.

Half title: *Pentellic Bilge for Bennet Cerf's Birthday.*

"As a feature of Random House Night at the Philadelphia Booksellers' Association, November 14, 1940, at the Penn A. C."

Verse, printed on two pages; unillustrated. The piece was printed after the event (late in 1940) under Cerf's direction and subsequently distributed. Perhaps 200 copies were printed. Dr. Seuss adapted this "ode" from an earlier poem entitled "Pentellic Bilge for Valentine's Day," which had appeared in *Jack o' Lantern* in 1936 [*see* C20].

1943

A13.0 *This Is Ann: She's Dying to Meet You* / [by W. Munro Leaf; illustrations by Dr. Seuss]. Washington, D.C.: War Dept., 1943.

"[U.S. Army field manual] A.G.300.7."

Colophon: U.S. Government Printing Office: 1943 — 543637. A booklet ([32] p.) for servicemen serving in the Pacific describing how malaria is contracted from mosquito bites. Reprinted repeatedly by the G.P.O. at least as late as 1945, with increasingly higher GPO document numbers.

1948

A14.0 *The Log of the Good Ship* / spawned by old Captain Taylor; aquatints by Dr. Seuss. [*S.l.*]: Esso Marine Products, [*ca.* 1948].

A sequel (36 p.; 26 cm.) to and in the style of *Secrets of the Deep, or, The Perfect Yachtsman* [*see* A7.0]; provides instructions, humorously, for maintaining a ship's log and includes pages of blank log forms for the reader's use.

1956

A15.0 *Signs of Civil-iz-ation* / by Dr. Seuss. La Jolla, Calif.: La Jolla Town Council, 1956.

1st printing: pink coloration. Subsequently issued in black-and-white without added color; a 3rd printing, with a revised ordinance on the pamphlet lower cover, appeared in blue. This illustrated pamphlet was published in support of the town's municipal sign ordinance and includes the Town Council Advertising Sign Code of La Jolla on the lower cover. Geisel, whose advertising art was appearing nationally on billboards when this piece first appeared, lost those contracts soon after. The text of this pamphlet was reprinted in Bennet Cerf's column "Trade Winds" in *The Saturday Review*, 40 (January 26, 1957): p. 6 [*see* C103].

1966

A16.0 *The Charity Ball of 1966* [Program] / sponsored by the San Diego Society for Crippled Children for the benefit of the Childrens [*sic*] Hospital Fund; ed. by Mary Glen Phalen; illustrated by Dr. Seuss. San Diego: Published by the Society, 1966.

Soft-cover program, with extensive illustrated advertising; 120 p. Dr. Seuss created an original drawing for the cover; all other illustrations represent previously published drawings by Dr. Seuss, revised with text to accommodate advertisers. The feature production of the ball, held at Hotel del Coronado on February 5, was: "Dr. Seuss at the Ball."

1982

A17 "Hail to Our Chief! (And I don't mean Ronald Reagan)." [By Dr. Seuss]. [*S.l.: s.n.*, 1982].
Broadside poem.
A humorous poem, unillustrated, commemorating the birthday celebration at Random House, New York City, of Random House president Bob Bernstein; signed by Dr. Seuss and dated December 13, 1982.

Books and Book Illustrations: Anthologies, Collections and Selections

The following listing describes anthologies and selected works published subsequent to their first appearance in book form, as well as works that contain substantial Dr. Seuss material in facsimile or reprint. For the works published by Random House and Collins during Geisel's lifetime, Dr. Seuss had artistic and editorial control; the remainder were compiled and produced independently (and during Geisel's lifetime sometimes objectionably) by others.

1929

B1.0 [*Flit Cartoons.*] New York: Stanco Inc., 1929–1932.
1929: *Flit Cartoons: As They Have Appeared in Magazines and Newspapers throughout the Country* (21 p.).
1930: *Flit Cartoons: As They Have Appeared in Magazines and Newspapers throughout the Country* ([16] p.).
1932: *Adventures with a Flit Gun: A Collection of Flit Cartoons by Dr. Seuss* ([24 p.]).
A series of booklets comprising reprints of advertising cartoons that appeared in magazines and newspapers promoting the insecticide Flit.

1967

B2.0 *Dr. Seuss' Lost World Revisited: A Forward-Looking Backward Glance.* New York: Award Books, Universal Publishing and Distributing Corporation; London: Tandem Books, 1967.
"Award Books A253."
"First Printing, 1967."
A paperback reprint collection of cartoon essays that first appeared in

Liberty magazine in 1932. Most of the cartoons are poorly reproduced, with lengthy captions printed on facing pages. For adults. Geisel brought suit against this reprint publication, claiming copyright infringement, but lost the case.

1974

B3.0 *Dr. Seuss Storytime.* New York: Random House, 1974.

A four-volume set (volumes unnumbered) issued in a slip case; collective title appears on spine of each volume and on slip case. [Vol. 1]: *McElligot's Pool*; *The Zax*; *The Lorax*; *Scrambled Eggs Super!* [Vol. 2]: *Bartholomew and the Oobleck*; *Yertle the Turtle*; *Horton Hears a Who!*; *I Can Lick 30 Tigers Today!*; *What Was I Scared Of?*; *Gertrude McFuzz.* [Vol. 3]: *The King's Stilts*; *King Looie Katz*; *Too Many Daves*; *How the Grinch Stole Christmas*; *The Sneetches*; *Dr. Seuss's Sleep Book.* [Vol. 4]: *Thidwick, the Big-Hearted Moose*; *I Had Trouble in Getting to Solla Sollew*; *Horton Hatches the Egg*; *Did I Ever Tell You How Lucky You Are?*

B3.1 [Dr. Seuss Storytime, vol. 1]

Dr. Seuss Storybook. London: Collins, 1979, c1974.

First published by Random House under the title: *Dr. Seuss Story-time*, [vol. 1] (*see* B3.0, above); included are: *McElligot's Pool*; *The Zax*; *The Lorax*; *Scrambled Eggs Super!*

1976

B4.0 *The Dr. Seuss Read Along Library* [set 1]. Westminster, Md.: Random House Educational Media, 1976.

Issued as a kit comprising 18 books (3 copies of 6 titles), 6 sound cassettes and a discussion guide. The titles are: *The Cat in the Hat*; *The Foot Book*; *Fox in Socks*; *Hop on Pop*; *Mr. Brown Can Moo! Can You?*; *There's a Wocket in My Pocket!*

1977

B4.1 *The Dr. Seuss Read Along Library*, set 2. Westminster, Md.: Random House Educational Media, 1977.

Issued as a kit comprising 18 books (3 copies of 6 titles), 6 sound cassettes and a discussion guide. The titles are: *Oh, the Thinks You Can Think!*; *The Cat in the Hat Comes Back!*; *Green Eggs and Ham*; *One Fish, Two Fish, Red Fish, Blue Fish*; *Dr. Seuss's ABC*; *Marvin K. Mooney, Will You Please Go Now!*

1978

B5.0 *Bright and Early Read Along Library* [set 1]. Westminster, Md.: Random House Educational Media, [1978?].

Issued as a kit comprising 18 books (3 copies of 6 titles), 6 sound cassettes and a discussion guide. Three of the works are by Dr. Seuss: *Great Day for Up!*; *Marvin K. Mooney, Will You Please Go Now!*; *There's a Wocket in My Pocket!* The others, by Stan and Jan Berenstain, are: *Bears on Wheels*; *He Bear, She Bear*; *Inside Outside Upside Down.*

B5.1 *Bright and Early Read Along Library*, set 2. Westminster, Md.: Random House Educational Media, 1978.

Issued as a kit comprising 18 books (3 copies of 6 titles), 6 sound cassettes and a discussion guide. Three of the works are by Dr. Seuss or Theo. LeSieg: *Hooper Humperdink...? Not Him!*; *The Shape of Me and Other Stuff*; *Would You Rather Be a Bullfrog?* The others, by S. and J. Berenstain, are: *The Berenstains' B Book*; *C Is for Clown*; *Old Hat, New Hat.*

1979

Dr. Seuss Storytime [see: B3.1 *Dr. Seuss Storybook* (vol. 1)]

1986

B6.0 *Dr. Seuss from Then to Now: A Catalogue of the Retrospective Exhibition.* San Diego, Calif.: San Diego Museum of Art, 1986.

Printed in 8,000 copies. Provides the best published source for facsimile reproductions of Dr. Seuss's original drawings. The exhibition was curated by Mary Stofflet and opened in San Diego on May 17, 1986, before traveling on a national tour. Reprinted by Random House [*see below* B6.1 and B10.0].

1987

B6.1 *Dr. Seuss from Then to Now: A Catalogue of the Retrospective Exhibition* / Organized by the San Diego Museum of Art, San Diego, California (New York: Random House, [1987], c1986).

A reprint of B6.0 [*see above*] by Random House, with minor changes on title page and t.p. *verso.*

Reprinted as *The Art of Dr. Seuss: The Illustration Art and Archive Collection* along with a reprint of *The Secret Art of Dr. Seuss* in one volume under the collective title: *The Art of Dr. Seuss* [deluxe cased limited ed., issued with a print: "The Singing Cats"; and trade ed. without case or print] (New York: Random House; distr. Northbrook, Ill.: The Chase Group, 2002) [*see* B10.0].

B7.0 *The Tough Coughs As He Ploughs the Dough: Early Writings and Cartoons by Dr. Seuss.* Ed. and with an introduction by Richard Marschall. New York: William Morrow and Co., 1987.

An anthology of selected writings and illustrations, all of which first appeared between 1927 and 1937, comprising contributions to popular magazines and advertising art from his "Quick, Henry — the Flit!" campaign. The title of this work comes from a subtitle to the cartoon essay "Ough! Ough! Or Why I Believe in Simplified Spelling," which appeared in *Judge* magazine (April 13, 1929) [*see also* F126–127].

1991

B8.0 *Six by Seuss* / [introduction by Clifton Fadiman]. New York: Random House, 1991.

"A Treasury of Dr. Seuss Classics" appears on the dust-jacket.

Includes: *And to Think That I Saw It on Mulberry Street; The 500 Hats of Bartholomew Cubbins; Horton Hatches the Egg; Yertle the Turtle and Other Stories; How the Grinch Stole Christmas; The Lorax.*

Also distributed by Grolier Enterprises as a "Book Club Edition."

This collection faithfully reprints the individual works, but with title pages for each story revised by Dr. Seuss specifically for this publication. The anthology was first issued as the main selection of the Book-of-the-Month Club in June, 1991.

1992

B9.0 *Dr. Seuss's Beginner Book Classics.* [New York]: Random House, [1992].

A five-volume set (volumes unnumbered) issued in a slip case; collective title appears on slip case only. Contents: *Fox in Socks; One Fish, Two Fish, Red Fish, Blue Fish; The Cat in the Hat; Green Eggs and Ham; Dr. Seuss's ABC.*

"Special Commemorative Set With Deluxe Cloth-Bound Editions" [golden label on shrink wrapping].

Each volume is specially bound in full cloth; *The Cat in the Hat, Green Eggs and Ham* and *Oh, the Places You'll Go!* were subsequently issued separately [*see* 14.20; 19.12; 62.3] with an added "Special Deluxe edition" statement; the other works are projected for separate issue likewise in the future.

1995

B10.0 *The Secret Art of Dr. Seuss.* With an Introduction by Maurice
Sendak. New York: Random House, 1995.

Reprinted as *The Art of Dr. Seuss: The Secret Art Collection* together
with a reprint of *Dr. Seuss from Then to Now* [see B6.0-.1] in one volume under
the collective title: *The Art of Dr. Seuss: A Retrospective on the Artistic Talent
of Theodor Seuss Geisel* [deluxe limited ed., in three issues (regular, patron,
and collaborator), issued in a slip case and with a print: "The Singing Cats";
trade ed., uncased and without the print] (New York: Random House; distr.
Northbrook, Ill.: The Chase Group, 2002).

Features paintings and other art work previously unpublished; objects
featured are chiefly privately held. Some of these art works, and select
drawings from Dr. Seuss's books, have been lithographically reproduced
and offered for sale by the Chase Group (Northbrook, Ill.), who also produced a "Seussentennial" traveling exhibition (2003-2005; William Dreyer,
curator) and published an exhibition catalog featuring a multiplicity of
Dr. Seuss's art work: *The Art of Dr. Seuss: The Illustration Art and Archive
Collections* (Northbrook, Ill.: The Chase Group, 2003).

1996

B11.0 *A Hatful of Seuss: Five Favorite Dr. Seuss Stories.* New York: Random House, 1996.

Includes: *Bartholomew and the Oobleck*; *If I Ran the Zoo*; *The Sneetches and
Other Stories*; *Dr. Seuss's Sleep Book*; and, *Horton Hears a Who!*

Like its predecessor anthology *Six by Seuss* [see B8.0], this collection
of stories was first issued as the main selection of the Book-of-the-Month
Club, in November 1996.

B12.0 *Read and Learn with Dr. Seuss.* London: HarperCollins Children's
Books, 1996.

Includes: *The Cat in the Hat*; *The Cat in the Hat Comes Back!*; *Dr. Seuss's
ABC.*

B12.1 *The Best of Dr. Seuss.* London: Collins Picture Lions, 2003.
Reissue, with new title, of *Read and Learn... .*

1997

B13.0 *The Big Green Book of Beginner Books* / by Dr. Seuss and Theo.
LeSieg; illustrated by Quentin Blake, George Booth, Roy McKie,

Michael J. Smollin, James Stevenson, and B. Tobey. New York: Random House, 1997.
Contents: *Great Day for Up!*; *Would You Rather Be a Bullfrog?*; *I Wish That I Had Duck Feet*; *Wacky Wednesday*; *Maybe You Should Fly a Jet! Maybe You Should Be a Vet!*; *I Am NOT Going to Get Up Today!*

B14.0 ***Dr. Seuss's Bright and Early Board Books.*** New York: Random House, 1997.
A four-volume set (volumes unnumbered) issued in a handled carrying case; collective title appears on case only. Contents: *Dr. Seuss's ABC*; *The Foot Book*; *Mr. Brown Can Moo! Can You?*; *There's a Wocket in My Pocket!*
"Special Commemorative Set With Deluxe Cloth-Bound Editions" [golden label on shrink wrapping].
Contents are identical to the individually issued board books, but in larger (19.5 cm.) size. They abridge or modify the original works.

B15.0 ***Seuss-isms: Wise and Witty Prescriptions for Living from the Good Doctor.*** Foreword by Audrey Geisel. New York: Random House, 1997.
A selection of quotations and accompanying illustrations from Dr. Seuss's works, arranged by suitable topic or occasion.

B15.1 *Seuss-isms: Wise and Witty Prescriptions for Living from the Good Doctor.* Foreword by Audrey Geisel. London: Collins, 1999.

1998

B16.0 ***Doktor Siuss.*** V perevodakh Vladimira Gandelsmana; khudozhnik Mikhail Belomlinski. New York: Slovo / Word, 1998.
Includes Russian translations of: *If I Ran the Zoo* [*Esli bi Ya Bil Direktorom Zooparka*— see 9.a]; *King Looie Katz* [*Korol Lui Kotoriy*— see 34.a]; *Dr. Seuss's Sleep Book* [*Sonnoe Tsarstvo*— see 23.e]; *I Can Lick 30 Tigers Today!* [*Segodnya Lzobyn 30 Tigrov*— see 34.a]; *Yertle the Turtle* [*Cherepashiy Korol*— see 17.k]. Also includes Gandelsman's *Ameriki.*
This selection of translations contains none of Dr. Seuss's illustrations, and the black-and-white drawings that accompany the text have no relation to the original pictures.

B17.0 ***Dr. Seuss's Book of Bedtime Stories.*** London: Collins, 1998.
Includes: *Dr. Seuss's Sleep Book*; *Thidwick, the Big-Hearted Moose*; and *Horton Hears a Who!*

B17.1 *Dr. Seuss's Book of Bedtime Stories.* London: Collins, 2003.

B18.0 *Just What I'd Do: If I Ran the Circus or If I Ran the Zoo* / by Dr. Seuss. New York: Random House, 1998.

Comprises reprints of: *If I Ran the Circus* and *If I Ran the Zoo*.

1999

B19.0 *The Cat in the Hat's Great Big Flap Book* / Dr. Seuss. New York: Random House, 1999.

"Over 70 Flaps Inside!" [on upper cover].

A board book (12 p.), incorporating peek-a-boo flaps, "inspired by" [*i.e.*, comprising selected images and text from]: *The Cat in the Hat*; *One Fish, Two Fish, Red Fish, Blue Fish*; *Mr. Brown Can Moo! Can You?*; *There's a Wocket in My Pocket!*; and, *Dr. Seuss's ABC*.

B19.1 *The Cat in the Hat's Great Big Flap Book* / Dr. Seuss. London: Collins, 1999.

Dr. Seuss Goes to War: The World War II Editorial Cartoons of Theodor Seuss Geisel [see: F135]

B20.0 *Reading Is Fun with Dr. Seuss*. London: Collins, 1999.

Includes: *Hop on Pop*; *Marvin K. Mooney, Will You Please Go Now!*; *Oh, the Thinks You Can Think!*; *I Can Read with My Eyes Shut!*

B20.1 *Reading Is Fun with Dr. Seuss*. London: Collins, 2001.

B21.0 *Seuss-isms for Success: Insider Tips on Economic Health from the Good Doctor [i.e. Dr. Seuss]*. Introduction by Tom Peters. New York: Random House, 1999.

"Life Favors" [on lower cover].

A selection of quotations and accompanying illustrations from Dr. Seuss's works, arranged by suitable topic or occasion.

B22.0 *Ten Tall Tales by Dr. Seuss*. London: Collins, 1999.

Comprises all of the stories in: *The Sneetches and Other Stories*; *Yertle the Turtle and Other Stories*; and, *I Can Lick 30 Tigers Today! and Other Stories*.

2000

B23.0 *Dr. Seuss Went to War: A Catalog of Political Cartoons by Dr.*

Seuss / Mandeville Special Collections Library [UCSD]; intro. by Richard Minear. [La Jolla, Calif.]: UC Regents, 2000.
<http://orpheus.ucsd.edu/speccoll/dspolitic/>
　Online exhibit of 388 of the political cartoons by Dr. Seuss published in the newspaper *PM* between 1941 and 1943. For a related work, see F135.

2001

B24.0 ***The Advertising Artwork of Dr. Seuss*** / [Mandeville Special Collections Library. La Jolla, Calif.: The Library, 2001?] .
<http://orpheus.ucsd.edu/speccoll/dsads/index.shtml>
　Online selection of ad art from the Dr. Seuss Collection, held by the Mandeville Special Collections Library, UCSD. For more reproductions of Dr. Seuss's advertising art work, see F38.

B25.0 ***Rhymes, Riddles and Nonsense*** / by Dr. Seuss. London: Collins, 2001.
Reprints of: *Fox in Socks*; *Oh Say Can You Say?*; *The Cat's Quizzer*. Reissued in 2003.

2002

The Art of Dr. Seuss [deluxe and trade reprint eds.] [see: B10.0]

B26.0 ***The Complete Cat in the Hat*** / by Dr. Seuss. London: HarperCollins Children's Books, 2002.
The Cat in the Hat and *The Cat in the Hat Comes Back!*, issued jointly.

B27.0 ***Dr. Seuss's Fabulous Fables***. London: Collins, 2002.
Reprints of: *The Lorax*; *I Had Trouble in Getting to Solla Sollew*; *Did I Ever Tell You How Lucky You Are?*

B28.0 ***Hop on Pop-Up!: How to Raise a Happy Father with a Little Help from the Good Doctor!*** / by Dr. Seuss. New York: Random House, 2002.
"First edition."
　A pop-up book adapted from *Hop on Pop* and *Oh Say Can You Say?*

2003

The Art of Dr. Seuss [exhibition catalog] [see: B10.0]

The Best of Dr. Seuss [see: B12.1]

B29.0 *The Dr. Seuss Miniature Collection*. London: Collins, 2003.
Reprints of: *The Cat in the Hat*; *How the Grinch Stole Christmas*; *Fox in Socks*; *Green Eggs and Ham*.
Issued in a slip case.

Rhymes, Riddles and Nonsense [see: B25]

2004

B30.0 *Your Favorite Seuss* / by Janet Schulman and Cathy Goldsmith; illustrated by Dr. Seuss and with photographs by miscellaneous photographers. New York: Random House Children's Books, 2004.
Reprints of: *And to Think That I Saw It on Mulberry Street*; *McElligot's Pool*; *If I Ran the Zoo*; *Horton Hears a Who!*; *The Cat in the Hat*; *How the Grinch Stole Christmas*; *Yertle the Turtle*; *Happy Birthday to You!*; *Green Eggs and Ham*; *The Sneetches*; *Dr. Seuss's Sleep Book*; *The Lorax*; *Oh, the Places You'll Go!*
Includes accompanying essays by Barbara Bader, Stan and Jan Berenstain, John Lithgow, Christopher Paolini, Richard H. Minear, Barbara Mason, Starr Latronica, Peter Glassman, and Audrey Geisel.

Contributions to Magazines and Newspapers

Listed below are published stories, poems, essays, speeches, and other brief writings, usually illustrated, that Dr. Seuss contributed to popular magazines and, occasionally, to newspapers. The listing also includes cartoon series by Dr. Seuss and brief contributions by others that Dr. Seuss illustrated. These works are arranged alphabetically by story title; for an index to the magazine and newspaper titles in which the works appear, please consult the Name Index. Excluded are brief notices and fillers written while Geisel was a student, advertising artwork, cover art, and single cartoons (for a selection of the latter, see: The Tough Coughs as He Ploughs the Dough *[B7.0]; for a checklist of many of the single cartoons published variously, see:* P. Nel, Dr. Seuss: American Icon *[F143]).*

C1 **"The 500 Hats of Bartholomew Cubbins."** Abridged with illustrations by Dr. Seuss. *Children's Digest* (December, 1950). Pp. 50–60.

C2 ["**A-Hunting We Must Go ....**" By] Dr. Seuss. *College Humor* (January, 1932). Pp. 14–15.

An untitled poem, illustrated [title derived from first line of text].

C3 "**American Insects: Golfus Americanus.**" [By Dr. Seuss]. *Life* (August, 1933). P. 33.

A taxonomic description in full, illustrated, published as an advertisement for *The American Golfer*.

C4 "**And They Call It Golf!**" By J. Eckert Goodman, Jr.; [illustrations by Dr. Seuss]. *Sports Illustrated and The American Golfer* (April and May, 1936). Pp. 20 *ff.*

In two installments; illustrated with six cartoons by Dr. Seuss.

C5 "**Animals Every Student Loves.**" By Doctor Theodophilus Seuss, Ph.D., I.Q., H2SO4. *College Humor* (October, 1930–1932). *Passim.*

This series appeared frequently and comprised sets of cartoons with lengthy prose captions.

C6 "**The B. and M. Timetable — A Book Review.**" [By Theodor Geisel]. *Jack o' Lantern* (June, 1924). P. 33.

A satirical review essay, originally composed for a writing class assignment at Dartmouth College and discussed years later in "Benfield Pressey" [*see* C7].

C7 "**Benfield Pressey: 'He Seemed to Like the Stuff I Wrote.'**" By Theodor S. Geisel. In Collins, James. *Mentors: Noted Dartmouth Alumni Reflect on the Teachers Who Changed Their Lives.* Hanover, N.H.: Dartmouth College, 1991. Pp. 3–4.

Written in homage to Pressey (and to fellow student Norman Maclean), who was on the English faculty while Geisel was a student at Dartmouth. This piece also discusses the motivation behind writing "The B. and M. Timetable — A Book Review" [*see* C6].

C8 "**The Big Brag.**" By Dr. Seuss. *Redbook* (December, 1950). Pp. 46–47.

A short story in verse, illustrated. A slightly different version appears in *Yertle the Turtle and Other Stories* [*see* 17.0].

C9 "**The Bippolo Seed.**" By Dr. Seuss. *Redbook* (June, 1951). Pp. 46–47.

A short story in verse, illustrated.

C10 "**Boids and Beasties.**" [By] Dr. Theophrastus Seuss. *Judge* (November 19, 1927–March 24, 1928). *Passim.*

This series represents the first of many works that Dr. Seuss contributed to this humor magazine. The feature appeared irregularly and comprised sets of cartoons with lengthy captions. The concept was continued under the title "Fish, Beast and Bird" [*see* C28].

C11 "... Boners — From the Indiana *Bored Walk.*" [Illustrations by Dr. Seuss]. *College Humor* (August, 1932). Pp. 50–53.

"Brat Books on the March." [see: C130. "Writing for Children: A Mission."]

C12 "Bring 'em Buck Alive!" [By Dr. Seuss *et al.*]. *Ballyhoo*, 3/2 (September, 1932). Pp. 16–17.
A montage of drawings and photographs depicting expeditions to trap animals for an imaginary zoo. Dr. Seuss contributed to various of the satirical pieces published in this humor magazine, but always anonymously or pseudonymously and rarely obviously. One exception is a single cartoon parodying his "Quick, Henry — The Flit!" ad campaign published under the name "Dr. Souss" (*Ballyhoo*, 1/3 [October, 1931] [reprinted in: *The Book of Ballyhoo*, ed. N. Anthony and G.T. Delacorte, Jr. (New York: Simon and Schuster, 1931)].

C13 "... But for Grown-Ups Laughing Isn't Any Fun." By Dr. Seuss. *The New York Times Review of Books* (November 16, 1952). Children's Book Section, p. 2.
A prose essay, illustrated, on writing for children and on the differences between children's humor and that of adults.

C14 "The Cat in the Hat Beginner Book Dictionary in French." *McCall's* (November, 1965). Pp. 66 *ff.*
An abridged version of the book [*see* 26.b].

C15 "The Class Prophecy." By Ruth Hamel, Elizabeth Spencer and James S. Memery; [illustrated by Theo. Geisel]. *Brown and Gold Recorder* [Yearbook]. Springfield, Mass.: Pupils of Central High School, 1921. Pp. 37–42.
A cartoon essay, unsigned by Geisel; he also contributed other illustrations in this issue, although he was not on the yearbook staff (*cf.* C88: Geisel served on the staff of the senior yearbook, *The Pnalka,* the same year).

C16 "The Clock Strikes 13! A New Serial of Love and Crime." By Henry McSeuss Webster [*i.e.*, Dr. Seuss]. *Judge* (February 25, 1928). Pp. 8, 16.
A humorous essay, illustrated by Jack Rose (a Dartmouth College classmate).

C17 "The Cutting of the Wedding Cnouth, or, Divorce among the Druids." By Dr. Seuss. *Judge* (June 16, 1928). P. 14.
A humorous essay, illustrated.

C18 "Did I Ever Tell You ...?" By Dr. Seuss. *Redbook* (February, 1956). P. 14.
A poem, illustrated.

C18.1 "The Zode." [By Dr. Seuss]. In Johnston, Ray. *Developing Student Leaders: How to Motivate, Select, Train, and Empower Your Kids to Make a Difference.* El Cajon, Calif.: Youth Specialties, 1992. Pp. 21–22.
Text only, without illustration. A reprint of the poem originally published as "Did I Ever Tell You ...?" but cited in this publication as being a previously unpublished manuscript (an early typescript of the poem, bearing the caption title "The Zode," is held in the Dr. Seuss Collection, Mandeville Special Collections Library, UCSD).

C19 "Doing England on Ninety Cents." By Dr. Seuss. *Judge* (September 1, 1928). P. 9.
A humorous essay, illustrated.

C20 "Dr. Seuss' Poetry Corner." *Jack o' Lantern*, Jackobite number (1936). Pp. 18–19.
Comprises two stylistically unusual drawings and five poems: "Pentellic Bilge for Valentine's Day"; "Hark!"; "Secret Society"; "Salt Spray .... Does It Pay?"; and, "Square-Dance for an Amateur Echo-Eater." The first of these formed the basis for his *An Ode in Commemoration of Bennet Cerf's Thirty-Ninth Birthday* (1940) [*see* A12.0].

"Dr. Seuss Speaks Out" [see: C77. "My Uncle Terwilliger on the Art of Eating Popovers."]

C21 "Dr. T.'s Dressing Song." In "Something to Talk About," by Leo Lerman. *Mademoiselle*, 37 (May 1953). P. 116.
Lyrics, without illustration, from the motion picture *The 5000 Fingers of Dr. T.* [*see* D2.0].

C22 "The Economic Situation Clarified: A Prognostic Re-evaluation." By the Dr. Seuss Surveys. *The New York Times Magazine* (June 15, 1975). P. 71.
An "Endpaper" editorial for adults, in verse, with an accompanying cartoon featuring "Uppers" and "Downers" that later appeared in *Oh, the Places You'll Go!* [*see* 62.0].

"Epic Poem." [see: C77. "My Uncle Terwilliger ..."; C104–C105. "Small Epic Poem ..."]

C23 **"An Essay on Toleration."** By T. S. Geisel. *The Dartmouth Bema* (March, 1925). P. 7.
A prose essay, without illustration, appearing in the college's literary magazine.

C24 **"The Facts of Life, or, How Should I Tell My Child?"** By Dr. Seuss. *Life* (February–May, 1934). Pp. 22 *ff.*
A lengthy humorous essay, in two parts; illustrated.

C25 **"Famous Presidential Campaigns: The Republican Split of 1867."** By Theo. Seuss, 2nd. *Judge* (December 31, 1927). P. 5.
A humorous essay, illustrated.

C26 **"Fan Mail: An Authors'** [*sic*] **Occupation."** [By] Dr. Seuss. *Authors League* (April 1963).
A brief article (1 p.) for fellow authors, written in prose; unillustrated.

C27 **"A Few Notes on […]."** By Dr. Seuss. *Liberty Magazine*, 8 (June–November, 1932). *Passim.*
A series of cartoon essays, in prose, on various topics (*e.g.*, "A Few Notes on Birds"; "… on Facial Foliage"; "… on Fires").

C28 **"Fish, Beast and Bird: A Piscozoöavistical Survey."** By Doctor Theophrastus Seuss. *Judge* (August 23–September 20, 1930). *Passim.*
This series appeared irregularly and comprised sets of cartoons with lengthy captions.

C29 **"The Flustards."** By Dr. Seuss. *Redbook* (August, 1953). P. 65.
A poem, illustrated.

C30 **"Fox in Socks."** By Dr. Seuss. *Ladies' Home Journal* (March, 1965). Pp. 66–69.
An abridged version of the book [*see* 27.0].

C31 **"A Gentleman in the Case: Sea Story."** By Dr. Seuss. *Judge* (July 21, 1928). P. 14.
A humorous short story, illustrated.

"Gerald McBoing Boing" [see: C109. "Speaking of Pictures …: These Show Film Star McBoing Boing."]

C32 **"Gertrude McFuzz."** By Dr. Seuss. *Redbook* (July, 1951). Pp. 46–47.
A short story in verse, illustrated. A slightly different version appears in *Yertle the Turtle and Other Stories* [*see* 17.0].

C33 "The Glunk That Got Thunk." By Dr. Seuss. *Woman's Day* (July, 1969). Pp. 45–50.

A reprint of the same story that appears in *I Can Lick 30 Tigers Today! and Other Stories* [*see* 34.0], but with illustrations colored differently from those in the book.

C34 "Goofy Olympics." By Dr. Seuss. *Liberty Magazine*, 8 (June 4, 1932). Pp. 44–45.

A cartoon essay, in prose.

C35 "The Great Diet Derby." By Dr. Seuss. *Judge* (September 8, 1928). Pp. 16, 24.

A humorous essay, illustrated.

C36 "The Great Henry McBride." By Dr. Seuss. *Redbook* (November, 1951). Pp. 54–55.

A short story in verse, illustrated.

C37 "The Great McGrew Milk Farm." By Dr. Seuss. *Children's Activities* (April, 1955). Pp. 12–13.

A poem, illustrated. The New-Cow-McGrew Cow in the story was prefigured in 1928 in a cartoon in *Judge* magazine and later re-cast as the Umbus in *On Beyond Zebra* [*see* 12.0].

C38 "Gustaav Schleswigh, 3rd, 'Hops Off' the Finnish Frigate ...." Special Wire to *Judge* by Seuss. *Judge* (August 25, 1928). P. 6.

A humorous essay, illustrated.

C39 "Gustav, the Goldfish." By Dr. Seuss. *Redbook* (June, 1950). Pp. 48–51.

A short story in verse, illustrated.

C40 "The Harassing of Habbakuk." By Dr. Seuss. *Judge* (October 13, 1928). Pp. 8, 31.

A humorous essay, illustrated.

C41 "Harpooner with a Gentle Barb." By Dr. Seuss. *The New York Times Book Review* (September 12, 1954). P. 3.

A book review of: Nathaniel Benchley, *The Benchley Roundup* (New York: Harper & Bros., 1954).

C42 "Hejji." By Dr. Seuss. New York: King Features Syndicate, 1935.

This syndicated Sunday color comic strip ran from April–June, 1935, and reflected Geisel's recent exposure to Peruvian culture. It was canceled when William Randolph Hearst, feeling the economic pressures of the Depression, ordered King Features to fire the last six Sunday comic strip artists who had been hired, including Geisel. Reprinted in *The Comic Strip Century: Celebrating 100 Years of an American Art Form*, vol. 2, ed. Bill Blackbeard and Dale Crain (Northampton, Mass: Kitchen Sink Press, 1995): 284–295.

C43 **"Hoobub and the Grinch."** By Dr. Seuss. *Redbook* (May, 1955). P. 19.
    A poem, illustrated; an early 1954 draft was entitled "Hoolrib and Guido." This "Grinch" differs from the better known character, which Dr. Seuss developed a short time later [*q.v.*, 15.0].

C44 **"Hooeyana — A Reverie."** By Theophrastus Seuss, 4th (Class Whimsey). *Judge* (June 9, 1928). P. 17.
    A humorous essay, illustrated.

C45 **"Horton and the Kwuggerbug."** By Dr. Seuss. *Redbook* (January, 1951). Pp. 46–47.
    A short story in verse, illustrated.

C46 **"Horton Hatches the Egg."** By Dr. Seuss. *Children's Digest* (September, 1953). Pp. 99–118.
    Abridged from the book [*see* 5.0], with Dr. Seuss's illustrations.

C47 **"How I Spied on General Grant in '61."** By Theophrastus Seuss. *Judge* (January 28, 1928). Pp. 10, 28.
    A humorous essay, illustrated.

C48 **"How Gerald McGrew Caught the Filla-ma-Zokk: A New McGrew Zoo Tale."** By Dr. Seuss. *Children's Activities* (December, 1954). Pp. 14–15.
    A short story in verse, illustrated.

C49 **"How Officer Pat Saved the Whole Town."** By Dr. Seuss. *Redbook* (October, 1950). Pp. 46–48.
    A short story in verse, illustrated.

C50 **"How Orlo Got His Book."** By Dr. Seuss. *The New York Times Book Review* (November 17, 1957). Children's Book Section, pp. 1, 60.
    An essay for adults vilifying publishers' word lists, illustrated.

C51 **"How the Grinch Stole Christmas."** By Dr. Seuss. *Redbook* (December, 1957). Pp. 53–64.
    An abridged version of the book [*see* 15.0], with vastly altered and

inferior coloration. Dr. Seuss was displeased with the quality of this printing, and it became the last of his many contributions to appear in *Redbook* magazine.

C51.1 "How the Grinch Stole Christmas." By Dr. Seuss. [Milford, N.J.]: Distributed by Spadea Syndicate, Inc., 1965.
> An abridged version of the book, distributed for newspaper publication; the story appeared in the *Chicago Tribune* and the *Washington Post*, among others, in their Sunday comics sections.

C52 **"How to Write a Book for Beginning Readers."** By Dr. Seuss. *Education Summary* (March 5, 1958). Pp. 5*ff*.
An article about writing from word lists.

C53 **"If At First You Don't Succeed — Quit!"** *Saturday Evening Post* (November 28, 1964). P. 6.
A "Speaking Out" editorial for adults, with an accompanying cartoon.

C54 **"If I Ran the Circus."** By Dr. Seuss. *Children's Activities* (June, 1955). Pp. 14–15.
A poem, illustrated, with text and drawing different from that of the book with the same title [*see* 13.0].

C55 **"If I Ran the Zoo."** By Dr. Seuss. *Redbook* (July, 1950). Pp. 56–58.
A short story in verse, illustrated. A later, revised version of this work appeared as a book with the same title [*see* 9.0].

C56 **"If I Ran the Zoo."** By Dr. Seuss. *Children's Digest* (March, 1953). Pp. 99–118.
Abridged from the book [*see* 9.0], with Dr. Seuss's illustrations.

C57 ***Jack o' Lantern.*** Vol. 14–17. Hanover, N.H.: Published by the Students of Dartmouth College, 1921–1925.
Dartmouth College's humor magazine, issued monthly during the academic year. Geisel was on the Art Staff for vol. 16 and served as Editor-in-Chief for vol. 17. His first contributions appear in vol. 14 (October, 1921), when he was barely a month into his freshman year, with four cartoons: "Two Arguments against Matrimony," "The Pied Piper," [untitled: six cats], and "Soc-cer!" Most writings in the magazine are unsigned, but many during his editorship, by Geisel's later admission, were by him or, jointly, with Norman Maclean. Most of Geisel's cartoons are signed (usually "T.," "T.G."or "Geisel"). When he was put on probation in the spring of his senior year for drinking, Geisel was relieved of his editorial duties

and his name removed from the publication's credits. Consequently, he published some of his drawings in the April 1925 issue under a variety of pseudonyms: Seuss (his middle name), Anton Lang, L. Burbank, Thos. Mott Osborne, L. Pasteur, and D.G. Rosetti.

C58 "**Jazz!**" [By Jim Walls; illustrated by Ted Geisel]. *Jack o' Lantern* (June, 1922). P. 33.
An illustrated essay.

C59 "**Japan's Young Dreams: Children's Drawings Show How Occupation Has Changed Their Aspirations.**" *LIFE* (March 29, 1954). Pp. 89 *ff*.
This collection of children's drawings, with captions and brief commentary, was the result of a project undertaken by Geisel during a visit to Japan. The piece was heavily edited, and Geisel's own writing is obscured by editorial rephrasing. Geisel consequently distanced himself from the project, which misspells "Seuss" as "Suess" throughout, but he drew from his Japanese experiences in developing the theme for *Horton Hears a Who!* [*see* 11.0].

C60 "**The Kindly Snather.**" By Dr. Seuss. *Redbook* (December, 1956). P. 100.
A poem, illustrated.

C61 "**King Grimalken and the Wishbones.**" Story and drawing by Dr. Seuss. *Junior Catholic Messenger* (October 29, November 5, 12, 19, 1948). Pp. 55–B *ff*.
A short story, illustrated; published in four parts.

C62 "**Latest News from Mulberry Street.**" By Dr. Seuss. *Children's Activities* (February, 1955). Pp. 12–13.
A poem, illustrated.

C63 "**Laugh Is Like That!**" By Rube Goldbrick [*i.e.*, Dr. Seuss]. *Judge* (May 19, 1928). Pp. 21, 26.
A humorous essay, illustrated, evoking Rube Goldberg.

C64 "**Laying Out the Garden.**" By Corey Ford; drawings by Dr. Seuss. *Vanity Fair* (June, 1932). Pp. 43, 71.

C65 "*Life*'s **Little Educational Charts.**" By Dr. S[euss]. *Life* (July 5, 1929–May 23, 1930). *Passim*.
This lengthy series appeared weekly and comprised briefly captioned cartoons.

C66 "**The Lorax.**" By Dr. Seuss. *Woman's Day* (August, 1971). Pp. 67–71.
    An abridged version of the book with the same title [*see* 39.0].

C67 "**Making Children Want to Read.**" By Dr. Seuss. *Book Chat*, 9/5
    (Fall, 1958). P. 29.
    A discussion of the urgency of literacy as motive for publishing the
Beginner Books series.

C68 "**Marco Comes Late.**" By Dr. Seuss. *Redbook* (September, 1950). Pp.
    58–59.
    A short story in verse, illustrated.

   C68.1 "Marco Comes Late." Written and illustrated by Dr. Seuss. In *Treat
        Shop*. Selected and ed. by Eleanor M. Johnson and Leland B. Jacobs.
        Columbus, Ohio: Charles E. Merrill Books, 1954. Pp. 119–124.
           Text and illustrations as in C68, but with different layout; some
        of the illustrations have been flipped and printed in four-color pro-
        cess.

C69 "**Matilda, the Elephant with a Mother Complex.**" A Dr. Seuss Fable.
    Judge (April, 1938). P. 17.
    A short story in prose, illustrated. This work was later developed into
the book *Horton Hatches the Egg* [*see* 5.0].

C70 "**McElligot's Pool.**" By Dr. Seuss. *Children's Digest* (December, 1955).
    Pp. 73–96.
    "Adapted from 'McElligot's Pool'" [*see* 6.0].

C71 "**Modern Melodrama and the Early Greeks.**" [By] Seuss. *Judge* (Jan-
    uary 28, 1928). P. 18.
    A humorous essay, illustrated.

C72 "**Mr. Brown Can Moo Like a Cow! Can You? Dr. Seuss's Book of
    Wonderful Noises.**" *McCall's* (October, 1970). Pp. 78–81.
    An abridged version of *Mr. Brown Can Moo! Can You?* [*see* 37.0].

C73 "**Mr. Mullik Begs to Introduce His Three Checks to Matrimony.**"
    [By Theodor Geisel]. *Jack o' Lantern* (May, 1924). Pp. 28–29.
    A humorous essay, illustrated, describing three patents.

C74 "**Mr. Sullivan's Times.**" By John Ridell [*i.e.,* Corey Ford]; [illustra-
    tions by Dr. Seuss]. *Vanity Fair* (January, 1933). P. 39.

C75 "**The Munkits.**" By Dr. Seuss. *Redbook* (January, 1954). P. 67.
    A poem, illustrated.

C76 **"My Hassle with the First Grade Language."** By Dr. Seuss. *Chicago Tribune* (November 17, 1957).
   Reprinted in: *Education*, 78/6 (February, 1958): 323–325.
   A partly humorous essay about Dr. Seuss's writing early Beginner Books.

C77 **"My Uncle Terwilliger on the Art of Eating Popovers."** [By] Dr. Seuss. *The New York Times* (June 30, 1977). P. A–19.
   Caption title: "Dr. Seuss Speaks Out." Reprinted in: *The New York Times* (May 21, 1989), p. E–27.
   Unillustrated text of a brief "Epic Poem" first delivered as a commencement address at Lake Forest College on June 4, 1977.

C78 **"*New* New Jersey: The Great New Jersey Rehabilitation Plan."** By Dr. Seuss. *Life* (March, 1933). Pp. 24–25.
   A humorous prose essay from a New Yorker's perspective, illustrated.

C79 **"OK, RMN, Get Out the Old Zike-Bike."** [By Dr. Seuss]. In "Capitol Punishment," by Art Buchwald. *Washington Post* (July 30, 1974).
   This issue of Buchwald's syndicated newspaper column features Dr. Seuss's paraphrase of his own *Marvin K. Mooney, Will You Please Go Now!* [*see* 41.0], replacing each reference to "Marvin K. Mooney" with "Richard M. Nixon"; with a reprint illustration from the book.

C80 **"On the Firing Line."** By Theodor S. Geisel. *Springfield* [Mass.] *Union* (July, 1925). *Passim.*
   A series of humorous notes and briefs submitted by Geisel while the columnist who normally wrote this feature was on vacation; without illustrations.

C81 **"The Origin of Contract Bridge."** An historical treatise by the eminent philologist, Dr. Seuss. *Judge* (February 11, 1928). P. 8.
   A humorous essay, illustrated.

C82 ***PM.*** New York, N.Y.: Newspaper *PM*, Inc., 1941–1943.
   As the daily newspaper's editorial cartoonist, Dr. Seuss drew three cartoons a week illustrating the newspaper's position opposing American isolationism and fascist aggression, especially in relation to Nazi Germany. 404 cartoons appeared between January 30, 1941, and January 6, 1943; during 1942, some cartoons lagged in publication by one day between the west and east coast editions. An advertising brochure from *PM* Syndicate promoting syndication of Dr.

Seuss's *PM* cartoons in other newspapers was issued separately in 1941 ([8] p. in accordion fold format, including six cartoons). A selection of reprint cartoons (approx. 200) appears in Richard M. Minear's *Dr. Seuss Goes to War: The World War II Editorial Cartoons of Theodor Seuss Geisel* (N.Y.: New Press, 1999) [*see* F135]; a digitized online collection of Dr. Seuss's *PM* cartoons, scanned from the holdings of the Mandeville Special Collections Library, UCSD, has also been prepared [*see* B23.0]; for a listing of Dr. Seuss's *PM* cartoon titles, see P. Nel, *Dr. Seuss: American Icon* [*see* F143].

C83 **"The Past Is Nowhere."** By Dr. Seuss. *The New York Times Book Review* (January 16, 1955). Pp. 4, 33.

A book review of: Jiro Osaragi, *Homecoming* (New York: Alfred A. Knopf, 1954).

"Pentellic Bilge for Valentine's Day." [see: C.18. "Dr. Seuss' Poetry Corner."]

C84 **"Perfect Present."** By Dr. Seuss. *Child Life* (December, 1953). P. 9.

A poem, illustrated.

The Pnalka, 1920½ [see: C88. "Prophecy on the Prophets."]

Political cartoons [see: C82. *PM* Newspaper; C124. *Victory*.]

C85 **"A Prayer for a Child."** By Dr. Seuss. *Collier's* (December 23, 1955). P. 86.

A Christmas season prayer for peace, illustrated.

C86 **"Presidential Possibilities."** [By Theodor Geisel]. *Jack o' Lantern* (March, 1924). Pp. 24–25.

A humorous essay, illustrated.

C87 **"Preying Guests."** By Victor G. Heiser, M.D.; illustrated by Dr. Seuss. *Collier's* (January 15, 1938). Pp. 50 *ff*.

An article concerning the transmission of elephantiasis, malaria and other parasitic diseases, with three illustrations by Dr. Seuss on p. 50.

C88 **"Prophecy on the Prophets."** By T. S. Geisel. *The Pnalka, 1920½* [Central High School senior yearbook, Springfield, Mass.]. P. 48.

A one-page essay evoking Rube Goldberg, among others; without illustrations. Geisel served as Grind and Jokes Editor for this issue (*cf.* C15 for other yearbook contributions in *The Brown and Gold Recorder*).

C89 **"A Pupil's Nightmare."** By T. S. Lesieg. *The Central Recorder* [Central High School newspaper, Springfield, Mass.] (Friday, January 21, 1920). P. 16.

This article in his high school newspaper represents Geisel's first use of a pseudonym (his surname spelled backwards), one which he later adapted as "Theo. LeSieg." Geisel contributed numerous essays, poems and news notes during the period 1919–1921, but no drawings.

C90 **"Quaffing with the Pachyderms: Why I Prefer the West Side Speak-Easies."** By Dr. Theo. Seuss. *Judge* (March 17, 1928). Pp. 16–17.

A cartoon essay, with lengthy captions.

C91 **"Quality."** By Dr. Seuss. *Judge* (March, 1938). Pp. 9–14.

"*The Judge*'s Cartoonovelette, Complete in this Issue."

In prose, illustrated.

C92 **"The Rabbit, the Bear and the Zinniga-Zinnaga [*sic*]."** By Dr. Seuss. *Redbook* (February, 1951). Pp. 46–47.

A short story in verse, illustrated. The name of the fanciful tree in the title was misprinted; Dr. Seuss intended it to be "... Zinniga-Zanniga," which is how the word is spelled in the text. The animal characters are the same as those in "The Big Brag" [*see* 17.0].

"Richard M. Nixon, Will You Please Go Now!" [see: C79. "OK, RMN, Get Out the Old Zike-Bike."]

C93 **"The Royal Housefly and Bartholomew Cubbins."** By Dr. Seuss. *Junior Catholic Messenger* (January 13, 20, 27, February 3, 1950). P. 126–B *ff*.

A short story, illustrated; published in four parts.

C94 **"The Ruckus."** By Dr. Seuss. *Redbook* (July, 1954). P. 84.

A poem, illustrated.

C95 **"Santa Claus's Beard through the Ages."** By Corey Ford; [illustrations by Dr. Seuss]. *Vanity Fair* (December, 1931). Pp. 68 *ff*.

C96 **"Science Gives Three New Boons to Society."** By Dr. Seuss. *Judge* (1931). *Passim.*

This series appeared irregularly and comprised sets of cartoons with lengthy captions.

C97 **"The Science of Everything."** By John Ridell [*i.e.*, Corey Ford]; [illustrations by Dr. Seuss]. *Vanity Fair* (June, 1931). Pp. 76–77.

C98 "Scrambled Eggs Super!" Written and illustrated by Dr. Seuss. *Children's Digest* (March, 1955). Pp. 75–98.
    An adaptation of the book [*q.v.* 10.0].

C99 "See Dr. Seuss for Social Publicity!" *The New York Woman* (October 7, 1936). P. 40.
    A cartoon essay, with lengthy captions.

C100 "Senator Heflin and the Presidency: A Superstitious Forecast." by Dr. Theophrastus Seuss. *Judge* (April 7, 1928). P. 8.
    A humorous essay, illustrated.

C101 "Sex and the Sea God: A Frothy Novelette." By Dr. Seuss. *Judge* (August 11, 1928). Pp. 15, 25.
    Illustrated.

C102 "A Short Condensed Poem in Praise of *Reader's Digest Condensed Books.*" By Dr. Seuss. Dust-jacket advertisement, *ca.* 1957.
    A promotional panel for *The Reader's Digest* Association, Inc., illustrated with the Cat in the Hat and used chiefly on *Reader's Digest Condensed Books* dust-jackets. Use of the advertisement in various media continued into the early 1980s.

C103 "Signs of Civilization." In "Trade Winds," by Bennett Cerf. *The Saturday Review*, 40 (January 26, 1957). P. 6.
    A reprint, without illustrations. Originally published as an illustrated pamphlet in support of the town's sign ordinance by the La Jolla [Calif.] Town Council in 1956 [*see* A15.0].

C104 "Small Epic Poem (Size 2¾ B)." Duplicated typescript, June, 1978. Reprinted in: *San Diego Union Tribune* (June 19, 1978), p. B-1.
    Text of a commencement address delivered before Revelle College, University of California, San Diego, June 18, 1978; unillustrated.

C105 "Small Epic Poem, Size 3½ B." *San Diego Union* (May 28, 1978). P. A-16.
    Reprinted in: *Publishers Weekly* (June 26, 1978), p. 93.
    An address delivered before the American Booksellers Association convention on May 27, 1978; unillustrated.

C106 "The Sneetches." By Dr. Seuss. *Redbook* (July, 1953). P. 77.
    A poem, illustrated. Later published in a different version in *The Sneetches and Other Stories* [*see* 21.0].

C107 **"Somebody's a-Comin' to Our House."** As dictated by Toney, Jr., to Antoinette Seuss; pictures by Dorothy Nohope Smith Barlow. *Judge* (February 28, 1928). P. 20.

A humorous essay.

C108 **"Speaking of Pictures …: Housing Problem Almost Eliminates Thidwick the Moose."** *LIFE* (November 22, 1948). Pp. 26–28.

A selection of illustrations from *Thidwick, the Big-Hearted Moose* [*see* 7.0] promoting the book's release.

C109 **"Speaking of Pictures …: These Show Film Star McBoing Boing."** *LIFE* (January 15, 1951). Pp. 8–9.

A selection of illustrations from *Gerald McBoing Boing* [*see* D19.0] promoting the film's release.

C110 **"Speedy Boy."** By Dr. Seuss. *Children's Activities* (March, 1955). Pp. 14–15.

A short story in verse, illustrated.

C111 **"Static City."** By Corey Ford; [illustrations by Dr. Seuss]. *Vanity Fair* (August, 1931). Pp. 50–51.

C112 **"Steak for Supper."** By Dr. Seuss. *Redbook* (November, 1950). Pp. 44–46.

A short story in verse, illustrated.

C113 **"The Strange Shirt Spot."** By Dr. Seuss. *Redbook* (September, 1951). Pp. 68–69.

A short story in verse, illustrated; an early draft bears the title "Young Homemakers."

C114 **"The Strangest Game I Ever Refereed."** By Dr. Theophrastus Seuss. *Judge* (November 10, 1928). P. 4.

A humorous essay, including a football team roster composed entirely of players named "Seuss"; illustrated.

C115 **"Tadd and Todd."** By Dr. Seuss. *Redbook* (August, 1950). Pp. 56–58.

A short story in verse, illustrated.

C116 **"Tardy Laurels for Forgotten Brows."** By Dr. Seuss. *Judge* (February 7–April 18, 1931). *Passim.*

This series appeared irregularly and comprised sets of cartoons with lengthy captions.

C117 **"Thidwick, the Big-Hearted Moose."** Written and illustrated by Dr. Seuss. *Children's Digest* (April, 1954). Pp. 81–100.
"An adaptation of the picture book illustrated by the author" [*q.v.* 7.0; see also: C108. "Speaking of Pictures ...: Housing Problem Almost Eliminates Thidwick the Moose"].

C118 **"To My Grandmother, My 'Buddy.'"** [By] Seuss. *Judge* (April 21, 1928). P. 17.
A poem, illustrated.

C119 **"To the Tallow-Chandler, the Grim Exponent of a Dying Gravy."** A sentimental lyric, with no harm meant, by Dr. Seuss. *Judge* (June 19, 1929). P. 6.
Illustrated.

C120 **"The Tragic Tale of the Turnbull Triplets, or, An Urgent Warning to the American Mother."** By Dr. Seuss, the Alienist. *Judge* (August 18, 1928). P. 8.
A humorous essay, illustrated.

C121 **"Tree Number 3."** By Dr. Seuss. *McCall's* (February, 1959). P. 28.
A poem, illustrated.

C122 **"Unsung Beasts Who Made Great Historical Events Possible."** [By] Dr. Seuss. *Life* (June 6–June 27, 1930). *Passim.*
This brief cartoon series was first captioned "Unsung Animals Who Made Great Historical Events Possible."

C123 **"Van Loon's Catalogue."** By John Ridell [*i.e.*, Corey Ford]; drawings by Dr. Seuss. *Vanity Fair* (January, 1933). Pp. 34–35.

C124 **_Victory._** Vol. 3. Washington, D. C.: Division of Information, Office for Emergency Management, 1942. *Passim.*
Dr. Seuss contributed cartoons frequently to this weekly bulletin during April–August, 1942.

C125 **"The Waiting Room at Dang-Dang."** [By Dr. Seuss]. *Judge* (September 15, 1928). Pp. 9, 28.
A humorous essay, illustrated.

C126 **"Wanted, $1,000,000 for Qincy Qilq."** By Qincy Qilq [*i.e.*, Dr. Seuss]. *Life* (January 11— February 8, 1929). *Passim.*
A series of humorous essays based on Qilq's appeal to the public for $1,000,000 so that he can become a philanthropist; illustrated.

C127 "'Wherever Did You Get Such an Idea Anyhow?' They Ask." By Dr. Seuss, otherwise Theodor Seuss Geisel. *Young Wings* (January, 1950). Pp. 8–9.

An article for children, illustrated, about composing *Bartholomew and the Oobleck.*

C128 "Who's Who in Bo-Bo." [By Theodor Geisel.] *Jack o' Lantern* (November, 1923). Pp. 24–25.

Descriptions, in prose, of "Bo-Boians," imaginary beasts from the "Isle of Bo-Bo"; illustrated.

C129 "Wife Up a Tree." By Dr. Seuss. *This Week* (May 17, 1953).

A poem, illustrated.

C130 "Writing for Children: A Mission." By Dr. Seuss. *Los Angeles Times* (November 27, 1960). Books: Fall and Winter [supplement], p. 11.

Preliminarily entitled "Brat Books on the March"; a prose essay about writing for juveniles, unillustrated.

C131 "Ye Knyghts of Ye Table Round: Being Ye Inside Dope on King Arthur's Court." Translated from Merlin's Memoirs by Doctor Theophrastus Seuss. *Judge* (March 31–June 23, 1928). Pp. 16 *ff.*

A series of prose essays, illustrated.

C132 "Yertle the Turtle." By Dr. Seuss. *Redbook* (April, 1951). Pp. 46–47.

A short story in verse, illustrated. A slightly different version from the story with the same title that appears in *Yertle the Turtle and Other Stories* [*see* 17.0].

C133 "The Zaks." By Dr. Seuss. *Redbook* (March, 1954). P. 84.

A poem, illustrated. The work was later published in a different version as "The Zax" in *The Sneetches and Other Stories* [*see* 21.0].

"The Zode" [see: C18. "Did I Ever Tell You ...?]

Screenplays, Film/Video, Multimedia and Theatrical/Musical Adaptations

Dr. Seuss wrote several screenplays directly for film, and he was intimately involved in the numerous animated adaptations of his works. When these productions are adaptations of books, they typically differ both in revised texts and in added songs and images; fuller character development often comes with animation as well.

Excluded from this listing are filmstrips and filmstrip kits, which were sold largely to institutions such as schools and libraries and essentially represent photoduplications of their respective books. Also excluded are most of the approximately forty documentary films and animated short features with which Geisel was anonymously involved, usually either by writing scripts or directing animation, while in the U.S. Army Signal Corps Information and Educational Division during World War II. In instances when Geisel's involvement in army productions was significant and unambiguous, however, those works are listed below.

D1.0 *The 500 Hats of Bartholomew Cubbins* / an Animated Puppetoon produced and directed by George Pal; based upon the story by Dr. Seuss. UM&M TV Corp., 1945.
16 mm b/w, 9 min.

D1.1 *The 500 Hats of Bartholomew Cubbins* [Theatre program] / based on the book by Dr. Seuss; adapted for the stage by Timothy Mason. [Minneapolis, Minn.]: Children's Theatre Company, 1980.

Theatre program ([20] p.) for the performance of an unpublished stage adaptation, written by Timothy Mason in 1980 and approved by Dr. Seuss. This work and *Dr. Seuss' How the Grinch Stole Christmas* [*see* D29.4–.51] were the only two Dr. Seuss books adapted for the stage (although Dr. Seuss was working on a theatrical adaptation of *The Seven Lady Godivas* at the time of his death). The performance premiered April 19, 1980, by The Children's Theatre Company, Minneapolis, Minn.

D2.0 *The 5,000 Fingers of Dr. T* / screenplay by Allan Scott and Dr. Seuss; directed by Roy Rowland; produced by Stanley Kramer; lyrics by Dr. Seuss. Columbia Pictures, 1953.
A Stanely Kramer Company Production.
Featuring: Peter Lind Hayes, Mary Healy, Hans Conried, Tommy Rettig, John Heasley, and Noel Cravat.
Live action motion picture, color; reissued as a videorecording; 90 min.

Young Bart Collins dreams of his piano teacher, Dr. Terwilliker [Dr. T], whose teaching method results in 500 boys playing the grandest piano ever built. Lyrics for "Dr. T's Dressing Song" were published in *Mademoiselle* magazine [*see* C21]. The film opened to mixed reviews and has since developed a cult following. The project soured Geisel on Hollywood productions, and he purposely excluded the work from his *résumé* for years.

ABC [see: D13.0. *Dr. Seuss's ABC*]

And to Think That I Saw It on Mulberry Street [see: D34.0. *Marco Takes a Walk*]

An Awfully Big Adventure: The Making of Modern Children's Literature: [Dr. Seuss] [see: F6. *An Awfully Big Adventure ...*]

Army-Navy Screen Magazine [see: D40.0. *Private S.N.A.F.U.*]

Army Orientation Film #8 [see: D43.0. *Your Job in Germany*]

Army Orientation Film #15 [see: D38.0. *"Our Job in Japan"*]

Bartholomew and the Oobleck [see: D14.0. *Dr. Seuss's Caldecotts*]

The Big Brag [see: D18.0. *Four by Seuss*; D42.0. *Yertle the Turtle and Other Stories*]

D3.0 ***The Butter Battle Book*** / written for television with lyrics by Dr. Seuss; produced by Ralph Bakashi; executive producer: Theodor Geisel. Turner Network Television, 1989.

A Bakashi production; voices: Charles Durning, Christopher Collins, Miriam Flynn, Clive Revill, and Joseph Cousins.

Animated feature originally produced for TNT-TV broadcast on November 13, 1989; reissued as a videocassette, 30 min.

Also issued jointly on videocassette with *Daisy-Head Mayzie* and *In Search of Dr. Seuss*.

D4.0 ***The Cat in the Hat*** / a CBS Television Network production, in association with DFE Films; directed by Hawley Pratt; produced by Chuck Jones and Ted Geisel; music by Dean Elliott. CBS-TV, 1971.

A DePatie-Freleng production; voices: Allan Sherman, Daws Butler, Tony Frazier, Pamelyn Ferdin, Gloria Camacho, Thurl Ravenscroft, and Lewis Morford.

Animated freature produced for CBS-TV broadcast on March 10, 1971; reissued as a videocassette, 24 min.

Issued subsequently with a study guide.

Also reissued jointly on videocassette with *Dr. Seuss on the Loose* in 1985.

D4.1 *The Cat in the Hat* [see: D9.0. *Dr. Seuss Beginner Book Video*]

D4.2 *The Cat in the Hat.* [And] *Maybe You Should Fly a Jet! Maybe You Should be a Vet!* New York: Random House Home Video, 1997.
Produced by Green Light Media.
Videocassette, ca. 30 min.

D4.3 *The Cat in the Hat* [interactive multimedia]. [Novato, Calif.]: Living Books, 1997.
Interactive computer disc, designed by Brøderbund Software, Inc.; issued with a copy of the book.
CD-ROM.

D4.4 *The Cat in the Hat* [interactive multimedia] [see: D12.0. *Dr. Seuss Reading Games*].

D4.5 *Dr. Seuss' The Cat in the Hat* [Motion picture, 2003] / Universal Pictures, DreamWorks Pictures and Imagine Entertainment; produced by Brian Grazer; directed by Bo Welch; screenplay by Alec Berg, David Mandell, and Marc Sherman; music by David Newman [and Marc Shaiman]. Universal City, Calif.: Universal, 2003.
Featuring Mike Meyers, Spencer Breslin, Dakota Fanning, Alec Baldwin, *et al.*
VHS and DVD; 88 min.
Also issued as a sound recording [*see* E8.02]
    Released fall 2003; based on *The Cat in the Hat;* sound track also issued separately [*see* E8.01]. Adapted to book format as: *Dr. Seuss' The Cat in the Hat Movie Storybook* / adapted by Justine & Ron Fontes [adapted from the screenplay by Alec Berg, David Mandel, and Jeff Schaffer] (N.Y.: Random House, 2003); *Do Not Open This Crate!* / by Stephen Krensky; illustrated by Aristides Ruiz [adapted from the screenplay by Alec Berg ...] (N.Y.: Random House, 2003); *Dr. Seuss' The Cat in the Hat* / adapted by Jesse Leon McCann; illustrated by Christopher Moroney [based on the motion-picture screenplay by Alec Berg ...] (N.Y.: Golden Books, 2003); and, *Dr. Seuss' The Cat in the Hat* / adapted by Jim Thomas [based on the motion picture screenplay by Alec Berg ...] (N.Y.: Random House, 2003) [translated into French as *Le chat chapeauté* (Paris: Pocket jeunesse, 2004)].

D4.5.a The Cat in the Hat [Motion picture, 2003] [Spanish].
El Gato de Dr. Seuss. Universal City, Calif.: AVH/Universal, 2004.

D5.0 *The Cat in the Hat Comes Back! Plus, There's a Wocket in My Pocket! and Fox in Socks* / produced by Praxis Media, Inc. New York: Random House Home Video, 1989.

Voices: Lynn Blair *et al.*
Videocassette, 30 min.

The Cat in the Hat Gets Grinched [see: D22.0. *The Grinch Grinches the Cat in the Hat*]

The Complete Uncensored Private Snafu [see: D40.0. *Private S.N.A.F.U.*]

D6.0 *Daisy-Head Mayzie* / written by Dr. Seuss; music by Philip Appleby; produced by Christopher O'Hare; directed by Tony Collingwood. Turner Network Television, 1995.
Produced by Hanna-Barbera Cartoons; voices: Tim Curry *et al.*
Animated feature produced for TNT-TV broadcast February 5, 1995; reissued as a videocassette (some cassettes show publication date "1994"), 25 min.
Also issued jointly on videocassette with *The Butter Battle Book* and *In Search of Dr. Seuss.*

Created originally in the 1960s for television production as a liveaction film, with the intention of also publishing a cartoon magazine version, but eventually produced posthumously as this animated feature based on Dr. Seuss's preliminary sketches and subsequently adapted in book form [*see* 63.0]. The book was released late in 1994, prior to the animated feature's premier.

D7.0 *Design for Death* / executive producer: Sid Rogell; screenplay by Theodor S. Geisel and Helen Palmer Geisel; produced by Theron Wrath and Richard O. Fleischer. Hollywood, Calif.: RKO, 1947.
Narrators: Kent Smith and Hans Conried.
35 mm b/w; 48 min.

Live-action; without animation. This feature, about the rise of war lords in Japan, won the 1947 Academy Award for the best feature-length documentary. The Geisels developed the script based on work that he had done in producing the film *Our Job in Japan* for the U.S. Army [*see* D38.0]. A copy survives at the Library of Congress Motion Picture, Broadcasting, and Recorded Sound Division; the script ("as *finally* recorded; May 23, 1947"), in typescript, is held in the Dr. Seuss Collection, Mandeville Special Collections Library, UCSD.

D8.0 *Did I Ever Tell You How Lucky You Are? Scrambled Eggs Super!* / produced by Tish Rabe; designed and directed by Ray Messecar. New York: Random House Home Video, 1993.
Produced by Green Light Media; voices: John Cleese and Brett Ambler.

Included in: *The Cat in the Hat and Other Dr. Seuss Favorites* [*see* E8.03].
Videocassette, 30 min.

D8.1 *Did I Ever Tell You How Lucky You Are? Scrambled Eggs Super!* / pro-
duced by Tish Rabe; directed by Ray Messecar. [Australia]: Golden
Press Video, 1995.
Produced by Green Light Media; voices: John Cleese and Brett
Ambler.
Videocassette, 30 min.
A reissue of D8.0.

D9.0 **Dr. Seuss Beginner Book Video** / produced and directed by Ken
Hoin. New York: Random House Home Video, 1994.
Includes: *Green Eggs and Ham*; *The Cat in the Hat*; *One Fish, Two Fish,
Red Fish, Blue Fish*; *Oh, the Thinks You Can Think!*; *The Foot Book*.
Produced by Praxis Media; voice: Lennie Stea.
Videocassette, 40 min.
Green Eggs and Ham and *The Cat in the Hat* also issued together sepa-
rately.

A Dr. Seuss Christmas [see: D28.0. *Horton Hears a Who!*]

D10.0 **Dr. Seuss Explores the Museum That Ought to Be.** In *Omnibus*
(IV/vol. 22) / TV-Radio Workshop of the Ford Foundation; produced by Robert Saudek. CBS Television Network, 1956.
Videoreel, 30 min.
The first of three *Omnibus* segments that aired on March 11, written
by and featuring Dr. Seuss, and hosted by Alistair Cooke. The program
intended to promote the concept of science museums.

A Dr. Seuss Film Festival [see: D28.0. *Horton Hears a Who!*]

Dr. Seuss' Halloween Is Grinch Night [see: D23.0. *Halloween Is Grinch Night*]

Dr. Seuss' How the Grinch Stole Christmas [see: D29.0. *How the Grinch
Stole Christmas*]

D11.0 **Dr. Seuss On the Loose** / made by DePatie-Freleng Enterprises;
produced by CBS Television Network; teleplay/lyrics by Dr. Seuss;
produced by Friz Freleng and Ted Geisel; directed by Hawley Pratt;
executive producer: David H. DePatie. CBS-TV, 1974.
Voices: Hans Conried, Bob Holt, Allan Sherman, and Paul Winchell.
Animated freature produced for CBS-TV broadcast on October 15, 1973;
reissued in 16mm and videocassette, 25 min.

Issued subsequently with a study guide.

Also reissued jointly on videocassette with *The Cat in the Hat* in 1985.

Subsequently issued under the title: *Green Eggs and Ham and Other Stories.*

An animated trilogy, with the Cat in the Hat as narrator, based on the stories *The Sneetches, The Zax* and *Green Eggs and Ham.*

D11.1 [Dr. Seuss On the Loose: Green Eggs and Ham]
Green Eggs and Ham. Brunswick, N.J.: BFA Educational Media, 1974.
Edited from the motion picture *Dr. Seuss On the Loose* [1974].
9 min.

D11.2 [Dr. Seuss On the Loose: The Sneetches]
The Sneetches. Brunswick, N.J.: BFA Educational Media, 1974.
Edited from the motion picture *Dr. Seuss On the Loose* [1974].
13 min.

D11.3 [Dr. Seuss On the Loose: The Zax]
The Zax. Brunswick, N.J.: BFA Educational Media, 1974.
Edited from the motion picture *Dr. Seuss On the Loose* [1974].
5 min.

Dr. Seuss' Pontoffel Pock & His Magic Piano [see: D39.0. *Pontoffel Pock, Where Are You?*]

D12.0 *Dr. Seuss Reading Games* [interactive multimedia]. Fremont, Calif.: Creative Wonders, 1999.
Interactive computer disc comprising *The Cat in the Hat* and *Dr. Seuss's ABC.*
CD-ROM.

Dr. Seuss' The Butter Battle Book [see: D3.0. *The Butter Battle Book*]

Dr. Seuss' The Cat in the Hat [see: D4. *The Cat in the Hat*]

Dr. Seuss' The Grinch Grinches the Cat in the Hat [see: D22.0. *The Grinch Grinches the Cat in the Hat*]

Dr. Seuss' The Hoober-Bloob Highway [see: D25.0. *The Hoober-Bloob Highway*]

Dr. Seuss' The Lorax [see: D33.0. *The Lorax*]

Dr. Seuss Video Festival [see: D28.0. *Horton Hears a Who!*]

D13.0 *Dr. Seuss's ABC* / produced by Praxis Media. New York: Random House Home Video, 1989.

Also includes: *I Can Read with My Eyes Shut!* and *Mr. Brown Can Moo! Can You?*
Videocassette, 30 min.

D13.1 *Dr. Seuss's ABC* [interactive multimedia]. Novato, Calif.: Living Books, 1995.
Interactive computer disc, issued with a copy of the book. Designed by Brøderbund Software, Inc.
CD-ROM.

D14.0 *Dr. Seuss's Caldecotts.* Westminster, Md.: Random House Video, 1985.
Adaptations of three Caldecott Honor books: *McElligot's Pool, Bartholomew and the Oobleck,* and *If I Ran the Zoo.*
Videocassette, 56 min.

D14.1 [Dr. Seuss's Caldecotts: Bartholomew and the Oobleck]
Bartholomew and the Oobleck. Westminster, Md.: Random House Video, 1986.
Edited from *Dr. Seuss's Caldecotts* [1985].
26 min.

D14.2 [Dr. Seuss's Caldecotts: If I Ran the Zoo.]
If I Ran the Zoo. Westminster, Md.: Random House Video, 1986.
Edited from *Dr. Seuss's Caldecotts* [1985].
12 min.

D14.3 [Dr. Seuss's Caldecotts: McElligot's Pool.]
McElligot's Pool. Westminster, Md.: Random House Video, 1986.
Edited from *Dr. Seuss's Caldecotts* [1985].
12 min.

Dr. Seuss's Gertrude McFuzz [see: D20.0. *Gertrude McFuzz*]

D15.0 *Dr. Seuss's Green Eggs and Ham for Soprano, Boy Soprano, and Piano* / text by Theodor Geisel (Dr. Seuss); music by Robert Kapilow. New York: G. Schirmer; Milwaukee: Distr. by Hal Leonard, 1995, c1993.
Musical score; 35 pp.; arrangements also exist in versions for chamber ensemble and full orchestra (N.Y.: Schirmer, 1995 and 1998 respectively).
Recorded performance: Port Washington, N. Y.: Koch International, 1995.

D16.0 *Dr. Seuss's My Many Colored Days* / narrated by Holly Hunter; featuring the Minnesota Orchestra; music by Richard Einhorn; con-

ducted by Eiji Oue. Minneapolis, Minn.: Minnesota Orchestral Visual Entertainment, 1999.
Videocassette; 45 min.
A story concert with 3-D animation.

Dr. Seuss's Pontoffel Pock, Where Are You? [see: D39.0. *Pontoffel Pock, Where Are You?*]

D17.0 *Dr. Seuss's Sleep Book, Plus Hunches in Bunches* / produced by Tish Rabe; directed by Ray Messecar. New York: Random House Home Video, 1993.
Produced by Green Light Media; narrated by Madeline Kahn.
Videocassette, 30 min.

D17.1 *Dr. Seuss's Sleep Book, Plus Hunches in Bunches* / produced by Tish Rabe; directed by Ray Messecar. [Australia]: Golden Press Video, 1995.
Produced by Green Light Media; narrated by Madeline Kahn.
Videocassette, 30 min.
A reissue of D17.0.

Dr. Seuss's The 5,000 Fingers of Dr. T [see: D2.0. *The 5,000 Fingers of Dr. T*]

Excursion, No. 19 [see: D36.0. *Modern Art on Horseback*]

The Foot Book [see: D9.0. *Dr. Seuss Beginner Book Video*; D37.0. *One Fish, Two Fish, Red Fish, Blue Fish* ...]

D18.0 *Four by Seuss.* Westminster, Md.: Random House Video, 1985.
Each story originally issued separately as filmstrips.
Includes: *Thidwick, the Big-Hearted Moose*; *Yertle the Turtle*; *The Big Brag*; *Gertrude McFuzz.*
Videocassette, 46 min.

Fox in Socks [see: D5.0. *The Cat in the Hat Comes Back! Plus,* ...]

D19.0 *Gerald McBoing Boing* / story by Theodor Geisel; musical score by Gail Kubik; produced by Stephen Bosustow; directed by Robert Cannon. Los Angeles: Churchill Films; Columbia Pictures, 1950.
"Jolly Frolics" series.
Produced by United Productions of America; voice: Marvin Miller.
Animated feature, subsequently issued with a study guide.
Score and story subsequently adapted and issued as a sound recording, with text [*see* D19.1–3; E19.0–2], and as an illustrated book.

Subsequently reissued in various formats both separately and with other adaptations featuring the same character, including: *Gerald McBoing Boing* [videorecording] / United Productions of America; Columbia Pictures, Inc. Burbank, Calif.: Columbia Pictures Home Entertainment, 1980 [4 shorts, 29 min.].
16 mm (reissued in Super 8mm and as a videorecording), 7–15 min.

    Geisel created the character, who speaks only in sound effects, with a sound recording in mind, but he was not intimately involved in the production or animation of this movie cartoon, which earned its producers the Academy Award for Short Subjects in 1951. Stills promoting the film appeared in *LIFE* magazine [*see* C109], and a book adaptation of the original film was published in 1952 [*Gerald McBoing Boing* (based on United Productions of America's Academy Award-winning motion picture) / pictures adapted by Mel Crawford. New York: Simon & Schuster, 1952 — republished by Random House, 2000, and as a "sound book," 2003]. U.P.A. adapted the character for several other cartoon shorts during the 1950s: *Gerald McBoing Boing's Symphony* [1953]; *How Now, Gerald McBoing Boing* [1954]; *Gerald McBoing Boing on the Planet Moo* [1956]. Subsequently, from December, 1956, through October, 1958, an animated variety show entitled *The Gerald McBoing Boing Show* aired Sunday evenings on CBS-TV. In addition, Dell Comics published a series of comic books entitled *Gerald McBoing Boing and the Near-Sighted Mr. Magoo* during 1952–1953. Geisel was not involved in the production of any of these adaptations or sequels.

D19.1 *Gerald McBoing Boing: A Children's Tale Based on the Columbia Pictures Release "Gerald McBoing Boing" for Narrator and Chamber Orchestra* / Gail Kubik; [words by] Dr. Seuss; [with additional lyrics by Gail Kubik]. New York: Southern Music Pub., 1952.
Performable also with narrator, piano, and percussion solo.
Musical score (86 p.).

D19.2 *Gerald McBoing Boing and Other Heroes*. Hollywood, Calif.: Delos International, 1990.
Includes *Gerald McBoing Boing* / music by Gail Kubik; text by Dr. Seuss (with additional lyrics by the composer).
Narrator: Werner Klemperer; musical accompaniment by Xtet, Adam Stern, conductor.
Audio CD ["DE-6001"], 12 min. [*see also* E19.1]
    Issued with accompanying text. The performance was recorded March 31 and April 1, 1990, at Faith Lutheran Church, Tujunga, California.

D19.3 *Peter and the Wolf* [including: *Gerald McBoing Boing* / Gail Kubik]. Ocean, N.J.: MusicMasters, 1991.
Comprises three stories narrated by different performers, including: *Gerald McBoing Boing* / music by Gail Kubik; text by Dr. Seuss; narrated by Carol Channing; musical accompaniment by the Little Orchestra Society, Dino Anagnost, conductor.
Audio CD, 13:43 min. [*see also* E19.2]
Issued with accompanying text.

D20.0 *Gertrude McFuzz* [vocal score] / text by Theodor Geisel (Dr. Seuss); music by Robert Kapilow. New York: G. Schirmer; Milwaukee: Distr. by Hal Leonard, 2000, c1996.
Vocal score (33 p.) For soprano, girl soprano and orchestra (piano reduction).
The original chamber version of this work was commissioned by the BankBoston Celebrity Series and the 92nd Street Y.

Gertrude McFuzz [see also: D18.0. *Four by Seuss*; D42.0. *Yertle the Turtle and Other Stories*]

Great Day for Up! [see: D30.0. *I Am NOT Going to Get Up Today!*]

D21.0 *Green Eggs and Ham* [interactive multimedia] / by Dr. Seuss. San Francisco: Living Books, 1996.
Interactive computer disc, designed by Brøderbund Software, Inc.; issued with a copy of the book.
CD-ROM.

Green Eggs and Ham [see also: D9.0. *Dr. Seuss Beginner Book Video*; D11.0. *Dr. Seuss on the Loose*; D15.0. *Dr. Seuss's Green Eggs and Ham for Soprano* ...]

The Grinch Big Note Christmas Collection [see: D29.2. *How the Grinch Stole Christmas*]

D22.0 *The Grinch Grinches the Cat in the Hat* / written by Dr. Seuss; produced by Ted Geisel, Audrey S. Geisel and Friz Freleng; directed by Bill Perez; teleplay and lyrics by Ted Geisel; music by Joe Raposo. ABC-TV, 1982.
Produced by Marvel Productions in association with DePatie-Freleng; voices: Mason Adams, Bob Holt, Frank Welker, Joe Eich, Marilyn Jackson, Melissa Mackay, and Richard B. Williams.
Produced as an animated feature for ABC-TV broadcast on May 20, 1982; reissued in 16 mm and as a videorecording, 25 min.

Also issued together with *Pontoffel Pock, Where Are You?* [videocassette, 49 min.].

Subsequently issued under the title: *The Cat in the Hat Gets Grinched.*

This production received the Emmy Award, Best Children's Special, in 1982. Work on the project began in 1979, and preliminary working titles included "The Cat in the Hat Meets the Grinch," "The Grinch Takes on the Cat in the Hat" and "The Grinch Schplotzes the Cat-in-the-Hat."

Grinch Night [see: D23.0. *Halloween Is Grinch Night*]

D23.0 *Halloween Is Grinch Night* / by Dr. Seuss; directed by Gerard Baldwin; produced by Ted Geisel and Audrey S. Geisel; executive producers: David H. DePatie and Friz Freleng; music by Joe Raposo. ABC-TV, 1977.

A DePatie-Freleng Production; voices: Hans Conried, Hal Smith, Irene Tedrow, and Gary Shapiro.

Produced as an animated feature for ABC-TV broadcast on October 29, 1977; reissued as a videorecording, 25 min.

Subsequently issued as: *Grinch Night* and *It's Grinch Night.*

This production, which drew heavily from several of Dr. Seuss's works but mainly from the story "What Was I Scared Of?" [*see* 21.0], received the Emmy Award, Best Children's Special, in 1977.

D24.0 *Hitler Lives* / written and produced by Theodor Geisel; directed by Frank Capra. Hollywood, Calif.: Warner Brothers, 1946.
Motion picture short; 18 min.

Live-action, without animation. An earlier version of this work, entitled *Your Job in Germany* [*see* D43.0], was part of the U.S. Army's *Why We Fight* film series, for which Geisel wrote the screenplay in 1944 to convey the U.S. Army's non-fraternization policy to occupation forces in Germany. That original version was directed by Frank Capra and narrated by John Beal as "Army Orientation Film #8"; the original notes and most of the preliminary screenplay drafts were burned because the project was classified "Secret"; the final recording typescript and one preliminary draft survive in the Dr. Seuss Collection, Mandeville Special Collections Library, UCSD, and a copy of the film is held by the National Archives. In 1946, Warner Brothers gained possession of the film from the U.S. Army, eliminated Beal's narration, added a short epilogue, and changed the title to *Hitler Lives.* The Warner Brothers production was awarded an Academy Award as the best documentary short in 1946.

D25.0 *The Hoober-Bloob Highway* / a CBS Television Network production in association with DFE Films; teleplay and lyrics by Dr. Seuss;

directed by Alan Zaslove; produced by Friz Freleng and Ted Geisel; music by Dean Elliott. CBS-TV, 1975, c1974.

Produced by DePatie-Freleng; voices: Bob Holt, Hal Smith.

Originally produced as an animated motion picture for CBS-TV broadcast on February 19, 1975; subsequently released in 16mm and videocassette; 24 min.

Issued subsequently with a study guide.

Also issued on videocassette together with *The Lorax*.

Dr. Seuss had become increasingly frustrated by the process of adapting books to motion pictures, and so he wrote this story specifically for film. The first draft of this work, entitled "The Dispatcher on High," reveals Dr. Seuss's initial plan for the project: "A Live-Action Ballet-Rock Opera utilizing Dr. Seuss Design with minor animation." Many of the creatures featured here are adapted from those that appear in *If I Ran the Zoo* [*see* 9.0].

D26.0 *Hop on Pop. Plus 2 More Dr. Seuss Classics* / written and illustrated by Dr. Seuss; produced and directed by Ken Hoin. New York: Random House Home Video, 1989.

Produced by Praxis Media, Inc.

Includes: *Marvin K. Mooney, Will You Please Go Now!* and *Oh Say Can You Say?*

Videocassette, 30 min.

D27.0 *Horton Hatches the Egg* / produced by Leon Schlesinger; story by Dr. Seuss; adaptation by Michael Maltese; animation by Robert McKimson. Hollywood, Calif.: Warner Bros., 1942.

Merrie Melody No. 15, in Technicolor.

Motion picture cartoon short; 7 min.

D27.1 *Horton Hatches the Egg. Plus, If I Ran the Circus* / produced by Tish Rabe; directed by Raymond Messecar. New York: Random House Home Video, 1992.

Produced by Green Light Media; voices: Billy Crystal [*Horton* ...]; Brett Ambler [*If* ...].

Videocassette, 30 min.

D27.2 *Horton Hatches the Egg. Plus, If I Ran the Circus* / produced by Tish Rabe; directed by Raymond Messecar. [Australia]: Golden Press Video, 1995.

Produced by Green Light Media; voices: Billy Crystal [*Horton* ...]; Brett Ambler [*If* ...].

Videocassette, 30 min.

A reissue of D27.1.

D28.0 *Horton Hears a Who!* / produced by Chuck Jones and Theodor Geisel; directed by Chuck Jones; music composed by Eugene Poddany. Culver City, Calif.: Metro-Goldwyn-Mayer, 1970.

Voices: Hans Conried, June Foray and Chuck Jones.

Originally released as an animated motion picture; subsequently broadcast on CBS-TV and issued as a videorecording; 26 min.

Also issued on videocassette together with *How the Grinch Stole Christmas* under various titles: *A Dr. Seuss Christmas*; *Dr. Seuss Film Festival*; *Dr. Seuss Video Festival* [videocassette, 48 min.].

Television premier on March 19, 1970. "Doc" was changed to "The Doctor" to avoid confusion with Disney characters.

D28.1 *Horton Hears a Who! Plus, Thidwick, the Big-Hearted Moose* / produced by Tish Rabe; directed by Ray Messecar. New York: Random House Video, 1992.

Produced by Green Light Media; voices: Dustin Hoffman [*Horton* ...]; Merwyn Goldstein, Ron Marshall, Larry Robinson [*Thidwick* ...]. Videocassette, 30 min.

D28.2 *Horton Hears a Who! Plus, Thidwick, the Big-Hearted Moose* / produced by Tish Rabe; directed by Ray Messecar. [Australia]: Golden Press Video, 1995.

Produced by Green Light Media; voices: Dustin Hoffman [*Horton* ...]; Merwyn Goldstein, Ron Marshall, Larry Robinson [*Thidwick* ...]. Videocassette, 30 min.

A reissue of D28.1.

D29.0 *How the Grinch Stole Christmas* [Animated feature] / produced by Chuck Jones and Theodor Geisel; directed by Chuck Jones; music composed by Eugene Poddany. Metro-Goldwyn-Mayer, 1966.

Voices: Boris Karloff, Thurl Ravenscroft and June Foray.

Originally released as an animated feature for broadcast on CBS-TV on December 18, 1966; issued subsequently as a videorecording (22 min.) and in DVD format (in multiple languages and with added features).

Also issued together with *Horton Hears a Who!* under two separate titles: *A Dr. Seuss Christmas;* and *Dr. Seuss Film Festival* [videocassette, 48 min.].

The sound track was also issued separately as a sound recording [*see* E28.0].

This project represents both Dr. Seuss's first book adaptation as a motion picture and the last recording that Boris Karloff made. Geisel had been reluctant to have any of his "better-known" books adapted for television but was persuaded to make the attempt with this work.

D29.a [Dr. Seuss' How the Grinch Stole Christmas [Animated feature] [Spanish].

Cómo el Odio se robó la Navidad = How the Grinch Stole Christmas /
producida por Chuck Jones y Thoedore (Dr. Seuss) Geisel. Mexico
City: Warner Home Video Mexico, 2000.

D29.1 How the Grinch Stole Christmas [Musical score]
You're a Mean One, Mr. Grinch / lyrics by Dr. Seuss; music by Albert
Hague. Miami, Fla.: Columbia Pictures Publications, 1966.
Musical score (3 p.) for the feature song.

D29.2 How the Grinch Stole Christmas [Musical score]
The Grinch Big Note Christmas Collection / arranged by Pamela Schultz.
Miami, Fla.: Columbia Pictures Publications, 1985.
Musical score (11 p.) for: "Trim Up the Tree," "Welcome Christmas"
and "You're a Mean One, Mr. Grinch."

D29.3 *How the Grinch Stole Christmas! Plus, If I Ran the Zoo* / produced
by Tish Rabe; directed by Ray Messecar. New York: Random House
Home Video, 1992.
Produced by Green Light Media; voices: Walter Matthau [*How the
Grinch* ...]; Brent Ambler [*If* ...].
Included in: *The Cat in the Hat and Other Dr. Seuss Favorites* [*see*
E8.03].
Videocassette, 30 min.

D29.4 *Dr. Seuss' How the Grinch Stole Christmas! November 17, 1994–January 3, 1995* [Theatre program] / book [*i.e.*, stage adaptation] and
lyrics by Timothy Mason; music by Mel Marvin. [Minneapolis,
Minn.]: The Children's Theatre Company, [1994].
"Based on the Book *How the Grinch Stole Christmas* by Dr. Seuss."
Theatre program ([10] p.) for the performance of an unpublished
musical stage adaptation. The performance featured Paul Boesing
in the role of the Grinch. This work and *The 500 Hats of Bartholomew Cubbins* [*see* D1.1] have been the only two Dr. Seuss books
adapted for the stage (although Dr. Seuss was working on a theatrical adaptation of *The Seven Lady Godivas* at the time of his death).

D29.5 *Dr. Seuss' How the Grinch Stole Christmas! November 15 [1998]–January 3 [1999]* [at the Old Globe Theatre] [Theatre program] / book
[*i.e.*, stage adaptation] and lyrics by Timothy Mason; music by Mel
Marvin; directed by Jack O'Brien. In *Performing Arts*, Southern California Edition, 32/11 (November 1998): P1-P24.
"Originally commissioned by Minneapolis Children's Theater, Minneapolis, Minnesota."

Theatre program [24 p.] issued as a special section of the magazine *Performing Arts*. The play is essentially the same adaptation as D29.4, above, but with different sets (by John Lee Beatty) and costumes (by Robert Morgan). The production, which premiered with Guy Paul in the role of the Grinch, is intended for a seasonal ten-year run at the Old Globe Theatre, San Diego, Calif.

D29.51   *The Grinch Gala! Saturday, November 21st, 1998, Old Globe Theatre, Who-ville Pavilion, Balboa Park* [Keepsake program] / Old Globe Theatre; Lisa Barket ... [*et al.*], co-chairs. San Diego, Calif.: Old Globe Theatre, 1998.

Gala program keepsake [42 p.] celebrating the West Coast premier of *How the Grinch Stole Christmas!* [*see* D29.5]; chiefly advertisements.

D29.6   *Dr. Seuss' How the Grinch Stole Christmas* [Motion picture, 2000] / Universal Pictures and Imagine Entertainment; a Brian Grazer Production; a Ron Howard film; produced by Brian Grazer and Ron Howard; directed by Ron Howard; screenplay by Jeffrey Price and Peter S. Seaman; music, James Horner. Universal City, Calif.: Universal, 2000.

Narrator: Anthony Hopkins; featuring Jim Carrey, Taylor Momsen *et al.*

Videocassette and DVD; 105 min.

Released fall of 2000. Issued variously in videocassette and DVD, sometimes with a copy of the book; sound track also issued separately [*see* E28.01]; adapted to book format (in several states with varying titles) as: *Grinch & Bear It!: Life According to the Supreme Green Meanie!* / based on the motion picture screenplay by Jeffrey Price & Peter S. Seaman [dialog lines from the motion picture] (N.Y.: Random House, 2000); *Dr. Seuss's How the Grinch Stole Christmas! Movie Storybook* / adapted by Louise Gikow (N.Y.: Random House, 2000) [and, London: HaperCollins, 2000; and, translated into French as *Le Grinch* (Paris: Pocket jeunesse, 2000); and, translated into German as *Der Grinch* (Nuremberg: BSV, 2000)]; and further adapted as: *Dr. Seuss' How the Grinch Stole Christmas!* / taken from the junior novelization adapted by Louise Gikow; adapted by Coleen Degnan-Veness (Harlow: Penguin, 2001); and as: *Who's Who in Whoville?* / illustrated by Robert Roper (London: HarperCollinsEntertainment, 2000).

D29.6a   [Dr. Seuss' How the Grinch Stole Christmas [Motion picture, 2000] [Spanish]].

Cómo el Grinch se robó la Navidad de Dr. Seuss. Universal City, Calif.: Universal, 2001.

Hunches in Bunches [see: D17.0. *Dr. Seuss's Sleep Book, Plus Hunches in Bunches*]

D30.0 *I Am NOT Going to Get Up Today! The Shape of Me and Other Stuff. Great Day for Up! In a People House* / produced and directed by Raymond Messecar. New York: Random House Home Video, 1991.
Produced by Praxis Media, Inc.; voices: Lorna List, Ron Marshall, Brendon Perry, Sascha Radetsky, Jim Thurman, and Mervina Goldsmith.
Videocassette, 25 min.

I Can Read with My Eyes Shut! [see: D13.0. *Dr. Seuss's ABC*]

D31.0 *If I Ran the Zoo* / produced by Paratore Pictures, Ltd. New York: Random House Video, 1985.
Previously produced as a film strip; also issued in the "Dr. Seuss's Caldecotts" series of the Caldecott Video Collection [*see* D14.0. *Dr. Seuss's Caldecotts*]. Voices: Skip Hinnant *et al.*
Videocassette, 18 min.

D31.1 *If I Ran the Zoo* / produced by Green Light Media. New York: Random House Home Video, 1992.
Issued with *How the Grinch Stole Christmas!* [*see* D29.3]

In a People House [see: D30.0. *I Am NOT Going to Get Up Today!*]

D32.0 *In Search of Dr. Seuss* / Turner Pictures; directed by Vincent Paterson; produced by Joni Levin; written by Keith R. Clarke. Turner Network Television, 1994.
A Joni Levin/Point Blank production; featuring Kathy Najimy and Matt Frewer.
Motion picture produced for Turner Network-TV broadcast on November 6, 1994; reissued as a videorecording, 90 min.
Also issued with *The Butter Battle Book* and *Daisy-Head Mayzie* [videorecording, 137 min.].
Produced posthumously and without any pre-production collaboration with Geisel, this television feature mixes biography, samplings of animated adaptations, as well as musical productions to reveal the life and works of Dr. Seuss.

It's Grinch Night! [see: D23.0. *Halloween Is Grinch Night*]

Know Your Enemy — Japan [see: D38.0. *"Our Job in Japan"*]

Know Your Job in Germany [see: D43.0. *Your Job in Germany*]

El libro de patas y pies [see: D37.a. One Fish, Two Fish ... [Spanish]]

D33.0 *The Lorax* / a CBS Television Network production in association
with DFE Films; teleplay and lyrics by Dr. Seuss; directed by Haw-
ley Pratt; produced by Friz Freleng and Ted Geisel; music by Dean
Elliott. CBS-TV, 1972.
Produced by DePatie-Freleng; voices: Eddie Albert, Bob Holt, Athena
Lorde, and Harlen Carraher.
Originally produced as an animated feature for CBS-TV broadcast on
February 14, 1972; subsequently released in 16mm and in videocassette; 25
min.
Also issued together with *The Hoober-Bloob Highway* in videocassette, 51
min.
Issued subsequently with a study guide.
This production received the Critics Award at the International Ani-
mated Cartoon Festival, Zagreb, 1972.

D34.0 *Marco Takes a Walk: Variations for Orchestra Op. 25* / composed
by Deems Taylor. [Unpublished score, 1942].
Described by the composer in: *The Philharmonic Symphony Society of New
York* [Program]: *Carnegie Hall, Sunday Afternoon, November 15,* [1942] *at 3:00.*
[New York: The Society, 1942]. Pp. [3]–[4].
These musical variations were inspired by *And to Think That I Saw
It on Mulberry Street* [*see* 1.0] and were originally composed to accompany
Sterling Holloway's reading of the story on *The Family Hour* (CBS Radio,
November 30, 1941) [*cf.* E2.0].

Marvin K. Mooney, Will You Please Go Now! [see: D26.0. *Hop on Pop,
Plus* ...]

Maybe You Should Fly a Jet! Maybe You Should be a Vet! [see: D4.2. *The
Cat in the Hat* ...]

D35.0 *McElligot's Pool* / produced and designed by Marian Stanley. New
York: Random House, 1985.
A Miller-Brody production; also issued in the "Dr. Seuss's Caldecotts"
series of the Caldecott Video Collection [see: D14.0. *Dr. Seuss's Caldecotts*].
A film, subsequently released in videocassette, 12 min.

D36.0 *Modern Art on Horseback.* In *Excursion,* No. 19/ TV-Radio Workshop of the Ford Foundation; directed by Daniel Petrie; written and
demonstrated by Dr. Seuss. New York: NBC-TV, 1954.

Broadcast January 31, 1954.

The program attempted to explain contemporary art to teenagers. Featured are Hans Conried, Dorothy Donahue, with Burgess Meredith as "the guide"; Cooper Union Art School students also participated in the production. A copy of the script (2nd version) and photographs of the production were published in: *The Cooper Union Art School Publication*, 1 ([1954]) [*see* F40].

Mr. Brown Can Moo! Can You? [see: D14.0. *Dr. Seuss's ABC*]

My Many Colored Days [see: D16.0. *Dr. Seuss's My Many Colored Days*]

Oh! las ideas que puedes idear! [see: D37.a. One Fish, Two Fish ... [Spanish]]

Oh Say Can You Say? [see: D26.0. *Hop on Pop, Plus ...*]

Oh, the Thinks You Can Think! [see: D9.0. *Dr. Seuss Beginner Book Video*; D37.0. *One Fish, Two Fish, Red Fish Blue Fish ...*]

Omnibus [see: D10.0. *Dr. Seuss Explores the Museum That Ought to Be*]

D37.0 ***One Fish, Two Fish, Red Fish, Blue Fish. Plus, Oh, the Thinks You Can Think! and The Foot Book*** / directed and produced by Ken Hoin. New York: Random House Home Video, 1989.
Produced by Praxis Media, Inc.; voices: Lynn Blair *et al.*
Videocassette, 30 min.

D37.1 *One Fish, Two Fish, Red Fish, Blue Fish* [see: D9.0. *Dr. Seuss Beginner Book Video*]

D37.a One Fish, Two Fish, Red Fish, Blue Fish [Spanish]
Un pez dos peces pez rojo pez azul. New York: Random House Video, 1994.
Includes: *Oh! las ideas que puedes idear!* and *El libro de patas y pies*.

D38.0 ***"Our Job in Japan"*** / [produced and directed by Theodor Geisel; script by Carl Foreman and Theodor Geisel; music by Dmitri Tiomkin]. [Washington, D.C.]: Signal Corps and Information and Education Division, U.S. Army, 1945.
"Army Orientation Film #15 [O.F.-15]."
16 mm b/w, 22 min.; subsequently converted for distribution on videocassette [Capitol Heights, Md.: National Audiovisual Center, 1982], 18 min.
Subsequently issued on videocassette jointly with *Your Job in Germany* [Chicago, Ill.: International Historic Films, 1984].

Live-action, without animation; also entitled *Know Your Enemy — Japan*. The film was prepared for release without credits and suppressed by Gen. Douglas MacArthur, who deemed it too sympathetic toward the Japanese people. A copy of the film is held by the National Archives. Geisel's work on this film formed the basis for *Design for Death* [*see* D7.0].

Pontoffel Pock & His Magic Piano [see: D39.0. *Pontoffel Pock, Where Are You?*]

D39.0 *Pontoffel Pock, Where Are You?* / produced by Ted Geisel and Audrey S. Geisel; executive producers: David H. DePatie and Friz Freleng; directed by Gerard Baldwin; teleplay and lyrics by Ted Geisel; music by Joe Raposo. ABC-TV, [1980], c1979.

A DePatie-Freleng production; voices: Ken Lundie, Joe Raposo, Wayne Morton, Hal Smith, Sue Allen, and Don Messick.

Animated feature originally produced for broadcast on ABC-TV on May 2, 1980; reissued as a videorecording, 25 min.

Also issued together with *The Grinch Grinches the Cat in the Hat* [videocassette, 49 min.].

Subsequently issued in videocassette under the title: *Pontoffel Pock & His Magic Piano*.

Written directly for animation; a preliminary title for this work was "The Peculiar Piano of Pontoffel Pock."

D40.0 *Private S.N.A.F.U.* / A Signal Corps production [written by Ted Geisel and Phil Eastman; directed by Chuck Jones, Friz Freleng *et al.*]. Washington, D.C.: U.S. War Dept. [Hollywood, Calif.: Warner Bros.], 1943–1944.

Animated cartoon shorts produced for *Army-Navy Screen Magazine*; voices by Mel Blanc.

16mm b/w.

Subsequently reissued on videocassette as: *The Complete Uncensored Private Snafu Cartoons from W.W.II* / [Warner Bros.] [[Cudahy, Wis.]: Bosko Video, c1990–1993 (2 VHS videocassettes; 115 min.)]; also reissued on videocassette variously by Bosko, *etc.* under various titles and comprising selected cartoons numbering between 10 and 14 episodes.

"Private S.N.A.F.U. [Situation Normal All Fouled Up]" was a cartoon character who personified the average serviceman's gripes and concerns, created for U.S. Army training film shorts during World War II. Twenty-eight episodes, which appeared in *Army-Navy Screen Magazine*, were produced: 1. *Coming! Snafu!*; 2. *Gripes*; 3. *Spies*; 4. *The Goldbrick*; 5. *The Infantry Blues*; 6. *Fighting Tools*; 7. *The Home Front*; 8. *Rumors*; 9. *Booby*

Traps; 10. *Snafuperman*; 11. *Snafu vs. Malaria Mike*; 12. *A Lecture on Camouflage*; 13. *Gas*; 14. *Going Home*; 15. *The Chow Hound*; 16. *Censored*; 17. *Outpost*; 18. *Payday*; 19. *Target Snafu*; 20. *A Few Facts: Inflation*; 21. *Three Brothers*; 22. *In the Aleutians*; 23. *A Few Quick Facts: Fear*; 24. *It's Murder She Says*; 25. *Hot Spot*; 26. *Operation Snafu*; 27. *No Buddy Atoll*; 28. *Private Snafu Presents Seaman Tarfu.*

The character was developed by Frank Capra, Chuck Jones and Art Heineman; Geisel wrote some of the episodes, and his cartooning appears in some of the scenes. Subsequently, the character was adapted by the Navy for a psychotherapy film program designed to treat patients suffering from combat fatigue.

A brief article describing this cartoon series appeared in *Business Screen* (December 30, 1945) [*see* F154]; see also: Eric Costello, "Private SNAFU & Mr. Hook," *ANiMATO!*, 37 (Spring 1997): 44–57 [*see* F42].

Scrambled Eggs Super! [see: D8.0. *Did I Ever Tell You How Lucky You Are? Scrambled Eggs Super!*]

D41.0 Seussical: The Musical / music by Stephen Flaherty; lyrics by Lynn Ahrens. Miami, Fla.: Warner Bros. Publ., 2001.
Vocal score; 103 p.
Vocal score for voice and piano. This project, which draws from characters and elements in most of Dr. Seuss's major books, premiered on Broadway in 2000.

D41.1 Seussical: The Musical [Selections]
Seussical: The Musical / lyrics by Lynn Ahrens; music by Stephen Flaherty. New York: Decca Broadway, 2001.
CD, with lyrics (46 p.) included in case; recorded December 18, 2000.

The Shape of Me and Other Stuff [see: D30.0. *I Am NOT Going to Get Up Today!*]

The Sneetches [see: D11.0. *Dr. Seuss On the Loose*]

There's a Wocket in My Pocket! [see: D5.0. *The Cat in the Hat Comes Back! Plus, ...*]

Thidwick, the Big-Hearted Moose [see: D28.0. *Horton Hears a Who! Plus, Thidwick ...*; D18.0. *Four by Seuss*]

Un pez dos peces pez rojo pez azul [see: D37.a. One Fish, Two Fish ... [Spanish]]

D42.0 *Yertle the Turtle and Other Stories. Plus, Gertrude McFuzz and The Big Brag* / produced by Tish Rabe; designed and directed by Ray Messecar. New York: Random House Video, 1992.
Produced by Green Light Media; voice: John Lithgow.
Videocassette, 30 min.

D42.1 *Yertle the Turtle and Other Stories, Plus, Gertrude McFuzz and The Big Brag* / produced by Tish Rabe; directed by Ray Messecar. [Australia]: Golden Press Video, 1995.
Produced by Green Light Media; voice: John Lithgow.
Videocassette, 30 min.
        A reissue of D42.0.

D42.2 [Yertle the Turtle and Other Stories]
Yertle the Turtle. The Big Brag. Gertrude McFuzz. [see: D18.0. *Four by Seuss*]

You're a Mean One, Mr. Grinch [see: D29.1. How the Grinch Stole Christmas [Musical score]

D43.0 *Your Job in Germany* / produced by Army Pictorial Service for Army Information Branch, Information and Education Division A.S.F.; [screenplay by Theodor Geisel; directed by Frank Capra]. [Washington, D.C.]: United States Office of War Information, 1944.
"Army Orientation Film #8 [O.F.- 8]."
Narrator: John Beal.
Motion picture short, distributed as one of the films in the Special Information Series.
Subsequently revised and released as *Hitler Lives* [*see* D24.0].
16mm b/w; 15 min.; subsequently converted for distribution on videocassette [Capitol Heights, Md.: National Audiovisual Center, 1982].
Subsequently reissued on videocassette jointly with "*Our Job in Japan*" [Chicago, Ill.: International Historic Films, 1984].
        Live-action, without animation; also entitled *Know Your Job in Germany*. For notes about this work and its relation to *Hitler Lives*, see D24.0.

The Zax [see: D11.0. *Dr. Seuss On the Loose*]

Sound Recordings

Commercial sound recordings, chiefly on phonograph records and magnetic tape, and recently also on compact discs, have been issued both separately and as kits that might also include copies of the book, often in paperback, or filmstrip adaptations. Subsequent issues of the same recording are common, as are releases of individual titles subsequent to their original appearance among a collection of titles. Works listed below generally indicate the original recording only. Excluded are the numerous radio productions of works that were broadcast but not published as audio recordings; recordings for the blind; and other non-commercial recordings.

E1.0 ***The 500 Hats of Bartholomew Cubbins*—**[194–?].
First issued as a Bluebird phonograph recording.
Voice: Paul Wing.

   E1.1 *The 500 Hats of Bartholomew Cubbins*— 2000.
     In *Classic Children's Tales* (vol. 2) (N.Y.: Imperial Intl.).

E2.0 ***And to Think That I Saw It on Mulberry Street*—**[194–?].
First issued as a Decca phonograph recording.
Music: Harry Sosnik; voice: Sterling Holloway (first performed as a reading of the story on *The Family Hour* [CBS Radio]) [*cf.* 1.0; D34.0].

   E2.1 *And to Think That I Saw It on Mulberry Street* [see: E22.0. *Happy Birthday to You!*; E11.0. *The Dr. Seuss Audio Collection*]

E3.0 ***Bartholomew and the Oobleck*—**1961.
First issued as an RCA Camden Children's Series phonograph album [CAL1035]; also includes *Yertle the Turtle & Other Stories*; both works subsequently also issued separately.
Included in: *Dr. Seuss Presents Favorite Children's Stories*—1972 [*see* E12.0].
Voice: Marvin Miller.

   E3.1 *Bartholomew and the Oobleck*—1981.

   E3.a Bartholomew and the Oobleck [Hebrew]—1982.
     Gedalyahu veha-mistuk / [songs] by Gary Eckstein, based on the Hebrew translation by Le'ah Na'or.

E4.0 ***Because a Little Bug Went Ka-CHOO!*—**1978.

The Big Brag [see: E54.0. *Yertle the Turtle & Other Stories*].

E5.0 ***Bright and Early Read Along Library*** [set 1]—[1978?].
Includes: *Great Day for Up!*; *Marvin K. Mooney, Will You Please Go Now!*; *There's a Wocket in My Pocket!* and three works by S. and J. Berenstain.
Issued with a discussion guide and copies of the books [*see* B5.0].

E6.0 *Bright and Early Read Along Library*, set 2 —1978.

Includes: *Hooper Humperdink...? Not Him!; The Shape of Me and Other Stuff; Would You Rather Be a Bullfrog?* and three works by S. and J. Berenstain.

Issued with a discussion guide and copies of the books [*see* B5.1].

E7.0 *The Butter Battle Book*—1984.

E8.0 *The Cat in the Hat*—1976.

Issued as a Beginner Books Read-Along Book & Cassette.

Included in: *The Dr. Seuss Read Along Library* [set 1]—1976 [*see* E13.0].

Also issued jointly with *Dr. Seuss's ABC* and *Green Eggs and Ham* in 1987.

E8.1   *The Cat in the Hat*—1981.

Issued by Fisher-Price, with blank space for personalized recording.

E8.2   *The Cat in the Hat*—1995.

Issued by HarperCollins (London) along with a copy of the book.
Voice: Adrian Edmondson.

E8.a   The Cat in the Hat [Hebrew]—1982.

Hatul ta'alul / Hebrew version by Le'ah Goldberg; narrated and sung by Yi'srael Guryon and Miri Aloni.

E8.b   The Cat in the Hat [Spanish]—1993.

Issued with: *El gato ensombrerado* / escrito por Dr. Seuss; traducido por Carlos Rivera. New York: Random House, 1993 [*see* 14.t].

E8.01 *The Cat in the Hat* [Motion picture]— 2003.

Dr. Seuss' The Cat in the Hat. New York: Decca/Universal, 2003.

Sound track; music by David Newman, Marc Shaiman, and Mike Myers; with Smash Mouth.

CD; 49 min.

E8.02 *The Cat in the Hat* [Motion picture]— 2003.

Dr. Seuss' The Cat in the Hat. New York: Imagination, 2003.

Sound recording of the motion picture, narrated by Spencer Breslin.

2 CDs; 1 hr., 53 min.

E8.03 *The Cat in the Hat and Other Dr. Seuss Favorites*— 2003.

New York: Random House Audio, 2003.

Collected works, some as reissues of earlier recordings, also including: *Horton Hears a Who!; How the Grinch Stole Christmas; Did I Ever Tell You How Lucky You Are?; The Lorax; Yertle the Turtle and Other Stories; Thidwick, the Big-Hearted Moose; Horton Hatches the Egg; The Cat in the Hat Comes Back!*

Voices: John Cleese, Billy Crystal Ted Danson, Kelsey Grammer, Dustin Hoffman, John Lithgow, Walter Matthau, and Mercedes McCambridge.

E9.0 *The Cat in the Hat Comes Back!*—1977.
Included in: *The Dr. Seuss Read Along Library* [set 2]—1977 [*see* E14.0].

  E9.1 *The Cat in the Hat Comes Back!*—1995.
  Issued by HarperCollins (London) along with a copy of the book.
  Voice: Adrian Edmondson.

The Cat in the Hat Comes Back!— 2003 [*see* E8.03]

E10.0 *The Cat in the Hat Song Book*—1967.
First issued as an RCA Camden Children's Series phonograph album.
Cassette title: *Dr. Seuss Presents The Cat in the Hat Song Book.*
Also issued jointly with *If I Ran the Zoo* and *Dr. Seuss's Sleep Book* [*see* E36.0].
Score by Eugene Poddany.

E11.0 *The Dr. Seuss Audio Collection*—1969.
Includes: *Happy Birthday to You!*; *The Big Brag*; *Gertrude McFuzz*; *Scrambled Eggs Super!*; *And to Think That I Saw It on Mulberry Street.*
Voice: Hans Conried.

Dr. Seuss Presents The 500 Hats of Bartholomew Cubbins [see: E1.0. *The 500 Hats of Bartholomew Cubbins*]

Dr. Seuss Presents Bartholomew and the Oobleck [see: E3.0. *Bartholomew and the Oobleck*]

Dr. Seuss Presents The Cat in the Hat Song Book [see: E10.0. *The Cat in the Hat Song Book*—1967]

Dr. Seuss Presents Dr. Seuss's Sleep Book [see: E36.0. *If I Ran the Zoo*—1966]

E12.0 *Dr. Seuss Presents Favorite Children's Stories*—1972.
Includes: *Fox in Socks*; *Green Eggs and Ham*; *Horton Hatches the Egg*; *Yertle the Turtle*; *The Sneetches*; *Bartholomew and the Oobleck.*
Voice: Marvin Miller.

Dr. Seuss Presents Fox in Socks ... [see: E18.0. *Fox in Socks*—1965]

Dr. Seuss Presents Green Eggs and Ham ... [see: E25.0. *Horton Hatches the Egg*—1960; E18.0. *Fox in Socks*—1965]

Dr. Seuss Presents Horton Hatches the Egg ... [see: E25.0. *Horton Hatches the Egg*—1960]

Dr. Seuss Presents If I Ran the Zoo ... [see: E36.0. *If I Ran the Zoo*—1966]

Dr. Seuss Presents Sleep Book [see: E36.0. *If I Ran the Zoo*—1966]

Dr. Seuss Presents The Sneetches, and Other Stories. [see: E25.0. *Horton Hatches the Egg*—1960]

Dr. Seuss Presents Yertle the Turtle and Other Stories [see: E3.0. *Bartholomew and the Oobleck*; E54.0. *Yertle the Turtle & Other Stories*]

E13.0 *The Dr. Seuss Read Along Library* [set 1]—1976.
Six cassettes, issued in a folder. Includes: *The Cat in the Hat*; *Fox in Socks*; *Hop on Pop*; *Mr. Brown Can Moo! Can You?*; *The Foot Book*; *There's a Wocket in My Pocket!*
Issued with a discussion guide and copies of the books [*see* B4.0].

E14.0 *The Dr. Seuss Read Along Library*, set 2—1977.
Includes: *Oh, the Thinks You Can Think!*; *The Cat in the Hat Comes Back!*; *Green Eggs and Ham*; *One Fish, Two Fish, Red Fish, Blue Fish*; *Dr. Seuss's ABC*; *Marvin K. Mooney, Will You Please Go Now!*
Issued with a discussion guide and copies of the books [*see* B4.1].

E15.0 *Dr. Seuss's ABC*—1977.
Issued as a Beginner Books Read-Along Book & Cassette.
Included in: *The Dr. Seuss Read Along Library*, set 2—1977 [*see* E14.0].
Also issued along with *The Cat in the Hat* and *Green Eggs and Ham* in 1987.

***Dr. Seuss's ABC*—** 2003 [*see* E21.2]

Dr. Seuss's Sleep Book [see: E36.0. *If I Ran the Zoo*—1966]

E'dal'yahu V'hamistuh [see: E3.a. Bartholomew and the Oobleck [Hebrew]]

E16.0 *The Eye Book*—1974.

E17.0 *The Foot Book*—1974.
Issued as a Bright and Early Read Along Library Book & Cassette.

  E17.1 *The Foot Book*—1976.
    Included in: *The Dr. Seuss Read Along Library* [set 1]—1976 [*see* E13.0].

E18.0 [*Fox in Socks*—1960].
Included, in two versions, in: *Dr. Seuss Presents Horton Hatches the Egg* ...—1960 [*see* E25.0].
Subsequently issued in 1965 in RCA's Camden Children's Series as: *Dr.*

Seuss Presents Fox in Socks; Green Eggs and Ham, which also includes *The Rabbit, the Bear and the Zinniga-Zanniga*; also issued separately.
Included in: *Dr. Seuss Presents Favorite Children's Stories*—1972 [*see* E12.0].
Included in: *The Dr. Seuss Read Along Library* [set 1]—1976 [*see* E13.0].
Issued as a Bright and Early Read Along Library Book & Cassette.
Voice: Marvin Miller.

E18.1 *Fox in Socks*—1995.
Issued by HarperCollins (London) along with a copy of the book.
Voice: Adrian Edmondson.

Fox in Socks— 2003 [*see* E21.2]

E19.0 *Gerald McBoing Boing*—1950.
Originally issued by Capitol Records.
Told by "The Great Gildersleeve" [*i.e.*, Harold Peary]; album jacket illustration by Dr. Seuss.

E19.1 *Gerald McBoing Boing*—1990.
Issued with printed text. Narrator: Werner Klemperer; musical accompaniment by Xtet, Adam Stern, conductor [*see* D19.2].

E19.2 *Peter and the Wolf* [including: *Gerald McBoing Boing*]—1991.
Issued with printed text. Narrator: Carol Channing; musical accompaniment by the Little Orchestra Society, Dino Anagnost, conductor [*see* D19.3].

Gertrude McFuzz [see: E54.0. *Yertle the Turtle & Other Stories*]

E20.0 *Great Day for Up!*—1975.
Issued as a Bright and Early Read-Along Library Book & Cassette.
Included in: *Bright and Early Read Along Library* [set 1]—[1978?] [*see* E5.0].

E21.0 [*Green Eggs and Ham*—1960].
Issued as a Beginner Books Read-Along Book & Cassette and as a Bright and Early Read Along Library Book & Cassette.
Included in: *Dr. Seuss Presents Horton Hatches the Egg ...*—1960 [*see* E25.0].
Included in: *Dr. Seuss Presents Fox in Socks ...*—1965 [*see* E18.0]; also issued separately.
Included in: *Dr. Seuss Presents Favorite Children's Stories*—1972 [*see* E12.0].
Included in: *The Dr. Seuss Read Along Library,* set 2—1977 [*see* E14.0].
Also issued along with *The Cat in the Hat* and *Green Eggs and Ham* in 1987.
Voice: Marvin Miller.

E21.1	*Green Eggs and Ham*—1995.
Issued by HarperCollins (London) along with a copy of the book.
Voice: Adrian Edmondson.

E21.2	*Green Eggs and Ham and Other Servings of Dr. Seuss*—2003.
Issued by Imagination Studio (N.Y.) and Random House Audio (N.Y.);
also includes: *One Fish, Two Fish, Red Fish, Blue Fish*; *Oh, the Thinks
You Can Think!*; *I Am NOT Going to Get Up Today!*; *Oh Say Can You
Say?*; *Fox in Socks*; *I Can Read with My Eyes Shut!*; *Hop on Pop*; *Dr.
Seuss's ABC*.
Voices: Jason Alexander, David Hyde Pierce and Michael McKean.

Green Eggs and Ham— 2003 [*see* E47.0]

**E22.0	Happy Birthday to You!**—1969.
Originally issued by Caedmon Records.
Also includes: *Gertrude McFuzz* and *The Big Brag* (from *Yertle the Turtle
& Other Stories)* [*see* E54.1]; *Scrambled Eggs Super!*; *And to Think That I Saw
It on Mulberry Street*.
Included in: *The Dr. Seuss Audio Collection* [*see* E11.0].
Voice: Hans Conried.

Hatul ta'alul [see: E8.a. The Cat in the Hat [Hebrew]]

**E23.0	Hooper Humperdink ...? Not Him!**—1978.
Included in: *Bright and Early Read Along Library*, set 2 —1978 [*see* E6.1].

**E24.0	Hop on Pop**—1974.
Issued as a Bright and Early Read Along Book & Cassette.
Included in: *The Dr. Seuss Read Along Library* [set 1]—1976 [*see* E13.0].

Hop on Pop— 2003 [*see* E21.2]

**E25.0	Horton Hatches the Egg**—1947.
Originally issued on two MGM phonograph albums.
Reissued in 1960 in RCA's Camden Children's Series with the title: *Dr.
Seuss Presents Horton Hatches the Egg, The Sneetches, and Other Stories*, and
also including: *Fox in Socks* [slow and fast versions]; *Green Eggs and Ham*;
and *The Rabbit, the Bear and the Zinniga-Zanniga*. Subsequently issued separately and in various combinations excluding one or more of the stories
(usually *The Rabbit, the Bear and the Zinniga-Zanniga*) as: *Dr. Seuss Presents
Horton Hatches the Egg* ...; *Dr. Seuss Presents Green Eggs and Ham* ...; *Dr.
Seuss Presents Fox in Socks* ...; *Dr. Seuss Presents The Sneetches, and Other Stories*.

Also included in: *Dr. Seuss Presents Favorite Children's Stories*—1972 [*see* E12.0].

This recording of *Horton Hatches the Egg* was also released with *Ali Baba and the Forty Thieves* (Leo the Lion Records) in 1966; with *Horton Hears a Who!* (Random House) in 1976.
Voice: Marvin Miller.

E25.1 *Horton Hatches the Egg*—1991.
Included in: *The Cat in the Hat and Other Dr. Seuss Favorites* [*see* E8.03].
Voice: Billy Crystal.

E26.0 *Horton Hears a Who!*—1976.
Also issued with *Horton Hatches the Egg*.

E26.1 *Horton Hears a Who!*—1981.

E26.2 *Horton Hears a Who!*—1990.
Included in: *The Cat in the Hat and Other Dr. Seuss Favorites* [*see* E8.03].
Voice: Dustin Hoffman.

***Horton Hears a Who!*—** 2003 [*see* E47.0]

E27.0 *How the Grinch Stole Christmas!*—1975.
Voice: Zero Mostel; side 2 includes a selection of Christmas songs.

E27.*1 How the Grinch Stole Christmas!*—1988.
Voice: Walter Matthau.

E28.0 *How the Grinch Stole Christmas!* [Animated feature]—[1966?]
Distributed by Leo the Lion Records; "The Original TV Sound Track" [*cf.* D29.0].
Voice: Boris Karloff.

E28.1 [*How the Grinch Stole Christmas*] [Animated feature]—1973.
Songs from "How the Grinch Stole Christmas" and Other Children's Christmas Songs / Marty Gold Children's Chorus. New York: RCA/ Camden, 1973.

E28.2 [*How the Grinch Stole Christmas*] [Animated feature]—1985.
Albert Hague Sings Selections from "How the Grinch Stole Christmas" / composed and sung by Albert Hague; with Renée Orin and the Rob Carlson Singers. Providence, R.I.: Sine Qua Non, 1985.

E28.01 *How the Grinch Stole Christmas* [Motion picture] — 2000.
How the Grinch Stole Christmas. Burbank, Calif.: Buena Vista Records, 2000.
Voices: Corey Burton, narrator; Jim Carrey, Taylor Momsen, *et al.*
CD-ROM, issued with audiocassette and copy of the book.

   E28.01.1 [*How the Grinch Stole Christmas*] [Motion picture] — 2000.
   Dr. Seuss' How the Grinch Stole Christmas / score by James Horner.
   Santa Monica, Calif.: Interscope, 2000.
   CD, 77 min.; recording of the motion picture score.

E29.0 *Hunches in Bunches* — 1982.

E30.0 *I Am NOT Going to Get Up Today!* — 1988.

I Am NOT Going to Get up Today! — 2003 [*see* E21.2]

E31.0 *I Can Lick 30 Tigers Today! and Other Stories* — 1982.

E32.0 *I Can Read with My Eyes Shut!* — 1978.

I Can Read with My Eyes Shut! — 2003 [*see* E21.2]

E33.0 *I Had Trouble in Getting to Solla Sollew* — 1982.

E34.0 *I Wish That I Had Duck Feet* — 1975.
Issued as a Beginner Books Read-Along Book & Cassette.

E35.0 *If I Ran the Circus* — 1981.

E36.0 *If I Ran the Zoo* — 1966.
Originally issued as an RCA Camden Children's Series phonograph album.
Title begins: *Dr. Seuss Presents "If I Ran the Zoo" and "Sleep Book."*
Also issued jointly with *The Cat in the Hat Song Book*; each title was also subsequently issued separately.
Voice: Marvin Miller; music composed by Marty Gold.

E37.0 *The Lorax* — 1981.

   E37.1 *The Lorax* — 1992.
      Included in: *The Cat in the Hat and Other Dr. Seuss Favorites* [*see* E8.03].
      Voice: Ted Danson.
      Issued as a Dr. Seuss Book and Cassette Classic.

   E37.2 *The Lorax* — 2004.
      Voice: Rik Mayall.
      Issued jointly with the book.

E38.0 *Marvin K. Mooney, Will You Please Go Now!*—1977.
Issued as a Bright and Early Read-Along Library Book & Cassette.
Included in: *The Dr. Seuss Read Along Library* [set 2]—1977 [*see* E14.0].
Included in: *Bright and Early Read Along Library* [set 1]—[1978?] [*see* E5.0].

E39.0 *Mr. Brown Can Moo! Can You?*—1976.
Issued as a Read-Along House Book & Cassette. Reissued in the same series, together with *There's a Wocket in My Pocket!*, in 1989.
Included in: *The Dr. Seuss Read Along Library* [set 1]—1976 [*see* E13.0].

E40.0 *Oh Say Can You Say?*—1981.
Distributed by the National Library Service, Washington, D.C., for the blind and physically handicapped; voice: Richard Braun.

    E40.1 *Oh Say Can You Say?*—1987.
    Issued as a Beginner Books Read-Along Book & Cassette.

Oh Say Can You Say?— 2003 [*see* E21.2]

E41.0 *Oh, the Thinks You Can Think!*—1977.
Included in: *The Dr. Seuss Read Along Library* [set 2]—1977 [*see* E14.0].

Oh, the Thinks You Can Think!— 2003 [*see* E21.2; E47.0]

E42.0 *On Beyond Zebra*—1982.
Issued as a Read-Along House Book & Cassette.

E43.0 *One Fish, Two Fish, Red Fish, Blue Fish*—1977.
Included in: *The Dr. Seuss Read Along Library* [set 2]—1977 [*see* E14.0].
Also distributed by Fisher-Price Toys in 1980.

One Fish, Two Fish, Red Fish, Blue Fish— 2003 [*see* E21.2]

E44.0 *Please Try to Remember the First of Octember!*—1978.
Issued as a Beginner Books Read-Along Book & Cassette.

The Rabbit, the Bear and the Zinniga-Zanniga [see: E25.0. *Dr. Seuss Presents Horton Hatches the Egg* ...; E18.0. *Dr. Seuss Presents Fox in Socks* ...]

E45.0 [*Scrambled Eggs Super!*—1969].
Included in: *Happy Birthday to You!*—1969 [*see* E22.0].
Included in: *The Dr. Seuss Audio Collection*—1969 [*see* E11.0].
Voice: Hans Conried.

    E45.1 *Scrambled Eggs Super!*—1982.

E46.0 *Seussical: The Musical*— 2001.

Lyrics by Lynn Ahrens; music by Stephen Flaherty. Issued with printed lyrics [see: D41.1].

E47.0 *Songs of Dr. Seuss and More*— 2003.

A collection of songs, many first published in *The Cat in the Hat Song Book*. Includes: "A Day for the Cat in the Hat"; "Horton Hears a Who!"; "You're a Mean One, Mr. Grinch"; "Green Eggs and Ham"; "Plinker Plunker"; Wickersham Brothers Song"; "The No Laugh Race"; "The Super Supper March"; "Oh, the Thinks You Can Think!"; "My Uncle Terwilliger Waltzes with Bears"; "How Lucky You Are"; "The Left Sock Thievers"; "Be Kind to Your Small Person Friends"; "Let Us All Sing."

Performed by Hit Crew.

E48.0 *The Shape of Me and Other Stuff*—1978.

Issued as a Beginner Books Read-Along Book & Cassette.

Included in: *Bright and Early Read Along Library* [set 2]—1978 [*see* E6.1].

E49.0 [*The Sneetches and Other Stories*—1960].

Included in: *Dr. Seuss Presents Horton Hatches the Egg ...*—1960 [*see* E25.0].

Included in: *Dr. Seuss Presents Favorite Children's Stories*—1972 [*see* E12.0]; also issued separately.

Voice: Marvin Miller.

E50.0 *Ten Apples Up on Top!*—1974.

Also includes P. D. Eastman's *Go, Dog, Go!*

Issued as a Beginner Books Read-Along Book & Cassette.

E51.0 *There's a Wocket in My Pocket!*—1976.

Issued as a Bright and Early Read Along Book & Cassette [*see* 46.0].

Included in: *The Dr. Seuss Read Along Library* [set 1]—1976 [*see* E13.0].

Included in: *Bright and Early Read Along Library* [set 1]—[1978?] [*see* E5.0].

E52.0 *Thidwick, the Big-Hearted Moose*—1975.

Included in: *The Cat in the Hat and Other Dr. Seuss Favorites* [*see* E8.03].

Voice: Mercedes McCambridge.

E52.1 *Thidwick, the Big-Hearted Moose*—1982.

E53.0 *Would You Rather Be a Bullfrog?*—1978.

Included in: *Bright and Early Read Along Library* [set 2]—1978 [*see* E6.1].

E54.0 *Yertle the Turtle & Other Stories*—1961.

Included in: *Dr. Seuss Presents Bartholomew and the Oobleck ...*—1961 [*see* E3.0]; subsequently issued with *Yertle the Turtle ...* named first in the title.

Included in: *Dr. Seuss Presents Favorite Children's Stories*—1972 [*see* E12.0];
also issued separately.
Voice: Marvin Miller.

E54.1 [*Yertle the Turtle and Other Stories*: Gertrude McFuzz; The Big
Brag—1969]
Included in: *Happy Birthday to You!*—1969 [*see* E22.0].
Included in: *The Dr. Seuss Audio Collection* [*see* E11.0].
Voice: Hans Conried.

E54.2 *Yertle the Turtle and Other Stories*—1992.
Included in: *The Cat in the Hat and Other Dr. Seuss Favorites* [*see* E8.03].
Voice: John Lithgow.

II. Writings About Dr. Seuss

The following listing cites selected biography, literary criticism, interviews, and works by others that center on or draw heavily from Dr. Seuss's writings and drawings. Excluded are cursory newspaper and news magazine articles and book reviews unless the piece reveals unique or substantive information. Also excluded are unpublished academic theses, adaptations produced after Geisel's death that draw only remotely from Dr. Seuss's creations (such as products and publications associated with the Jim Henson production The Wubbulous World of Dr. Seuss*), as well as the various work books for school children that evoke Dr. Seuss's style but contain none of his own creations; workbooks that contain Dr. Seuss material are included.*

Because of the increasingly comprehensive coverage of online periodical indexes, articles concerning Dr. Seuss that have been published since 2000 are not included in the listing below. Readers should consult online databases available at most public and academic libraries for a search of those works. For additional articles about Geisel, please note particularly the bibliographies and reprinted articles that appear respectively in P. Nel's Dr. Seuss: American Icon *[F143] and* Of Sneetches and Whos and the Good Dr. Seuss *[F147].*

For compilations and anthologies essentially comprising selections of Dr. Seuss materials but compiled or issued by others, please consult "Books and Book Illustrations: Anthologies, Collections and Selections" in Part I [B1–B30].

F1 "3 Elephants Newest 'Find' of Dr. Seuss." *Richmond Times-Dispatch* (December 1, 1940). Books for Christmas [tabloid insert], p. 21.

Includes extensive quotations from Dr. Seuss in which he discusses three elephant characters: Norton, Morton and Horton; illustrated with three drawings by Dr. Seuss. The piece essentially promotes *Horton Hatches the Egg*.

F2 "The 25th Anniversary of Dr. Seuss." *Publishers Weekly*, 182 (December 17, 1962). Pp. 11–14.

F3 Alderson, Brian. "A Perfect 'Parent's Assistant.'" *Times* (London) (August 23, 1972). P. 16.
  Includes Geisel's discussion about sexism in his books.

F4 Anderson, Celia Catlett, and Marilyn Fain Apseloff. *Nonsense Literature for Children: Aesop to Seuss*. Hamden, Conn.: Library Professional Publications, 1989.
  Discusses and cites Dr. Seuss's works *passim.*, providing both textual criticism (with emphasis on phonics) and interpretation of his drawings.

F5 Arakelian, Paul G. "Minnows into Whales: Integration across Scales in the Early Styles of Dr. Seuss." *Children's Literature Association Quarterly*, 18/1 (Spring, 1993). Pp. 18–22.
  Discusses the integration of text and illustrations, with special emphasis on the added levels of meaning that accrue when artist and author are the same person.

The Art of Dr. Seuss [*see* B10.0]

F6 *An Awfully Big Adventure: The Making of Modern Children's Literature: [Dr. Seuss]*. Produced and directed by Roger Parsons; narrator: Connie Booth; series editor: Michael Poole. [London]: BBC-TV, 1998.
  One of a broadcast series; biographical feature (50 min.) first broadcast on British television on February 28, 1998. Includes interviews with: Audrey Geisel, Christopher Cerf, Robert Sullivan, Chuck Jones, Herb Cheyette, Judith and Neil Morgan, Margarita [*i.e.* Margaretha (Peggy)] Owens, Phyllis Cerf Wagner, Michael Frith, and Bernice Cullinan.

F7 Bader, Barbara. "Dr. Seuss." In *American Picture Books from Noah's Ark to the Beast Within*. New York: Macmillan, 1976. Pp. 302–312.
  Literary criticism.

F8 Bailey, John P., Jr. "Three Decades of Dr. Seuss." *Elementary English*, 42/1 (January, 1965). Pp. 7–12.

F9 Baldacci, Leslie. "The Dr. Is In." *Chicago Sun-Times* (October 15, 1998). Pp. 33 *ff*.

Includes an interview with Audrey Geisel emphasizing "Seuss!", a ten-city traveling exhibition at the Chicago Children's Museum, originally developed by the Children's Museum of Manhattan.

F10 Bandler, Michael J. "Dr. Seuss: Still a Drawing Card." *American Way* (December, 1977). Pp. 23 *ff*.

Includes an interview with Geisel.

F11 Bandler, Michael J. "Portrait of a Reading Man." *Washington Post Book World* (May 7, 1972). P. 2.

Includes an interview with Geisel centering on his reading habits and preferences.

F12 Bandler, Michael J. "Seuss on the Loose." *Parents* (September, 1987). Pp. 116 *ff*.

F13 Barone, Diane. "*The Butter Battle Book*: Engaging Children's Thoughts of War." *Children's Literature in Education*, 24/2 (June, 1993). Pp. 123–135.

Discusses children's responses to reading the book.

F14 "Beginner Books: New Trade Learn-To-Read Juveniles." *Publishers Weekly* (June 2, 1958). Pp. 116–117.

F15 Bell, Terry. "The Saga of Dr. Seuss." *New Zealand Women's Weekly* (June 7, 1976). Pp. 20–21.

Includes an interview with Geisel concerning his earlier works.

F16 Bernstein, Peter W. "Unforgettable Dr. Seuss." *Reader's Digest*, 140 (April 1992). Pp. 60–64.

F17 Beyette, Beverly. "Seuss: New Book on the Tip of His Tongue." *Los Angeles Times* (May 29, 1979). Sec. 5, pp. 1 *ff*.

Includes an interview with Geisel.

F18 Bodmer, George R. "The Post-Modern Alphabet: Extending the Limits of the Contemporary Alphabet Book, from Seuss to Gorey." *Children's Literature Association Quarterly*, 14/3 (Fall 1989). Pp. 115–117.

F19 Boekhoff, P. M., and Stuart A. Kallen. *Dr. Seuss*. San Diego: KidHaven Press, 2002.

A biography for juveniles.

F20 Bracey, Earnest N. "American Popular Culture and the Politics of Race in Dr. Seuss' The Sneetches." *Popular Culture Review,* 10/2 (August, 1999). Pp. 131–137.

F21 Brown, A. S. "When Dr. Seuss Did His Stuff for Exxon." *The Lamp,* 69/1 (Spring, 1987). Pp. 28–29.
    Discusses Dr. Seuss's advertising campaigns for Essolube and Essomarine.

F22 Bunzel, Peter. "Wacky World of Dr. Seuss." *LIFE* (April 6, 1959). Pp. 107 *ff.*
    Reprinted in *Of Sneetches and Whos* ... [*see* F147].

F23 Burchell, Sam. "*Architectural Digest* Visits: Dr. Seuss." *Architectural Digest* (December, 1978). Pp. 88–93.
    Includes photographs of Geisel's studio and some of his paintings.

F24 Burns, Thomas A. "Dr. Seuss' *How the Grinch Stole Christmas*: Its Recent Acceptance into the American Popular Christmas Tradition." *New York Folklore*, 2/3–4 (Winter, 1976). Pp. 191–204.
    Considers reasons for the success and popularity of the animated feature broadcast annually on television.

F25 Butler, F. "Seuss as a Creator of Folklore'" *Children's Literature in Education*, 20/3 (September 1989). Pp. 175–181.

F26 Cahn, Robert. "The Wonderful World of Dr. Seuss." *Saturday Evening Post*, 46 (July 6, 1957). Pp. 18 *ff.*
    An interview with Geisel; includes a caricature self-portrait.

F27 Caitlin, Dover. "Juicing Seuss." *Print*, 52/5 (September-October, 1998). Pp. 10–11.
    An interview with Lane Smith concerning his illustrating *Hooray for Diffendoofer Day!*

F28 Calhoun, Richard. "Geisel, Theodor Seuss." In *Contemporary Graphic Artists*. Vol. 3. Ed. by Maurice Horn. Detroit: Gale Research Co., 1988. Pp. 75–78.

F29 "Campaigns: Darn ... another Dragon." *Tide* (July, 1930). P. 3.
    Discusses Dr. Seuss's advertising art.

F30 Carlinsky, Dan. "The Wily Ruse of Doctor Seuss, or, How Ted Geisel

Has Done Real Well." *The Magazine of the Boston Herald American* (March 4, 1979). Pp. 12 *ff.*

    Includes an interview with Geisel.

F31 Carlsson-Paige, N., and D. E. Levin. "*The Butter Battle Book*: Uses and Abuses with Young Children." *Young Children*, 41 (1986). Pp. 37–42.

F32 Carpenter, Humphrey, and Mari Prichard. "Seuss, Dr." In *Oxford Companion to Children's Literature*. New York: Oxford Univ. Press, 1999. Pp. 477–478.

F33 Carratello, John, and Patty Carratello. *Dr. Seuss*. Huntington Beach, Calif.: Teacher Created Materials, 1992.

    Illustrated by Cheryl Buhler, Sue Fullam, and Keith Vasconcelles.

F34 "The Cat in the Hat and Seuss." In "Up Front." *Retail Ad Week* (March, 1976). Pp. 3 *ff.*

    Concerns the marketing and promotion of Dr. Seuss products.

F35 Cech, John. "Some Learning, Blurred, and Violent Edges of the Contemporary Picture Book." *Children's Literature*, 15 (1987). Pp. 197–206.

    Discusses *The Butter Battle Book* within a broader literary context.

F36 Clifford, Jane. "A Farewell to Dr. Seuss." *San Diego Tribune* (September 25, 1991). Pp. C1–C2.

F37 Coglon, Kari. *Dr. Seuss and His Stories*. Bothell, Wash.: Wright Group, 2000.

    A biography for juveniles.

F38 Cohen, Charles. *The Seuss, the Whole Seuss, and Nothing But the Seuss: June 1, 2002–January 5, 2003*. Springfield, Mass.: Connecticut Valley Historical Museum, 2002.

    An exhibition catalog ([9] p.) focusing on Dr. Seuss drawings and artifacts in the context of popular culture. Subsequently substantially expanded (309 p.), especially with emphasize on Dr. Seuss's magazine and advertising art, and published as:

    • *The Seuss, the Whole Seuss, and Nothing But the Seuss: A Visual Biography of Theodor Seuss Geisel*. New York: Random House, 2004.

The Comic Strip Century [*see* C42]

F39 Cook, Timothy. "Another Perspective on Political Authority in Children's Literature: The Fallible Leader in L. Frank Baum and Dr. Seuss." *Western Political Quarterly*, 36/2 (June, 1983). Pp. 326–336.
A scholarly article on the political socialization of children.

F40 *Cooper Union Art School Publication*, 1 ([1954]).
Includes script and photographs of, as well as documentation of student participation in, *Modern Art on Horseback*, a television workshop written and demonstrated by Dr. Seuss that was broadcast on NBC-TV in the series *Excursion* (no. 19, January 31, 1954) [*see* D36.0].

F41 Coover, Robert. *A Political Fable.* New York: Viking Press, 1980.
Originally published in slightly different form as: "The Cat in the Hat for President," *New American Review*, 4 (1968): 7–45. Political satire on American politics and the national campaign process, employing the Cat in the Hat as the candidate and including imagery and parody of Dr. Seuss's works. For commentary on Coover's work, see: Marc Chénetier, "Robert Coover for President! (A Turning of Fables, 'flaunting the rules of the game')," *Delta: Revue du Centre d'Etudes et de Recherche sur les Ecrivains du Sud aux Etats-Unis*, 28 (June 1989): 53–62.

F42 Costello, Eric O. "Private SNAFU & Mr. Hook." *ANiMATO!*, 37 (Spring, 1997). Pp. 44–57.
Discusses production and provides synopses for the *Private S.N.A.F.U.* animated shorts [*see also* D40, F154].

F43 Cott, Jonathan. "The Good Dr. Seuss." In *Pipers at the Gates of Dawn: The Wisdom of Children's Literature.* New York: Random House, 1983. Pp. 1–37.
Literary criticism incorporating an interview with Geisel. Reprinted in *Of Sneetches and Whos ...* [*see* F147].

F44 Crichton, Jennifer. "Dr. Seuss Turns 80." *Publishers Weekly* (February 10, 1984). Pp. 22–23.
Includes an interview with Geisel.

F45 Davis, David C. "What the Cat in the Hat Begat." *Elementary English*, 39/7 (July, 1962). Pp. 677 *ff*.
Discusses Dr. Seuss's influence on controlled vocabulary trade books for children.

F46 Dean, Tanya. *Theodor Geisel.* Philadelphia: Chelsea House, 2002.
For juveniles.

F47 Dempsey, David. "The Significance of Dr. Seuss." *The New York Times Book Review* (May 11, 1958). P. 30.

F48 Dickinson, Howard W. "Let's Borrow the Flit Blunderbuss of Humor." *Printers' Ink* (October 11, 1928). Pp. 10, 12.
Discusses Dr. Seuss's advertising art.

F49 Diehl, Digby. "Dr. Seuss' Q&A." *The Los Angeles Times WEST Magazine* (September 17, 1972). Pp. 37 *ff.*
Reprinted in Diehl's collection of interviews: Digby Diehl, *Supertalk* (Garden City, N.J.: Doubleday, 1974), pp. 169–179.
An interview with Geisel.

F50 Dohm, J. H. "The Curious Case of Dr. Seuss." *The Junior Bookshelf,* 27/6 (December, 1963). Pp. 323–329.
Literary criticism in a British context.

F51 Dow, A., and J. Slaughter. "*The Butter Battle Book* and a Celebration of Peace." *Childhood Education,* 66/1 (1989). Pp. 25–27.

F52 "Dr. Seuss." *Wilson Library Bulletin* [Readers' Choice of Best Books], 14/250 (November 1939).
An early biographical encapsulation.

F53 "Dr. Seuss." In *Children's Literary Review.* Vol. 9. Ed. by G. Senick and M. Hug. Detroit: Gale Research, 1985. Pp. 160–197.
Includes extracts from book reviews and works on commentary and literary criticism.

F54 "Dr. Seuss." In *Pauses: Autobiographical Reflections of 101 Creators of Children's Books.* Ed. by Lee Bennett Hopkins. New York: HarperCollins, 1995. Pp. 111–114.
An autobiographical essay by Geisel, published posthumously.

Dr. Seuss Forever [see: F181. *Theodor Seuss Geisel: Reminiscences ...*]

Dr. Seuss from Then to Now: A Catalogue of the Retrospective Exhibition [see: B6.0–.1]

F55 *Dr. Seuss Is on the Loose: Dr. Seuss's Classroom Uses: A Guide for Inspiring Students to Analyze, Author/Illustrate, Perform with Dr. Seusss Stories.*

Prepared by the Children's Museum of Denver. Denver, Colo.: Children's Museum of Denver, [1988?].

Dr. Seuss' Lost World Revisited: A Forward-Looking Backward Glance [*see* B2.0]

F56 "Dr. Seuss Puts Stethoscope to Humorous Copy." *Advertising Age* (July 8, 1933).
Discusses Dr. Seuss's advertising art.

F57 "Dr. Seuss Remembered." *Publishers Weekly* (October 25, 1991). Pp. 32–33.
Reprinted in *Of Sneetches and Whos ...* [*see* F147].

F58 "The Dr. Seuss School of Unorthodox Taxidermy: Seussoligical Zoologica." *Vanguard Press* [Publisher's catalog] (Spring, 1938). Pp. 9–11.
Prospectus for wall-mounted sculptures of Dr. Seuss creatures: Tufted Gustard, Mulberry Street Unicorn and Blue-Green Abelard. Sizes ranged from 1–2½ feet high [*cf.* F193].

Dreyer, William. *The Art of Dr. Seuss: A Retrospective on the Artistic Talent of Theodor Seuss Geisel* [exhibition catalog] [see: B10.0]

F59 Dugan, Anne. "Seuss, Dr." In *Oxford Companion to Fairy Tales*. Ed. Jack Zipes. New York: Oxford Univ. Press, 2000.

F60 Fadiman, Clifton. "Children's Literature Then and Now: From Kenneth Grahame's *Wind in the Willows* to Dr. Seuss' *Cat in the Hat*." *Holiday* (April, 1959). Pp. 11 *ff*.
Reprinted as: "Professionals and Confessionals: Dr. Seuss and Kenneth Grahame," in *Only Connect: Readings on Children's Literature*, 2nd ed., ed. by Sheila Egoff *et al.* (New York: Oxford U. Press, 1969), pp. 316–322.
Contrasts the literary styles of Grahame and Dr. Seuss.

F61 Fensch, Thomas. *The Man Who Was Dr. Seuss: The Life and Work of Theodor Geisel*. Woodlands, Tex.: New Century Books, 2000.
A biography written for adults.

F62 Fisher, Margery. "Bartholomew Cubbins" and "Marco." In *Who's Who in Children's Books: A Treasury of the Familiar Characters of Childhood*. New York: Holt, Rinehart and Winston, 1975.

F63 Fleischer, Leonore. "Theodor Seuss Geisel." In "Authors & Editors." *Publishers Weekly*, 194 (December 2, 1968). Pp. 7–8.
Discusses the "Bright and Early Books" series.

F64 Foran, Jill. *Dr. Seuss.* Mankato, Minn.: Weigl Publ., 2003.
For juveniles; subsequently recorded for the blind and dyslexic (Princeton, N.J., 2004).

F65 Ford, Carin T. *Dr. Seuss: Best-loved Author.* Berkeley Heights, N.J.: Enslow Publ., 2003.
For juveniles.

F66 Freeman, Don[ald]. "Dr. Seuss at 72 — Going like 60." *Saturday Evening Post* (March, 1977). Pp. 8 *ff.*

F67 Freeman, Don[ald]. "Dr. Seuss from Then to Now." *San Diego Magazine* (May, 1986). Pp. 132 *ff.*
Includes a review of the exhibition with the same title [*cf.* B6].

F68 Freeman, Donald. "The Nonsensical World of Dr. Seuss." *McCall's*, 92 (November, 1964). Pp. 115 *ff.*

F69 Freeman, Donald. "Who Thunk You Up, Dr. Seuss?" *Parade* [newspaper magazine] (June 15, 1969). Pp. 12 *ff.*
Reprinted in: *Authors and Illustrators of Children's Books: Writings on Their Lives and Works,* ed. by Miriam Hoffman and Eva Samuels (New York: R. R. Bowker, 1972), pp. 165–171.

F70 Gaines, Ann Graham. *Dr. Seuss.* Bear, Del.: Mitchell Lane, 2002.
Brief book for juveniles.

F71 "Geisel, Theodor Seuss." In *Children's Literature Review.* Vol. 1. Ed. by A. Block and C. Riley. Detroit: Gale Research, 1976.
Extracts from reviews of Dr. Seuss's books.

F72 "Geisel, Theodor Seuss." In *Something About the Author.* Vol. 28. Ed. by A. Commire. Detroit: Gale Research, 1982.
Bio-bibliography in the form of extracts from other works.

F73 Gordon, Arthur. "The Wonderful Wizard of Soledad Hill." *Woman's Day* (September, 1965). Pp. 74 *ff.*

F74 Gough, John. "The Unsung Hero: Theo. Le Sieg." *Children's Literature Association Quarterly,* 11/4 (Winter, 1986/87). Pp. 183–186.
Includes an excerpt from a letter written by Geisel in which he explains the need for "LeSieg" as another pseudonym.

F75 Gray, William S., and May Hill Arbuthnot. "The Five Hundred Hats." In *More Streets and Roads.* Chicago: Scott, Foresman and Co., 1942. Pp. 156–166.

An abridged adaptation of *The 500 Hats of Bartholomew Cubbins*, substantially altered and simplified for inclusion in this basic elementary school reader; neither the text nor the color illustrations are by Dr. Seuss.

F76 Gray, William S., and May Hill Arbuthnot. "The King's Stilts." In *Days and Deeds*. Chicago: Scott, Foresman and Co., 1943. Pp. 196–214.

An abridged adaptation of *The King's Stilts*, substantially altered and simplified for inclusion in this basic elementary school reader; neither the text nor the color illustrations are by Dr. Seuss. This adaptation appeared in numerous reprintings of *Days and Deeds* as late as the mid–1950s. *Days and Deeds* was also published in a large print edition (Pittsburgh, Pa.: Stanwix House Publishers, [n.d.]).

F77 Greene, Carol. *Dr. Seuss: Writer and Artist for Children*. Chicago: Children's Press, 1993.
"A Rookie Biography."
For juveniles.

F78 Greenleaf, Warren T. "How the Grinch Stole Reading: The Serious Nonsense of Dr. Seuss." *Principal* (May, 1982). Pp. 6–9.
Reprinted in *Of Sneetches and Whos ... [see* F147].

F79 *Hanover Hears a Who: A Tribute to Dr. Seuss. Official Program. Jack o' Lantern*, 73/2 (Winter Carnival, 1981).
This issue of the Dartmouth College humor magazine, which Geisel had edited when he was a senior, served as the 1981 Winter Carnival program and includes tributes, essays and parodies in honor of Dr. Seuss [*cf.* F165].

F80 Hayward, Linda, and Cathy Goldsmith, adapted from the works of Dr. Seuss. *Boom Boom Boom!: Learn About the Sound of B and Other Stuff*. New York: Random House, 1995.
Dr. Seuss Beginner Fun Book series.
A phonics work book adapted from *Mr. Brown Can Moo! Can You?*

F81 Hayward, Linda, and Cathy Goldsmith, adapted from the works of Dr. Seuss. *Did I Ever Tell You How High You Can Count?: Learn About Counting Beyond 100*. New York: Random House, 1996.
Dr. Seuss Beginner Fun Book series.
A counting work book containing illustrations previously published in various Dr. Seuss books.

F82 Hayward, Linda, and Cathy Goldsmith, adapted from the works of Dr. Seuss. *I Am Not Going to Read Any Words Today!: Learn About Rhyming Words*. New York: Random House, 1995.
Dr. Seuss Beginner Fun Book series.
A rhyming work book adapted from *Hop on Pop*.

F83 Hayward, Linda, and Cathy Goldsmith, adapted from the works of Dr. Seuss. *I Can Add Upside Down!: Learn About Easy Addition*. New York: Random House, 1995.
Dr. Seuss Beginner Fun Book series.
An arithmetic work book adapted from *There's a Wocket in My Pocket!*

F84 Hayward, Linda, and Cathy Goldsmith, adapted from the works of Dr. Seuss. *Oh, the Things You Can Count from 1–10: Learn About Counting*. New York: Random House, 1995.
Dr. Seuss Beginner Fun Book series.
A counting work book containing illustrations previously published in various Dr. Seuss books.

F85 Hayward, Linda, and Cathy Goldsmith, adapted from the works of Dr. Seuss. *Oh, the Things You Can Say from A–Z: Learn About Big and Little Letters*. New York: Random House, 1995.
Dr. Seuss Beginner Fun Book series.
An alphabet work book containing illustrations previously published in various Dr. Seuss books.

F86 Hayward, Linda, and Cathy Goldsmith, adapted from the works of Dr. Seuss. *Sneetches Are Sneetches: Learn About Same and Different*. New York: Random House, 1995.
Dr. Seuss Beginner Fun Book series.
A work book stressing concepts, loosely adapted from the story *The Sneetches*.

F87 Hayward, Linda, and Cathy Goldsmith, adapted from the works of Dr. Seuss. *Wet Foot, Dry Foot, Low Foot, High Foot: Learn About Opposites and Different*. New York: Random House, 1995.
Dr. Seuss Beginner Fun Book series.
A work book stressing concepts, adapted from *The Foot Book*.

F88 Hearn, Michael Patrick, Trinkett Clark and H. Nicholas B. Clark. *Myth, Magic, and Mystery: One Hundred Years of American Children's Book Illustration*. Nofolk [Va.]: Roberts Rinehart Publ. and the Chrysler Museum of Art, 1996.

An exhibition catalog, including discussion and manuscript facsimiles of Dr. Seuss's works.

F89 Holden, James W. "'Quick, Henry—The Flit!'" *The American Press* (January, 1934). P. 4.
Discusses Dr. Seuss's advertising art.

F90 Hopkins, Lee Bennett. "Dr. Seuss (Theodor S. Geisel)." In *Books Are By People: Interviews with 104 Authors and Illustrators of Books for Young Children.* New York: Citation Press, 1969. Pp. 255–258.

F91 Horn, Laurence R. "Boats, Birds, and Beans: The Birth of Pragmatics and the Genealogies of Morays: Allusion and Reality in the Seussian Epic.'" *Style*, 24/4 (Winter 1990). Pp. 628–634.
Textual criticism of *Scrambled Eggs Super!*, involving linguistics and the philosopher H. Paul Grice.

F92 Hulbert, Ann. "The Man Who Invented The Cat in the Hat." *The New York Times Book Review* (April 23, 1995). Pp. 11–12.

F93 Humphrey, Hal. "Zoo's Who? Dr. Seuss, That's Who." *Cornet* (December, 1964). Pp. 114–120.
Includes an interview with Geisel.

F94 "In Giving New Note to Poster Art Dr. Seuss Often Draws the Line." *The Esso Dealer* (March, 1934).

In Search of Dr. Seuss [*see* D32.0]

F95 Ingalls, Zoë. "*The Cat in the Hat, The Butter Battle Book*, and Other Soupçons of Seuss!" *The Chronicle of Higher Education* (July 28, 1993). Pp. B4–B5.
Features the Dr. Seuss Collection, held by the Mandeville Special Collections Library, University of California, San Diego; illustrated.

F96 Jenkins, Henry. "'No Matter How Small:' The Democractic Imagination of Dr. Seuss." In *Hop on Pop: The Politics and Pleasures of Popular Culture.* Ed. H. Jenkins, Tara McPherson and Jane Shattuc. Durham, N.C.: Duke Univ. Press, 2002. Pp. 187–208.
Discusses political ideals and influences in Dr. Seuss's books.

F97 Jennings, Anne F. "Cases of Note: Dr. Seuss Enterprises, L.P., v. Penguin Books USA, Inc., and Dove Audio, Inc." *Against the Grain*, 9 (June 1997). Pp. 49–51.

Discusses the suit filed to block distribution of the parody *The Cat Not in the Hat!*, which concerns the murder trial of O.J. Simpson [*see* F101].

F98 Jennings, C. Robert. "Dr. Seuss: 'What Am I Doing Here?'" *Saturday Evening Post*, 238 (October 23, 1965). Pp. 105–109.
Includes an interview with Geisel.

F99 Johnson, Tim. "Dr. Seuss: Architect of Social Change." *Whole Earth Review*, 59 (Summer 1988). Pp. 120–122.
Discusses superficially the influence of "The Sneetches" in the context of the civil rights movement in the South.

F100 Jordan, Clifford L. "Dr. Seuss." *Dartmouth Alumni Magazine* (October, 1962). Pp. 24–27.

F101 Juice, Dr. *The Cat Not in the Hat!* (as told to Alan Katz and illustrated by Chris Wrinn). Beverley Hills, Calif.: Dove Books, 1996.
A parody of *The Cat in the Hat* and the murder trial of O. J. Simpson; distribution was blocked by court order on grounds of infringement, and the work was never released. For a discussion of the litigation surrounding this publication, see Anne F. Jennings's "Cases of note ..." [F97].

F102 Kahn, E. J., Jr. "Profiles: Children's Friend." *The New Yorker*, 36 (December 17, 1960). Pp. 47 *ff*.
A biographical feature of exceptional depth. Reprinted in *Of Sneetches and Whos ...* [*see* F147].

F103 Kasper, M. "In Memoriam / Dr. Seuss." *North American Review*, 277/1 (January–February, 1992). P. 46.
Prose fiction exemplifying the acceptance of the word "grinch" in the English language.

F104 Kemp, James W. *The Gospel According to Dr. Seuss*. Valley Forge, Pa.: Judson Press, 2004.
Parallels between thirteen Dr. Seuss stories and lessons found in the Scriptures.

F105 Kibler, Myra. "Theodor Seuss Geisel." In *American Writers for Children Since 1960* [*Dictionary of Literary Biography*, vol. 61]. Ed. by G. E. Estes. Detroit: Gale Research Co., 1987. Pp. 75–86.
A succinct bio-bibliography; revised in 1992: "Theodor Seuss

Geisel (Dr. Seuss, Theo. LeSieg)," *Dictionary of Literary Biography Yearbook, 1991* (Detroit: Gale Research Co., 1992), pp. 254–258.

F106 Krull, Kathleen. *The Boy on Fairfield Street: How Ted Geisel Grew Up to Become Dr. Seuss*. Paintings by Steve Johnson & Lou Fancher, with decorative illustrations by Dr. Seuss. New York: Random House, 2004.
Illustrated biography, focusing on Geisel's childhood and youth in Springfield, Mass.

F107 Kupferberg, Herbert. "A Seussian Celebration." *Parade* [newspaper magazine] (February 26, 1984). Pp. 4–6.
Includes a quote from Dr. Seuss about the source of his ideas: a "Retired Thunderbird."

F108 Lanes, Selma G. "Seuss for the Goose Is Seuss for the Gander." In *Down the Rabbit Hole: Adventures and Misadventures in the Realm of Children's Literature*. New York: Atheneum, 1971. Pp. 79–89.
Literary criticism. Reprinted in *Of Sneetches and Whos ...* [*see* F147].

F109 Lathem, Edward C. *Who's Who & What's What in the Books of Dr. Seuss*. Hanover, N.H.: Dartmouth College, 2000.
An iconographical dictionary for the terms, characters, and objects that appear in the major books written by Dr. Seuss (including posthumous publications); excluded are works written by Geisel under other pseudonyms; a publication commemorating the 75th anniversary of Geisel's graduation from Dartmouth College.

F110 Lathem, Edward C. "Words and Pictures Married: The Beginnings of Dr. Seuss." *Dartmouth Alumni Magazine* (April, 1976). Pp. 16–21.
Includes an interview with Geisel and selections of Dr. Seuss's illustrations. A more extensive transcript of the interview is held by the Rauner Special Collections Library, Dartmouth College [AlumniG277mi]. Reprinted in *Of Sneetches and Whos ...* [*see* F147].

F111 Lebduska, Lisa. "Rethinking Human Need: Seuss's *The Lorax*." *Children's Literature Association Quarterly*, 19/4 (Winter, 1994–1995). Pp. 170–176.
Considers *The Lorax* within the context of contemporary children's environmental literature.

F112 Lenburg, Jeff. *The Encyclopedia of Animated Cartoons*. Rev. ed. New York: Facts on File, 1991. *Passim*.
Includes descriptions and bibliographic data for Dr. Seuss's animated works.

F113 Levine, Stuart P. *Dr. Seuss*. San Diego, Calif.: Lucent Books, 2001.
For juveniles.

F114 Lindsay, Cynthia. "The Miracle of Dr. Seuss." *Good Housekeeping* (December, 1960). Pp. 32 *ff*.
Includes an interview with Geisel.

F115 Lingeman, Richard. "Dr. Seuss, Theo. Le Sieg." *The New York Times Book Review* (November 14, 1976). Pp. 23, 48.

F116 Lipez, Richard. "I Do Not Like Thee, Dr. Seuss, the Reason Why I Can't Deduce." *Atlantic Monthly* (August, 1977). P. 91.
Doggerel verse attacking Dr. Seuss's meter and rhyme.

F117 "The Logical Insanity of Dr. Seuss." *Time* (August 11, 1967). Pp. 58–59.
Describes a children's workshop at the La Jolla [Calif.] Museum of Art featuring Dr. Seuss and his works.

F118 Lurie, Alison. "The Cabinet of Dr. Seuss." *The New York Review of Books* (December 20, 1990). Pp. 50–52.
Reprinted in: *Popular Culture: An Introductory Text*, ed. J. Nachbar and K. Lausé (Bowling Green, Ohio: Bowling Green State University Popular Press, 1992), pp. 68–79.
Includes literary criticism in addition to a review of *Oh, the Places You'll Go!* Reprinted in *Of Sneetches and Whos* ... [*see* F147].

F119 Lynch, Wendy. *Dr. Seuss*. Chicago: Heinemann, 2000.
Also published Oxford: Heinemann, 2000; reprinted 2001.
Brief biography for juveniles.

F120 Lystad, Mary. *From Dr. Mather to Dr. Seuss: 200 Years of American Books for Children*. Boston: G. K. Hall, 1980.
Literary history and criticism emphasizing societal aspects; discussion of Dr. Seuss's works appears on pp. 196, *passim. Cf.* her "From Dr. Mather to Dr. Seuss: Over 200 Years of American Children's Books," *Children Today*, new ser., 5/3 (May-June, 1976): 10–15.

F121 Lystad, Mary. "The World According to Dr. Seuss." *Children Today*, 13/3 (May-June, 1984). Pp. 19–22.
Literary criticism focusing on child development.

F122 MacDonald, Ruth K. *Dr. Seuss*. Boston: Twayne Publishers, 1988.
Literary criticism and interpretation in depth from an academic perspective.

F123 MacEoin, Dottie. "It's on the Loose, It's on the Loose! It's Not a Triple-Crested Swoose, It's Not a Moose–It's Dr. Seuss." *Stars and Stripes* (March 26, 1967). Pp. 14–16.

Includes an interview with Geisel.

F124 "Malice in Wonderland." *Newsweek*, 19/6 (February 9, 1942). Pp. 58–59.

Includes discussion of Dr. Seuss's editorial cartooning for *PM* newspaper; illustrated [*cf.* C82, F135–136].

F125 Marcus, Jon. "Seeking Seuss in Springfield." *Yankee Traveler* (November-December, 1995). P. 6.

Discusses influence on Geisel of his home town, Springfield, Mass.

F126 Marschall, Richard. "The Forgotten Seuss: Just What the Doctor Disordered." *Nemo Annual: The Classic Comics Library*, 1 (1985). Pp. 39–44.

Discusses Dr. Seuss's early cartooning; illustrated. This is a revised version of an article entitled: "The Forgotten Seuss," *The Comics Journal*, 72 (May 1982): 121–123. The article, further revised, appears as the introduction to *The Tough Coughs as He Ploughs the Dough* [*see* B7.0].

F127 Marschall, Richard. "Geisel, Theodor Seuss." In *The World Encyclopedia of Cartoons*. Ed. by M. Horn. New York: Chelsea House Publ., 1980. P. 252.

F128 Marshall, Ian. "The Lorax and the Ecopolice." *ISLE: Interdisciplinary Studies in Literature and Environment*, 2/2 (Winter, 1996). Pp. 85–92.

For a response to this article, see Suzanne Ross, "Response to 'The Lorax and the Ecopolice' by Ian Marshall," *ISLE*, 2/2 (Winter, 1996): 99–104.

F129 Martin, Edwin. "Dr. Seuss Has Prolific Pen." *San Diego Union* (August 30, 1953). Pp. E1–E2.

Centers on the release of *The 5,000 Fingers of Mr. T.*

F130 Martin, Patricia Stone. *Dr. Seuss, We Love You.* Vero Beach, Fla.: Rourke Enterprises, 1987.

Illustrated by Karen Park; a Spanish translation was published in 1992 by the same publisher: *El Dr. Seuss, lo queremos.* For juveniles.

F131 Mass, Wendy. "Dr. Seuss." In *Great Authors of Children's Literature.* San Diego, Calif.: Lucent Books, 2000.

F132 McArthur, Tom. "English to Order." *English Today*, 5 (January–March, 1986). Pp. 27–29.

Focuses on the didacticism of "English to order" methods, used chiefly in English-as-foreign-language texts.

F133 Mensch, Betty, and Alan Freeman. "Getting to Solla Sollew: The Existentialist Politics of Dr. Seuss." *Tikkun*, 2/2 (1987). Pp. 30–34, 113–117.

Reprinted in: *Alternative Library Literature: A Biennial Anthology* (1986/1987): 151–160.

F134 Miklowitz, Gloria D. *Dr. Seuss*. Carlsbad, Calif.: Dominie Press, 2002. Spanish translation: Dominie Press, 2003.

For juveniles.

F135 Minear, Richard H. *Dr. Seuss Goes to War: The World War II Editorial Cartoons of Theodor Seuss Geisel*. New York: New Press, 1999. "Published in Cooperation with the Dr. Seuss Collection at the University of California at San Diego."

Also published London: I.B. Taurus, 2000; London: Verso, 2002; York: Distr. Signature Book Services, 2003.

Introduction by Art Spiegelman [which was reprinted, abridged, in the *New Yorker* (July 12, 1999): 62*f.*]; includes facsimile reprints of approximately 200 of the 404 editorial cartoons that Dr. Seuss created for *PM* newspaper between 1941–1943 [*cf.* B23.0; C82; F124].

F136 Minear, Richard H. *The Political Dr. Seuss*. Springfield, Conn.: Connecticut Valley Historical Museum, 2000.

An exhibition catalog (11 p.).

F137 Moebius, William. "The Poetry of Theodor Seuss Geisel." *Poets of New England, Episode 114*. Produced by Academic Instructional Media Services, University of Massachusetts at Amherst. 2000. Videocassette, 27 min.

A production of the University of Massachusetts Academic Television channel UMATV.

F138 Moje, Elizabeth B., and Woan Ru Shyu. "Oh, the Places You've Taken US: *RT*'s Tribute to Dr. Seuss." *Reading Teacher*, 45/9 (May 1992). Pp. 670–676.

Reprinted in: *Education Digest*, 58/4 (December 1992): 26–31.

Biography and literary criticism, with special emphasis on Dr.

Seuss's contributions to children's literature. Reprinted in *Of Sneetches and Whos ...* [*see* F147].

F139   Morgan, Judith, and Neil Morgan. *Dr. Seuss & Mr. Geisel: A Biography.* New York: Random House, 1995.
Also republished in paperback: New York: Da Capo Press, 1996.
An exhaustive biography written for adults.

F140   Morgan, Judith, and Neil Morgan. "Dr. Seuss & Theodor Geisel." *California State Library Foundation Bulletin*, 54 (January, 1996). Pp. 32–38.
Based on a presentation made at the Los Angeles Public Library on November 5, 1995.

F141   Moynihan, Ruth B. "Ideologies in Children's Literature: Some Preliminary Notes." *Children's Literature*, 2 (1973). Pp. 166–172.
Considers the political ideology in *Horton Hears a Who!* as well as works by other authors.

F142   Nel, Philip. "Dada Knows Best: Growing up 'Surreal' with Dr. Seuss." In *The Avant-Garde and American Postmodernity: Small Incisive Shocks.* Jackson, Miss.: U. Press of Mississippi, 2002. Pp. 41–72.
Revised from an article previously published in *Children's Literature*, 27 (1999).

F143   Nel, Philip. *Dr. Seuss: American Icon.* New York: Continuum, 2004.
Literary criticism and interpretation in depth from an academic perspective, with an extensive annotated bibliography, including citations for reviews and criticism organized by Dr. Seuss's book titles.

F144   *Newbery and Caldecott Medalists and Honor Book Winners: Bibliographies and Resource Material through 1977.* Jim Roginski, compiler. Littleton, Colo.: Libraries Unlimited, 1982. Pp. 233–236.

F145   Nichols, Lewis. "'Then I Doodled a Tree.'" *The New York Times Book Review* (November 11, 1962). Children's Book Section, pp. 2, 42.
Reprinted in *Of Sneetches and Whos ...* [*see* F147].

F146   Nilsen, Don L. F. "Dr. Seuss as Grammar Consultant." *Language Arts*, 54/5 (May, 1977). Pp. 567–572.
Discusses Dr. Seuss's use and misuse of grammar.

F147   *Of Sneetches and Whos and the Good Dr. Seuss: Essays on the Writings and Life of Theodor Geisel.* Ed. by Thomas Fensch. Jefferson, N.C.: McFarland & Co., 1997.

A collection of twenty-six reprint articles about Dr. Seuss, chiefly literary criticism but also including biography and several newspaper obituaries. Although some of the original articles were illustrated, none of those illustrations is reprinted in this anthology.

F148 Olton, Carol. "To a Living Literary Legend ...." *San Diego Union* (April 17, 1984. Pp. D1 *ff.*
      Includes an interview with Geisel.

F149 "The One and Only Dr. Seuss and His Wonderful Autography Tour." *Publishers Weekly* (December 8, 1958). Pp. 12–15.
      Discusses marketing of Dr. Seuss's works.

F150 Opdyke, W. K. "Dr. Seuss Features Telchron House Organ." *Printed Salesmanship*, 61/2 (April, 1933). P. 84.

F151 Ort, Lorrene L. "Theodore [*sic*] Seuss Geisel — The Children's Dr. Seuss." *Elementary English*, 32/3 (March, 1955). Pp. 135–142.
      Discusses the rhetoric in Dr. Seuss's writings.

F152 "The Other Cool Cat." *Early Years* (April, 1973). Pp. 22–24.
      Includes an interview with Geisel.

F153 Parravano, Martha V. "Dr. Seuss." In *Children's Books and Their Creators*. Ed. Anita Silvey. New York: Houghton Mifflin, 1995.

F154 "Private SNAFU." *Business Screen*. The Army Pictorial Issue, 7/1 (December 30, 1945). P. 89.
      Describes the character and the cartoon series, and considers their effect on the war effort [*see also* D40, F42].

F155 Rabe, Tish. *Oh, Baby, the Places You'll Go! A Book to Be Read in Utero*. Adapted by Tish Rabe from the works of Dr. Seuss [with an introductory letter to the reader by Audrey Geisel]. New York: Random House, 1997.
      First distributed in 1998. "— for doting parents-to-be to read aloud to their adorable baby-to-be" [dust-jacket]. A collection of illustrations, characters and verbiage evoking most of Dr. Seuss's books, but in verse written by the author.

F156 Raddatz, Leslie. "Dr. Seuss Climbs Down from His Mountain to Bring the Grinch to Television." *TV Guide* (December 17, 1966). Pp. 12–14.
      Includes an interview with Geisel.

F157 Rau, Dana Meachen. *Dr. Seuss.* New York: Children's Press, 2003.
For juveniles.

F158 Raymo, Chet. "Dr. Seuss and Dr. Einstein: Children's Books and Scientific Imagination." *Horn Book Magazine,* 68/5 (September-October, 1992). Pp. 560–567.
Reprinted in: *Only Connect: Readings on Children's Literature,* 3rd ed., ed. by Sheila Egoff *et al.* (New York: Oxford U. Press, 1996), pp. 184–191.
Adapted from a speech given at Bridgewater State College. Reprinted in *Of Sneetches and Whos ...* [*see* F147].

F159 Reimer, Mavis. "Dr. Seuss' *The 500 Hats of Bartholomew Cubbins*: Of Hats and Kings." In *Touchstones: Reflections on the Best in Children's Literature.* Vol. 3: *Picture Books.* West Lafayette, Ind.: Children's Literature Assoc., 1989. Pp. 132–142.
Literary criticism.

F160 Richardson, Barbara. "Dr. Seuss: Creator of 'The Cat in the Hat.'" *Book and Magazine Collector,* 202 (January, 2001). Pp. 44–58.
Discusses printing history and resale values for Dr. Seuss books in Great Britain, with a British imprint checklist; checklist should be viewed with caution, especially imprint dates.

F161 Rogers, W. G. "Local Color." *Springfield* [Mass.] *Union* (May 11, 1933).
Provides unique information about Geisel's early career.

F162 Roth, Rita. "On Beyond Zebra with Dr. Seuss." *New Advocate* (Fall, 1989). Pp. 213–225.
Discusses the use of Dr. Seuss texts for teaching children about individualism, critical literacy and improved social awareness. Reprinted in *Of Sneetches and Whos ...* [*see* F147].

F163 Sadler, Glenn Edward. "Maurice Sendak and Dr. Seuss: A Conversation." *Horn Book Magazine* (September/October, 1989). Pp. 582–588.
Transcript of an interview conducted in 1982 at Balboa Park, San Diego. Reprinted in *Of Sneetches and Whos ...* [*see* F147].
Reprinted, with added commentary as:
• "A Conversation: Maurice Sendak and Dr. Seuss," *Carver,* 9/1 (Spring, 1990): 25–34.
• "A Conversation: Maurice Sendak and Dr. Seuss," in *Teaching Children's Literature: Issues, Pedagogy, Resources,* ed. G. E. Sadler (New York: Modern Language Assoc. of America, 1992), pp. 241–250.

F164 Sale, Roger. *Fairy Tales and After*. Cambridge: Harvard U. Press. Pp. 8–12, *passim*.

Literary criticism, especially of Dr. Seuss's early books, placing him within a broad context of children's writers.

F165 Salzhauer, Mike. "A Carnival Cavort with Dr. Seuss." *The Dartmouth Review* (February 2, 1981). Pp. 6–7.

An interview with Geisel in celebration of Dartmouth College's Winter Carnival, which had a "Seussian" theme in 1981 [*cf.* F79].

F166 Schroth, Evelyn. "Dr. Seuss and Language Use." *The Reading Teacher*, 31/7 (April, 1978). Pp. 748–750.

Discusses using Dr. Seuss books in the classroom for teaching reading.

The Secret Art of Dr. Seuss [*see* B10.0]

F167 See, Carolyn. "Dr. Seuss and the Naked Ladies." *Esquire*, 81/6 (June, 1974). Pp. 118 *ff*.

Generally biographical, but with emphasis on Dr. Seuss's anomalous *The Seven Lady Godivas*. Reprinted in *Of Sneetches and Whos* ... [*see* F147].

*Seuss-isms for Success: Insider Tips on Economic Health from the Good Doctor [*i.e. *Dr. Seuss*] [*see* B21.0]

Seuss-isms: Wise and Witty Prescriptions for Living from the Good Doctor [*see* B15.0]

F168 "Seussology." *Advertising & Selling* (April, 1939). Pp. 42–45.

Discusses Dr. Seuss's advertising art; illustrated.

F169 Sheff, David. "Seuss on Wry ...." *Parenting Magazine* (February, 1987). Pp. 52–57.

An interview with Geisel.

F170 Shepherd, Kenneth R. "Geisel, Theodor Seuss." In *Contemporary Authors*, New Revision Series, 32. Detroit: Gale Research, 1991. Pp. 168–171.

Supercedes several earlier bio-bibliographies published by Gale Research.

F171 Silverman, Betsy Marden. "Dr. Seuss Talks to Parents." *Parents Magazine*, 35/11 (November, 1960). Pp. 44 *ff*.

Includes an interview with Geisel.

F172 Smith, James Steel. "The Comic Style of Dr. Seuss." In *A Critical Approach to Children's Literature*. New York: McGraw-Hill, 1967. Pp. 313–314.

Other references to Dr. Seuss appear *passim*.

F173 Snyder, C. R., and Kimberley Mann Pulvers. "Dr. Seuss, the Coping Machine, and 'Oh the Places You'll Go.'" In *Coping with Stress: Effective People and Process*. Ed. C. R. Snyder. Oxford: Oxford Univ. Press, 2001. Pp. 3–29.

Discusses *Oh, the Places You'll Go!* And *Oh, the Thinks You Can Think!* in a psychological context.

F174 Steig, Michael. "Dr. Seuss's Attack on Imagination: *I Wish that I Had Duck Feet* and the Cautionary Tale." In *The Child and the Story: An Exploration of Narrative Forms* [Proceedings of the Ninth Annual Conference of the Children's Literature Association, University of Florida, March 1982]. Ed. by Priscilla A. Ord. Boston, Mass.: Children's Literature Association, 1983. Pp. 137–141.

Literary criticism emphasizing subliminal psychological interpretations.

F175 Steinberg, Sybil S. "What Makes a Funny Children's Book? Five Writers Talk About Their Methods." *Publishers Weekly*, 213 (February 27, 1978). Pp. 87–89.

Includes an interview with Geisel.

F176 Stewart-Gordon, James. "Dr. Seuss: Fanciful Sage of Childhood." *Reader's Digest*, 100 (April, 1972). Pp. 141–145.

F177 Stong, Emily. "Juvenile Literary Rape in America: A Post-Coital Study of the Writings of Dr. Seuss." *Studies in Contemporary Satire*, 4 (1977). Pp. 34–40.

Satirical essay suggesting sexual innuendo in Dr. Seuss's writings.

F178 Sullivan, Emilie P. "Brightening Our Years: A Half Century of Laughter and Learning with Dr. Seuss." *Delta Kappa Gamma Bulletin*, 59 (Fall 1992). Pp. 47–51.

F179 Sullivan, Robert. "The Boy Who Drew Wynnmphs." *Yankee*, 59 (December 1995). Pp. 54 *ff*.

F180 Sullivan, Robert. "Oh, the Places He Went." *Dartmouth Alumni Magazine* (Winter, 1991). Pp. 18–45.

A biographical feature, illustrated, of exceptional depth.

F181 *Theodor Seuss Geisel: Reminiscences & Tributes.* By Victor H. Krulak, Jed Mattes, Judith & Neil Morgan, Herbert Cheyette, Chuck Jones, and Robert L. Bernstein; together with an introductory note by Audrey S. Geisel, and edited by Edward Connery Lathem. Hanover, N.H.: Dartmouth College, 1996.

Cover title: *Theodor Seuss Geisel, 1904–1991 | Dr. Seuss Forever.*

Published remarks first delivered at the San Diego Museum of Art on November 18, 1991. Edition limited to 2,000 copies, printed at the Stinehour Press during November 1996 and distributed in part to Friends of the Dartmouth Library and to Friends of the UCSD Library; gray lettering on cover.

A special second printing at the Stinehour Press during August 1997, limited to 500 copies and identical to F181 except for the colophon and green lettering on the cover, was prepared for selected donors to the Dartmouth Alumni Fund.

The Tough Coughs as He Ploughs the Dough: Early Writings and Cartoons by Dr. Seuss [*see* B7.0]

F182 Van Cleaf, David W., and Rita J. Martin. "Seuss's Butter Battle Book: Is There a Hidden Harm?" *Childhood Education*, 62/3 (January/February 1986). Pp. 191–194.

F183 Warren, Bob. "Dr. Seuss, Former *Jacko* Editor, Tells How Boredom May Lead to Success." *The Dartmouth* (May 10, 1934). P. 3.

A college newspaper article summarizing Geisel's activities since his being graduated in 1925.

F184 Waugh, John C. "Kingdom of Seuss." *Christian Science Monitor* (January 29, 1964). Pp. 9.

Includes an interview with Geisel and his wife Helen.

F185 Webb, Marian A. "Author of the Month: Dr. Seuss." *Juvenile Book Fare*, 5/3 (November, 1960). P. 1.

A cursory biographical summary but with a "Letter from Dr. Seuss" in which the author discusses the significance and importance of writing children's books.

F186 Weidt, Maryann N. *Oh, the Places He Went: A Story About Dr. Seuss—Theodor Seuss Geisel.* Ill. by Kerry Maguire. Minneapolis: Carolrhoda Books, 1994.

Subsequently issued in braille and as a sound recording.

A biography for juveniles.

F187 Wheeler, Jill C. *Dr. Seuss.* Edina, Minn.: Abdo & Daughters; Minneapolis: Distr. by Rockbottom Books, 1992.

A biography for juveniles. From the series: A Tribute to the Young at Heart.

F188 *Who's Dr. Seuss?: Meet Ted Geisel.* A Miller-Brody Video Production. Highstown, N.J.: Macmillan/McGraw-Hill School Publishing; American School Publishers, 1991, c1981.

Videocassette, 14 min.

An adaptation of the film strip/cassette sound recording issued originally as a kit by Random House in 1981.

F189 Wilder, Rob. "Catching Up with Dr. Seuss." *Parents Magazine* (June, 1979). Pp. 60–64.

Includes an interview with Geisel.

F190 Wintle, Justin, and Emma Fisher. *The Pied Pipers: Interviews with the Influential Creators of Children's Literature.* New York and London: Paddington Press, 1974.

Includes an interview with Geisel (pp. 113–131) in the form of written responses to questions submitted in writing in September, 1974.

F191 Wolf, Tim. "Imagination, Rejection, and Rescue: Recurrent Themes in Dr. Seuss." *Children's Literature*, 23 (1995). Pp. 137–164.

Literary criticism emphasizing psychological aspects of Dr. Seuss's writings.

F192 Woods, Mae. *Dr. Seuss.* Edina, Minn.: Abdo, 2000.

A brief biography for juveniles.

F193 "The World's Most Eminent Authority on Unheard-Of Animals." *Look* (June 7, 1938). Pp. 46–47.

Includes illustrations of Dr. Seuss's animal sculptures, which were marketed during the 1930s [*cf.* F58].

Your Favorite Seuss [*see* B30.0]

F194 Younger, Helen, Marc Younger and Dan Hirsch. *First Editions of Dr. Seuss Books: A Guide to Identification.* Saco, Me.: Custom Communications, 2002.

Bibliographic descriptions geared for book dealers and collectors, with illustrations of covers and dust-jackets and a discussion of "first printing points," focusing primarily on dust-jacket and binding variants [*i.e.* issues] rather than printings.

F195 Zicht, Jennifer. "In Pursuit of the Lorax: Who's in Charge of the Last Truffula Seed?" *EPA Journal* (September-October 1991). Pp. 27–30.

F196 Zornado, Joseph. "Swaddling the Child in Children's Literature." *Children's Literature Association Quarterly*, 22/3 (1997). Pp. 105–112. Compares characters in the animated version of *How the Grinch Stole Christmas* and the film version of *The Wizard of Oz*.

III. A Dr. Seuss
Iconography

"When I can't find the word I want, I think one up."— Dr. Seuss

Fictional names, terms and places listed below appear in the books, films and short stories created by Dr. Seuss and his various aliases. Excluded are creatures and characters depicted in single cartoons, in advertising campaigns, and those that are only mentioned in passing without illustration. Bracketed numbers refer to the corresponding bibliographical entries.

Abdulla Bullah Bull Bull Ben-eer [*see* King Abdulla ...]
Abercrombie
    Water beast in: "Bring 'em Buck Alive!" [C12].
Abrasion-Contusions
    Race cars in: *If I Ran the Circus* [13.0].
Acoustical Anti Audial Bleeper
    The Grinch's contraption, also named a Vacu-Sound Sweeper, that sucks sound out of the air and "gargles the sound waves for 50 miles around" in: *The Grinch Grinches the Cat in the Hat* [D22.0].
Aethelstan the Clam
    Contestant in: "The Great Diet Derby" [C35].
Alaric, Sir [*see* Sir Alaric]
Ali
    Peter Hooper's helper in: *Scrambled Eggs Super!* [10.0].
Ali ben Giseh [*see* Shiek Ali ben Giseh]
Alice
    Name of both Hooded Klopfers in: *Happy Birthday to You!* [18.0].

Andalusian Feeney Fowl
   Bird who has 1¾ inches trimmed from his tail to use as a party favor in:
   "Quality" [C91].
Ann
   Mosquito who carries malaria in: *This Is Ann* [A13.0].
Antrims
   Long-eared herd animals in: "Bring 'em Buck Alive!" [C12].
Apartment 12-J [*see* Fairfax Apartments]
Arabella
   One of the seven Lady Godivas in: *The Seven Lady Godivas* [3.0].
Aunt Annie's Alligator
   Dr. Seuss's ABC [24.0]
Aunt ... [*see* ..., Aunt]
Aw-Waw Hoo
   Setting for the story: *The Sneetches and Other Stories*: "The Sneetches"
   [21.0].

Baako
   Mountainous country and setting for the comic strip "Hejji" [C42].
Bad-Animal-Catching-Machine
   If I Ran the Zoo [9.0]
Banks, Miss
   School teacher in: *I Wish That I Had Duck Feet* [29.0].
Bar-ba-loots [*see* Brown Bar-ba-loots]
Bartholomew [*see* Cubbins, Bartholomew; Collins, Bartholomew]
Bass, Miss
   School teacher in: *Wacky Wednesday* [47.0].
Baumgrass the Cat
   Contestant in: "The Great Diet Derby" [C35].
Beagle-Beaked-Bald-Headed Grinch
   Eggless bird in: *Scrambled Eggs Super!* [10.0].
Bear, Mr.
   Gym teacher in: *Hooray for Diffendoofer Day!* [65.0].
Becker, Miss
   Medical receptionist in: *You're Only Old Once!* [60.0].
Bee-Watcher [*see* Hawtch-Hawtch]
Beeze, Mr.
   Art instructor, who paints pictures while hanging by his knees, in: *Hooray
   for Diffendoofer Day!* [65.0].
Beetlelion
   Hump-nosed aquatic creature in: "Bring 'em Buck Alive!" [C12].

Beezle-Berry
Sweet berry that grows from the Beezle-Berry vine (a "Beezle-Berry Day" represents a happy, sunny cheerful day) in: *The Grinch Grinches the Cat in the Hat* [D22.0].

Beezle-Nut oil
Boiling oil (also referred to as "juice") that threatens Who-ville in: *Horton Hears a Who!* [11.0].

Beezlenut tree
Sweet-blossomed nut tree in: "Horton and the Kwuggerbug" [C45]; *Scrambled Eggs Super!* [10.0].

Befft
Coiffed creatures who only go left in: *Oh, the Thinks You Can Think!* [49.0].

Bellar
Cellar dweller in: *There's a Wocket in My Pocket!* [46.0].

Bellows and Candle
Diagnostic hearing test in: *You're Only Old Once!* [60.0].

Ben [*see* Bim and Ben]

Bickelbaum, Benjamin B., Mr.
Object of a lullaby in: *The Cat in the Hat Song Book* [31.0].

Biffer-Baum Birds
Dr. Seuss's Sleep Book [23.0]

Big Bill [*see* Brown, Bill]

Big-Boy Boomeroo
Bomb, filled with Moo-backa-Moo and symbolizing atomic weapons, that causes a stand-off of doubtful outcome between Grandpa Yook and Van-Itch in: *The Butter Battle Book* [59.0].

Biggel-Balls
Tallying mechanism to count sleepers in: *Dr. Seuss's Sleep Book* [23.0].

Billings, Billy
Boy who gobbles junk-food and has fifty fillings in: *The Tooth Book* [57.0].

Bim and Ben
Sweatered creatures who bring a broom and lead a band in: *Fox in Socks* [27.0].

Bingle Bug
Bug who rides in Thidwick's antlers in: *Thidwick, the Big-Hearted Moose* [7.0].

Binn, Kingdom of [*see* Kingdom of Binn]

Bippo-no-Bungus
Flock of wild birds from the Jungles of Hippo-no-Hungus in: *If I Ran the Zoo* [9.0].

Bippolo Seed
  Magic seed from the Bippolo Tree in: "The Bippolo Seed" [C9].
Birthday Bird
  Brainy bird who is in charge of all birthday celebrations in: *Happy Birthday to You!* [18.0].
Birthday Flower Jungle
  Place where Who-Bups live in: *Happy Birthday to You!* [18.0].
Birthday Honk-Honker
  Man who blows the birthday horn on Mt. Zorn in: *Happy Birthday to You!* [18.0].
Birthday Pal-alace
  Building, which includes 65 rooms just for "Sweeping-Up-After-Brooms," where the Big Birthday Party is held in: *Happy Birthday to You!* [18.0].
Birtram [*see* King Birtram]
Bix, Mr.
  Man whose Borfin "goes shlump every night" in: *Did I Ever Tell You How Lucky You Are?* [42.0].
Black Light Machine [*see* Dark Machine]
Blern, Alfred Bummel Flooder Hillary Billary (Sir)
  Historical figure in: *The Hoober-Bloob Highway* [D25.0].
Blindfolded Bowman
  Creature archer from Brigger-ba-Root in: *If I Ran the Circus* [13.0].
Blinn
  Father of twins, who fixes Dinn's shin with pins, in: *Oh Say Can You Say?* [55.0].
Blinx
  Hound-sort of beast who gives heavenly rides in: "To My Grandmother, My 'Buddy'" [C118].
Bliss Street
  Intersects with Mulberry Street, where a traffic jam is likely, in: *And to Think That I Saw It on Mulberry Street* [1.0].
Block, Miss
  Marco's school teacher in: "Marco Comes Late" [C68].
Blogg
  Bulbous creature that blows by in: *Oh, the Thinks You Can Think!* [49.0].
  Moose-snouted creature in: *The Shape of Me and Other Stuff* [44.0].
Bloogle Bird
  Pink and yellow bird in: *Would You Rather Be a Bullfrog?* [50.0].
Blooie Katz
  Hooie Katz's tail-bearer in: *I Can Lick 30 Tigers Today! and Other Stories*: "King Looie Katz" [34.0].

Bloop-Bleepers
Horn-snouted creatures that live in Mini-Moons in: *The Hoober-Bloob Highway* [D25.0].

Bloozer [*see* Three-Nozzled Bloozer]

Blue Goo
Sprinkled substance designed to gum up the enemy's butter in: *The Butter Battle Book* [59.0].

Blue Hoo-Fish
I Can Draw It Myself: By Me, Myself [36.0]

Bo-Bo [*see* Isle of Bo-Bo]

Bo-Boians
Beasts from the Isle of Bo-Bo in: "Who's Who in Bo-Bo" [C128].

Bobble, Miss
Listening teacher in: *Hooray for Diffendoofer Day!* [65.0].

Bodja-Nodja-Stan
Arabian locale infested with tigers in: *The Hoober-Bloob Highway* [D25.0].

Bofa
Avuncular yellow creature on the sofa in: *There's a Wocket in My Pocket!* [46.0].

Bolster
Horn-blowing creature in: *If I Ran the Circus* [13.0].

Bombastic Aghast
Frightful bird in: *Scrambled Eggs Super!* [10.0].

Bonkers, Miss
Teacher who teaches "EVERYTHING," but in a different style than the rest, in: *Hooray for Diffendoofer Day!* [65.0].

Boober Bay at Bum Ridge
Site of the Bunglebung Bridge in: *Did I Ever Tell You How Lucky You Are?* [42.0].

Boola Boo Ball
City even more idyllic than Solla Sollew in: *I Had Trouble in Getting to Solla Sollew* [28.0].

Borfin
Mr. Bix's machine, which goes "shlump" every night, in: *Did I Ever Tell You How Lucky You Are?* [42.0].

Bouncing Queen Maeve
Peeping Jack's ship in: *The Seven Lady Godivas* [3.0].

Brice, Mr.
Man whose house is inhabited by twenty-six mice in: *The Many Mice of Mr. Brice* [43.0].

Brice-Mice house
  Mr. Brice's house, which is full of mice, in: *The Many Mice of Mr. Brice* [43.0].
Brickle bush
  Prickly bush in: *The Sneetches and Other Stories*: "What Was I Scared Of?" [21.0]; *Halloween Is Grinch Night* [D23.0]
Brigger-ba-Root
  Home of the Blindfolded Bowman in: *If I Ran the Circus* [13.0].
Briggs, Pete
  Farmer who pats pigs in: *Oh Say Can You Say?* [55.0].
Bright Dwight Bird-Flight Night-Sight Light
  Oh Say Can You Say? [55.0]
Brothers Ba-zoo
  Monastic characters joined by their beards in: *Did I Ever Tell You How Lucky You Are?* [42.0].
Brown, Bill (Big Bill)
  Bully in: *I Wish That I Had Duck Feet* [29.0].
Brown (farmer)
  Victim who has a bucket stuck on his head in: *Because a Little Bug Went Ka-CHOO!* [48.0].
Brown, Mr.
  Protagonist in: *Mr. Brown Can Moo! Can You?* [37.0].
Brown Bar-ba-loots
  Bear-like creatures in: *The Lorax* [39.0].
Bru Na Boinn
  Port of call in: *The Seven Lady Godivas* [3.0].
Bruce [*see* King Bruce]
Brutus
  Arabella's besotted horse in: *The Seven Lady Godivas* [3.0].
Bub
  Nickname for the nameless baby in: *The Hoober-Bloob Highway* [D25.0].
Buck, Gin
  Great animal catcher in: "Bring 'em Buck Alive!" [C12].
Bumble-Boat
  Motorized paddle boat in: *Marvin K. Mooney, Will You Please Go Now!* [41.0].
Bumble-Tub Creek
  Stream where the Bumble-Tub Club floats in: *Dr. Seuss's Sleep Book* [23.0].
Bunglebung Bridge
  Hazardous construction site in: *Did I Ever Tell You How Lucky You Are?* [42.0].

Bup
Bird-like creature in: "Bring 'em Buck Alive!" [C12].
Burp, Mr.
Mr. Buck's assistant in: "Bring 'em Buck Alive!" [C12].
Bus Driver's Blight
Ailment in: *You're Only Old Once!* [60.0].
Bustard
Fluffy bird who only eats custard with mustard sauce in: *If I Ran the Zoo* [9.0].

Casbahmopolis
Arabian oasis city where Neefa Feefa lives, and destination of Pock and his magic piano when he pushes the violet knob, in: *Pontoffel Pock, Where Are You?* [D39.0].
Cat A, B, C ... [*see* Little Cat A, B, C ...]
Cat in the Hat
"Grown-up" size cat characterized with a red-and-white striped hat and a red bow tie; protagonist in: *The Cat in the Hat* [14.0]; *The Cat in the Hat Comes Back!* [16.0]; *The Cat's Quizzer* [51.0]; *The Grinch Grinches the Cat in the Hat* [D22.0].
Associated through the work's title with *The Cat in the Hat Beginner Book Dictionary* but not a featured character in that book.
Featured in illustrations throughout: *The Cat in the Hat Song Book* [31.0]; *I Can Read with My Eyes Shut!* [54.0].
Narrator in: *Daisy-Head Mayzie* [D6.0; 63.0].
Cat in the Hat (daughter of)
Unnamed character in: *I Can Lick 30 Tigers Today! and Other Stories*: "The Glunk That Got Thunk" [34.0].
Cat in the Hat (great great great great grandpa of) [*see* King Looie Katz]
Cat in the Hat (son of)
Unnamed character in: *I Can Lick 30 Tigers Today! and Other Stories*: "I Can Lick 30 Tigers Today!" and "The Glunk That Got Thunk" [34.0].
Featured in illustrations throughout: *I Can Read with My Eyes Shut!* [54.0].
Cat-in-the-Hat-mobile
The Cat in the Hat's clean-burning automobile in: *The Grinch Grinches the Cat in the Hat* [D22.0].
Cat Manor
The name of the Cat in the Hat's abode in: *The Grinch Grinches the Cat in the Hat* [D22.0].
Catfish
McElligot's Pool [6.0]

Chantz, Charlie
Boy with no body from the waist up in: *I Can Draw It Myself: By Me, Myself* [36.0].

Chimney Sweep's Stupor
Ailment in: *You're Only Old Once!* [60.0].

Ching Chung Chose
Historical figure in: *The Hoober-Bloob Highway* [D25.0].

Chippendale Mupp
Creature who bites his own very long tail in: *Dr. Seuss's Sleep Book* [23.0].

Chooie Katz
Kooie Katz's tail-bearer in: *I Can Lick 30 Tigers Today! and Other Stories*: "King Looie Katz" [34.0].

Chuggs
Bean-shooter bugs in: *If I Ran the Zoo* [9.0].

Cindy-Lou
Girl Who in: *How the Grinch Stole Christmas* [15.0].

Circus Fish
Acrobat fish in: *McElligot's Pool* [6.0].

Circus McGurkus
Morris McGurk's imaginary circus in: *If I Ran the Circus* [13.0].

Clark
Tusked aquatic creature brought home as a pet in: *One Fish, Two Fish, Red Fish, Blue Fish* [20.0].

Clementina
One of the seven Lady Godivas, nicknamed "Teenie," in: *The Seven Lady Godivas* [3.0].

Clinic Fish [*see* Norval]

Clotte, Miss
School nurse in: *Hooray for Diffendoofer Day!* [65.0].

Collapsible Frink
Creature in: *Dr. Seuss's Sleep Book* [23.0].

Colliding-Collusions
Race car driving team in: *If I Ran the Circus* [13.0].

Collins, Bartholomew ["Bart"]
The piano student in: *The 5,000 Fingers of Mr. T* [D2.0].

Collins, Eloise
Bart's mother, who initially is enamored with Dr. Terwilliker, in: *The 5,000 Fingers of Mr. T* [D2.0].

Cooker-mobile
Motorized chuckwagon in: *If I Ran the Zoo* [9.0].

County of Keck
   Setting for the story in: *Dr. Seuss's Sleep Book* [23.0].
Cow [*see* New-Cow-McGrew Cow; Umbus]
Crandalls [*see* Curious Crandalls]
Craneo-Bulgis (species)
   The taxonomy assigned to human geniuses in: *Are You a Genius?* (Second
   Series) [A5.0].
Creeping Katie
   Racing snail in: *The Hoober-Bloob Highway* [D25.0].
Crunk-Car
   Robotic vehicle in: *Marvin K. Mooney, Will You Please Go Now!* [41.0].
Cubbins, Bartholomew
   Protagonist page boy in: *The 500 Hats of Bartholomew Cubbins* [2.0];
   Bartholomew and the Oobleck [8.0]; "King Grimalken and the Wishbones"
   [C60]; "The Royal Housefly and Bartholomew Cubbins" [C93].
Culpepper Springs
   Place where stilt-walkers sleep in: *Dr. Seuss's Sleep Book* [23.0].
Curious Crandalls
   Sleepwalkers with candles on their heads in: *Dr. Seuss's Sleep Book* [23.0].

Da-Dake
   Daytime locale in: *Oh, the Thinks You Can Think!* [49.0].
Daisy-Head Mayzie [*see* McGrew, Mayzie]
Dake, Dr.
   Physician and Gertrude's uncle in: *Yertle the Turtle and Other Stories*:
   "Gertrude McFuzz" [17.0].
Dang-Dang
   "Where the D[elerium] T[remens] Animals Stay When They're Not Out
   On Jobs" in: "The Waiting Room at Dang-Dang" [C125].
Daniel
   Kick-a-Poo spaniel in: *The Butter Battle Book* [59.0].
[Dark Machine]
   The Grinch's contraption [unidentified in the script but termed "Dark
   Machine" and "Black Light Machine" in the typescript stage directions]
   that sends a shadow beam (and other disturbing light patterns) over great
   distance in: *The Grinch Grinches the Cat in the Hat* [D22.0].
Dave [*see* McCave, Mrs.]
Dawf
   Small red mountain bird in: *Scrambled Eggs Super!* [10.0].
de Breeze, Prof.
   Instructor who teaches Irish ducks to read Jivvanese in: *Did I Ever Tell
   You How Lucky You Are?* [42.0].

Dellar
  Cellar dweller in: *There's a Wocket in My Pocket!* [46.0].
Derring, Dr.
  Directs his chorus of Dr. Derring's Singing Herring in: *Happy Birthday to You!* [18.0].
Derwin [*see* King Derwin]
Desert of Dayd
  Setting for the poem: "The Kindly Snather" [C61].
Desert of Dreer
  Setting for the poem: "The Munkits" [C75].
Desert of Drize
  Setting for the story: *Did I Ever Tell You How Lucky You Are?* [42.0].
Desert of Zind
  Habitat of the scraggle-foot Mulligatawny in: *If I Ran the Zoo* [9.0].
Didd, Kingdom of [*see* Kingdom of Didd]
Diet-Devising Computerized Sniffer [*see* Wuff-Whiffer]
Diffendoofer Day
  Holiday proclaimed by Principal Lowe to celebrate the splendid outcome of the students' test in: *Hooray for Diffendoofer Day!* [65.0].
Diffendoofer School
  Fanciful school in: *Hooray for Diffendoofer Day!* [65.0].
Diffendoofer Song
  Alma mater of Diffendoofer School in: *Hooray for Diffendoofer Day!* [65.0].
Dinkerville
  Town that serves as the setting for: *Hooray for Diffendoofer Day!* [65.0].
Dike Trees
  Trees with knotted roots in: *The King's Stilts* [4.0].
Dingoe
  Long-tailed creature in: "Bring 'em Buck Alive!" [C12].
Dinkzoober and Dinkzott
  Street corner address of Diffendoofer School in: *Hooray for Diffendoofer Day!* [65.0].
Dinn
  Dinosaur skeleton (similar in appearance to the Rumfa-Ramfa Rinko-Dinko Pod-u-lotta Pike-us, *q.v.*) in: *Oh Say Can You Say?* [55.0].
Diplo-Duppla-Dykus
  "T-rex" type dinosaur skeleton in: *The Hoober-Bloob Highway* [D25.0].
Disptacher [*see* Hoober-Bloob, Mr.]
District of Dofft
  Place where Offt reside in: *Dr. Seuss's Sleep Book* [23.0].

Diver Getz and Diver Gitz
  Divers who catch Time-Telling Fish as birthday pets in: *Happy Birthday to You!* [18.0].

Do-Gooding Fairies
  Rotor-capped creatures, including McGillicuddy, Humbolt, Higbee, and Heuckendorf, who help Pock in: *Pontoffel Pock, Where Are You?* [D39.0]

Dofft [*see* District of Dofft]

Dog Fish
  Fish that chase Catfish in: *McElligot's Pool* [6.0].

Doo, David Donald
  Dr. Seuss's ABC [24.0]

Doodle Delight
  Green soft drink packaged in six-packs in: *Please Try to Remember the First of Octember!* [53.0].

Dooklas
  Unit of currency in: *Did I Ever Tell You How Lucky You Are?* [42.0].

Dorcas J.
  One of the seven Lady Godivas in: *The Seven Lady Godivas* [3.0].

Doubt-trout
  Fish who inhabit Roover River in: *The Sneetches and Other Stories*: "What Was I Scared Of?" [21.0].

Downers
  Birds who "droob down" and reflect bad economic trends in: "The Economic Situation Clarified" [C22].

Dr. ... [*see* ..., Dr.]

Drakmids [*see* Pastoolas]

Drew, Donald Driscoll
  Man whose family all grew teeth in: *The Tooth Book* [57.0].

Droon, Lord [*see* Lord Droon]

Drum-Tummied Snumm
  Creature whose stomach is used as a musical instrument in: *If I Ran the Circus* [13.0].

Dutter and Dutter
  Birthday cake slicers in: *Happy Birthday to You!* [18.0].

Dwight
  Daddy who likes to look at birds at night in: *Oh Say Can You Say?* [55.0].

East Beast
  Worst beast on the beach in: *Oh Say Can You Say?* [55.0].

Eiffelberg Tower
  Tower in Who-ville where the shirker shouts "YOPP!" in: *Horton Hears a Who!* [11.0].

Eight-Nozzled, Elephant-Toted Boom-Blitz
  Zook weapon contraption devised to combat the Kick-a-Poo Kid in: *The Butter Battle Book* [59.0].
Eisenbart, Dr.
  Physician in: *Daisy-Head Mayzie* [D6.0; 63.0].
Elephant-Bird
  Progeny of Mayzie's Egg and Horton's efforts in: *Horton Hatches the Egg* [5.0].
Elephant-Cat
  If I Ran the Zoo [9.0]
Ellie's Elegant Elephant
  The Cat's Quizzer [51.0]
Eric
  King Birtram's page boy in: *The King's Stilts* [4.0].
Eskimo Fish
  McElligot's Pool [6.0]

Fa-Zoal
  Locale ten miles beyond the North Pole in: *Scrambled Eggs Super!* [10.0].
Fairfax Apartments (Apartment 12-J)
  Residence of the shirker Who in: *Horton Hears a Who!* [11.0].
Falkenberg (Farmer)
  Raddish farmer in: *Did I Ever Tell You How Lucky You Are?* [42.0].
Fepp
  Three-toed creature in: "Bring 'em Buck Alive!" [C12].
Fibble
  Creature who carries the Flummox's tail in: *If I Ran the Circus* [13.0].
Fiddle Disters
  Suds blowers in: *The Hoober-Bloob Highway* [D25.0].
Filla-ma-Zokk
  Ram-Tazzled beast who follows the music played on an o'Grunth in: "How Gerald McGrew Caught the Filla-ma-Zokk" [C48].
Finagle the Agent
  Talent agent in: *Daisy-Head Mayzie* [D6.0; 63.0].
Finch the Florist
  Daisy-Head Mayzie [D6.0; 63.0]
Findow
  Antlered, long-eared creature in the window in: *There's a Wocket in My Pocket!* [46.0].
Finney's Diner
  Fresh fish establishment run by Finney in: *Oh Say Can You Say?* [55.0].

Finnigan Fen
   Locale whose residents include the Hoop-Soup-Snoop-Group in: *Dr. Seuss's Sleep Book* [23.0].
Fix-it-Up Chappie [*see* McBean, Sylvester McMonkey]
Fizza-ma-Wizza-ma-Dill
   World's biggest bird in: *If I Ran the Zoo* [9.0].
Flannel-Wing Jay
   Eggless bird in: *Scrambled Eggs Super!* [10.0].
Flobbertown
   Nearby dreary town where Diffendoofer School students will be transferred if they fail their important pop-test in: *Hooray for Diffendoofer Day!* [65.0].
Floob
   The letter Floob is for "Floob-Boober-Bab-Boober-Bups" in: *On Beyond Zebra* [12.0].
Floob-Boober-Bap-Boober-Bups
   Bobbing creatures unsuited for eating but useful as stepping stones in: *On Beyond Zebra* [12.0].
Flooble-Dooble [*see* Home Town Selection Contraption]
Floogel horn
   Twisted tuba-type horn in: *Pontoffel Pock, Where Are You?* [D39.0].
Flummox
   Tailed creature who carries a Three-Snarper-Harp on its back in: *If I Ran the Circus* [13.0].
Flunn
   The letter Flunn is for "Flunnel" in: *On Beyond Zebra* [12.0].
Flunnel
   Soft rabbit-like creature who hides in a tunnel and only comes out to the sound of music played on the o'Grunth in: *On Beyond Zebra* [12.0].
Flustard(s)
   Beast who eats mustard with custard sauce in: *If I Ran the Zoo* [9.0].
   Creatures who stand around waiting for things that can't come in: "The Flustards" [C29].
Foddle
   Six-footed blue poodle-like creature (termed a "Foodle" in some story boards) in: *The Hoober-Bloob Highway* [D25.0].
Foice
   Undefined career choice in: *Maybe You Should Fly a Jet! ...* [56.0].
Foo-Foo the Snoo
   Horned and snouted creature in: *I Can Read with My Eyes Shut!* [54.0].
Foodle [*see* Foddle]

Fooie Katz
King Looie's tail-bearer in: *I Can Lick 30 Tigers Today! and Other Stories*: "King Looie Katz" [34.0].

Foon
Creature who eats hot moon pebbles in: *If I Ran the Circus* [13.0].

Foona-Lagoona
Locale of the Foona-Lagoona Baboona, who are fuzzy-maned creatures hanging on vines, in: *Dr. Seuss's Sleep Book* [23.0].

Fort Knox
Town of Mr. and Mrs. J. Michael Krox in: *Dr. Seuss's Sleep Book* [23.0].

Fotta-fa-Zee
Distant land without illness or the ravages of old age in: *You're Only Old Once!* [60.0].

Fox, Mrs.
Music teacher in: *Hooray for Diffendoofer Day!* [65.0].

Fred
Boy without a head in: *I Can Draw It Myself: By Me, Myself* [36.0].
Dog who feeds Fritz, his master, in: *Oh Say Can You Say?* [55.0].

Fribble, Miss
Laughing teacher in: *Hooray for Diffendoofer Day!* [65.0].

Fritz
Man who feeds Fred, his dog, in: *Oh Say Can You Say?* [55.0].

Fronk, Mr.
Dispatcher of D.T. animals in: "The Waiting Room at Dang-Dang" [C125].

Fros [*see* To-an-Fro Marchers]

Frumm
Home country of the Drum-Tummied Snumm in: *If I Ran the Circus* [13.0].

Fuddle
The letter Fuddle is for "Fuddle-dee-Duddle" in: *On Beyond Zebra* [12.0].

Fuddle-dee-Duddle, Miss
Bird with a long fancy tail in: *On Beyond Zebra* [12.0].

Fudnuddler Brothers
Balancing act, with Lud on the bottom, in: *Oh Say Can You Say?* [55.0].

Fun-In-A-Box
A sort of "Pandora's Box" from which Thing One and Thing Two emerge to upset the household in: *The Cat in the Hat* [14.0].

Funicular Goats
Provide air transport in: *Happy Birthday to You!* [18.0].

Future-Viewing Contraption
The Hoober-Bloob Highway [D25.0]
Futzenfell, Fredric
The Cat in the Hat Song Book [31.0]

Ga-Dopps
Port-of-call in: *Please Try to Remember the First of Octember!* [53.0].
Ga-Zair [*see* Ga-Zar]
Ga-Zar
Locale where bedrooms and bathrooms are *far* apart in: *Did I Ever Tell You How Lucky You Are?* [42.0] (also used as a locale named Ga-Zair in: *The Hoober-Bloob Highway* [D25.0]).
Ga-Zayt
Locale of traffic jam on "Zayt Highway Eight" in: *Did I Ever Tell You How Lucky You Are?* [42.0].
Ga-Zoom
Cannon contraption in: *Marvin K. Mooney, Will You Please Go Now!* [41.0].
Gack
Moose-like creature whose antlers are used in a ring-toss game called "Ring the Gack" in: *One Fish, Two Fish, Red Fish, Blue Fish* [20.0].
Gadipulator
Magical box that produces a variety of contraptions for Mr. Hoober-Bloob's use in: *The Hoober-Bloob Highway* [D25.0].
Galla-ma-Gook
Furry creature who juggles a fish, a clock, a raddish, and other odd objects in: "Latest News from Mulberry Street" [C62].
Gasket
Creature from Nantasket in: *If I Ran the Zoo* [9.0].
Geeling
Peanut-munching creature who hangs from the ceiling in: *There's a Wocket in My Pocket!* [46.0].
Gekko
Locale where Gekko grottos are found in: *On Beyond Zebra* [12.0].
Gellar
Cellar dweller in: *There's a Wocket in My Pocket!* [46.0].
General Genghis Kahn Schmitz [*see* Schmitz, Genghis Kahn, Gen.]
George Washington School
Locale in: *Wacky Wednesday* [47.0].
Ghair
Green, long-tailed dog-like creature under the chair in: *There's a Wocket in My Pocket!* [46.0].

Gherkin
   Creature from Nantasket in: *If I Ran the Zoo* [9.0].
Giant White-Tufted Condor
   Rare bird from the Andes, captured at the cost of three fingers and a thumb, in: "Quality" [C91].
Gibney Grackle
   Rare bird from the Belgian Congo, captured at the expense of 298 men, in: "Quality" [C91].
Gickler, Gil
   Pock's boss and master dill pickler in: *Pontoffel Pock, Where Are You?* [D39.0].
Ginns, Dr.
   An "A and S Man" who specializes in antrums and shins in: *You're Only Old Once!* [60.0].
Gish
   Fisherman in: *I Can Draw It Myself: By Me, Myself* [36.0].
Gleeks
   Disease that afflicts the camel in: *I Had Trouble in Getting to Solla Sollew* [28.0].
Glikk
   The letter Glikk is for "Glikker" in: *On Beyond Zebra* [12.0].
Glikker
   Tiny creature who lives in weeds and juggles cinnamon (or cucumber) seeds in: *On Beyond Zebra* [12.0].
Glotz
   Goat-like creature with black spots in: *Oh Say Can You Say?* [55.0].
Glotz, Mr.
   Dumb man who breaks his teeth untying knots in: *The Tooth Book* [57.0].
Glunk
   Green foul creature in: *I Can Lick 30 Tigers Today! and Other Stories*: "The Glunk That Got Thunk" [34.0].
Glunker Stew
   Dish which recipe the Glunk "tele-foams" to his mother in: *I Can Lick 30 Tigers Today! and Other Stories*: "The Glunk That Got Thunk" [34.0].
Gluppity-Glupp
   Toxic liquid by-product of the Thneed factory in: *The Lorax* [39.0].
Godiva family
   When Lord Godiva dies in an equestrian accident, his seven nudist daughters (Clementina ["Teenie"], Dorcas J., Arabella, Mitzi, Lulu, Gussie, and Hedwig) swear to abstain from marriage until each of them discovers a "horse truth" in: *The Seven Lady Godivas* [3.0].

Golden Years Clinic on Century Square for Spleen Readjustment and Muffler Repair
  You're Only Old Once! [60.0]
Goo-Goose
  Goose that chews gooey goo in: *Fox in Socks* [27.0].
Goomy gun
  Wheeled cannon used by the citizens of Groogen to chase away Pock and his piano in: *Pontoffel Pock, Where Are You?* [D39.0].
Gootch
  Creature from Nantasket in: *If I Ran the Zoo* [9.0].
Gown, Gucky
  Boy who lives all alone in the Ruins of Runk in: *Did I Ever Tell You How Lucky You Are?* [42.0].
Gox
  Bear-like creature who boxes in: *One Fish, Two Fish, Red Fish, Blue Fish* [20.0].
Grackle [*see* Gibney Grackle]
Gree-Grumps
  Tree-dwelling growlers in: *Halloween Is Grinch Night* [D23.0].
Green eggs and ham
  Green ham and eggs with green yolks; the object of Sam's pestering in: *Green Eggs and Ham* [19.0].
Green grape cakes
  Ape cakes in: *Oh Say Can You Say?* [55.0].
Gretchen, Aunt
  The perservering aunt who spent 22 futile years applying for membership in the Daughters of the American Revolution in: "If at First You Don't Succeed — Quit!" [C53].
Grew-Grasters
  Yellow-tufted pink amorphous creatures (termed Grew-Gusters in some story boards) that float in outer space in: *The Hoober-Bloob Highway* [D25.0]
Grice
  Bird who lays eggs on ice in: *Scrambled Eggs Super!* [10.0].
Grickily Gractus
  Large bird who lays her eggs in prickly cactus in: *Scrambled Eggs Super!* [10.0].
Grickle
  Creature in: "Steak for Supper" [C112].
Grickle-grass
  Wild ground cover in: *The Lorax* [39.0].

Grimalken [*see* King Grimalken]

Grin-itch

Locale with Grin-itch spinach in: *The Sneetches and Other Stories*: "What Was I Scared Of?" [21.0].

Grinch [*see also* Beagle-Beaked-Bald-Headed Grinch]

Creature, personifying the spoiler and eventually established as being green, who:

• personifies the huckster in: "The Hoobub and the Grinch" [C43].

• lives just north of Who-ville and attempts to ruin the Whos' Christmas in: *How the Grinch Stole Christmas* [15.0].

• plagues the people of Whoville in: *Halloween Is Grinch Night* [D23.0].

• tries to get even with the Cat in the Hat in: *The Grinch Grinches the Cat in the Hat* [D22.0].

Grinchmobile

The Grinch's sooty automobile in: *The Grinch Grinches the Cat in the Hat* [D22.0].

Gritch

Creature in: "Steak for Supper" [C112].

Grizzly-Ghastly

Bear-like creature in: *If I Ran the Circus* [13.0].

Groogen

Balloon-flying Bavarian/Tyrolean locale where every day is the 15th of May, in: *Pontoffel Pock, Where Are You?* [D39.0].

Grooz

Place with tall flag poles in: *Did I Ever Tell You How Lucky You Are?* [42.0].

Grox

Pet creature, whose pet carrier is a "Grox Box," in: *Oh Say Can You Say?* [55.0].

Guff

Fuzz-balled creature in: *Oh, the Thinks You Can Think!* [49.0].

Gumm, Gregory, Mr.

School principal in: *Daisy-Head Mayzie* [D6.0; 63.0].

Gump, Mr.

Owner of a seven-hump Wump in: *One Fish, Two Fish, Red Fish, Blue Fish* [20.0].

Gunk

Saw-toothed beast in: "Bring 'em Buck Alive!" [C12].

Guss

Cave man retailer in: *Signs of Civil-iz-ation* [A15.0].

Guss-ma-Tuss

Unidentified product invented and marketed by Guss in: *Signs of Civil-iz-ation* [A15.0].

Gusset
Creature from Nantasket in: *If I Ran the Zoo* [9.0].
Gussie
One of the seven Lady Godivas in: *The Seven Lady Godivas* [3.0].
Gussie, Aunt
Gerald McGrew's aunt in: "If I Ran the Circus" [C54].
Gustav the Goldfish
Pet goldfish, also called "Gus," in: "Gustav, the Goldfish" [C39].
Gwark [*see* Island of Gwark]

Habbakuk
Failed inventor and grandfather in: "The Harassing of Habbakuk" [C40].
Haddow, Harry
Boy who can't make a shadow in: *Did I Ever Tell You How Lucky You Are?* [42.0].
Hakken-Kraks
Howling water beasts in: *Oh, the Places You'll Go!* [62.0]; *Halloween Is Grinch Night* [D23.0].
Ham-ikka-Schnim-ikka-Schnam-ikka Schnopp
Large horse-like creature in: *Scrambled Eggs Super!* [10.0].
Hamicka-Schlippika-Schloppika-Schlow
Large furry dog-like creature in: *The Hoober-Bloob Highway* [D25.0].
Hamika-Snamika-Bamika-Bunt
Rear-halfed creature in: *I Can Draw It Myself* [36.0].
Happy Way Bus
Out-of-commission transport in: *I Had Trouble in Getting to Solla Sollew* [28.0].
Harp-Twanging Snarp
Harpists in: *If I Ran the Circus* [13.0].
Hart, Herbie
Boy who has taken his Throm-dim-bu-lator apart and is now confronted with the daunting task of reassembling it in: *Did I Ever Tell You How Lucky You Are?* [42.0].
Hawtch-Hawtch
Locale of the Hawtch-Hawtcher Bee-Watcher and his Bee-Watch-Watchers in: *Did I Ever Tell You How Lucky You Are?* [42.0].
Heironimus, Thidwick
Someone who cares in: "Dr. Seuss' Poetry Corner: Pentellic Bilge ..." [C20]; *An Ode in Commemoration of Bennet Cerf's Thirty-Ninth Birthday* [A12.0].

Hejji
  Boy traveler who finds adventure in the Andean-like country of Baako in: "Hejji" [C42].
Hen, Hilda
  The Tooth Book [57.0]
Herk-Heimer Sisters
  Dr. Seuss's Sleep Book [23.0]
Herman
  Squirrel who nests in holes drilled by a woodpecker in Thidwick's antlers in: *Thidwick, the Big-Hearted Moose* [7.0].
Hernando
  One of the do-gooding fairies in: *Pontoffel Pock, Where Are You?* [D39.0].
Heukendorf
  One of the do-gooding fairies in: *Pontoffel Pock, Where Are You?* [D39.0].
Hewig
  One of the seven Lady Godivas in: *The Seven Lady Godivas* [3.0].
Hi!
  The letter Hi! stands for "High-Gargel-orum" in: *On Beyond Zebra* [12.0].
Higbee
  One of the do-gooding fairies (named Hymie in early story board drafts) in: *Pontoffel Pock, Where Are You?* [D39.0].
High-Gargel-orum
  Huge fuzz-collared creatures who, attached by a basket, serve as transport in: *On Beyond Zebra* [12.0].
Hinkle-Horn Honkers
  Dr. Seuss's Sleep Book [23.0]
Hinklefoos, Hobart Heinrich
  Magistrate in: *Pontoffel Pock, Where Are You?* [D39.0].
Hippo-Heimers
  Pack animals that carry birthday snacks on their backs and their heads in: *Happy Birthday to You!* [18.0].
Hippo-no-Hungus [*see* Jungles of Hippo-no-Hungus]
Hippocras
  Dog-like creature as big as a horse who scares the Linnix in: "The Royal Housefly and Bartholomew Cubbins" [C93].
Hock-Zocker court
  New sport court, combining tennis, basketball, skate hockey, jai alai, and lacrosse, in: *Please Try to Remember the First of Octember!* [53.0].
Home Town Selection Contraption
  "One-armed bandit" machine with a spinning "Flooble-Dooble" in: *The Hoober-Bloob Highway* [D25.0].

Hoo-to Foo-to Boo-to Bah
   Undescribed pet that is missing in: *The Cat in the Hat Song Book* [31.0].
Hoober-Bloob, Mr.
   Also named "The Dispatcher"; the protagonist, who sends babies to Earth,
   in: *The Hoober-Bloob Highway* [D25.0].
Hoober-Bloob Highway
   A twisted ribbon of light that transports babies from outer space to Earth
   in: *The Hoober-Bloob Highway* [D25.0].
Hoobub
   Creature who personifies the gullible consumer in: "The Hoobub and the
   Grinch" [C43].
Hooded Klophers
   Two creatures used as transport to the Birthday Pal-alace in: *Happy Birth-
   day to You!* [18.0].
Hoodwink
   Winking bird in: *If I Ran the Circus* [13.0].
Hooey
   Parrot in: *Oh Say Can You Say?* [55.0].
Hooie Katz
   Chooie Katz's tail-bearer in: *I Can Lick 30 Tigers Today! and Other Sto-
   ries*: "King Looie Katz" [34.0].
Hoop-Soup-Snoop-Group
   Group of hoop-rolling creatures in: *Dr. Seuss's Sleep Book* [23.0].
Hooper, Liz
   Peter's sister in: *Scrambled Eggs Super!* [10.0].
Hooper, Peter T.
   Boy cook in: *Scrambled Eggs Super!* [10.0].
Horton, the Elephant
   Protagonist, developed from the precursor character Matilda the Elephant
   (*q.v.*), who: hatches the abandoned Egg in *Horton Hatches the Egg* [5.0];
   plays the role of protector in *Horton Hears a Who!* [11.0]; tries to help the
   Kwuggerbug in "Horton and the Kwuggerbug" [C45]. In promoting *Hor-
   ton Hatches the Egg*, Dr. Seuss discussed Horton in the context of two
   other elephants that he had met: Norton, whose trunk grew ten inches
   each time he ate strawberry ice cream sodas; and Morton, who as Marco's
   pet could be walked on a leash [*see* F1].
Humbolt
   One of the do-gooding fairies (named Herman in early story board drafts)
   in: *Pontoffel Pock, Where Are You?* [D39.0].
Humming-Fish
   The Lorax [39.0]

Humperdink, Hooper
   Party pooper in: *Hooper Humperdink–? Not Him!* [52.0].
Humpf
   The letter Humf is for "Humpf-Humpf-a-Dumpfer" in: *On Beyond Zebra*
   [12.0].
Humpf-Humpf-a-Dumpfer
   Pond-dwelling creature in: *On Beyond Zebra* [12.0].
Hunches
   Creatures, including Happy Hunch, Real Tough Hunch, Better Hunch,
   Homework Hunch, Sour Hunch, Very Odd Hunch, Spookish [Four-Way]
   Hunch, Nowhere Hunch, Up Hunch, Down Hunch, Wild Hunches,
   Super Hunch, and Munch Hunch, imagined by the unnamed boy char-
   acter in: *Hunches in Bunches* [58.0].
Hut-Zut
   Musical instrument (strings and horn) in: *I Can Read with My Eyes Shut!*
   [54.0].

Igloo Ice Cream Company
   Hooper Humperdink–? Not Him! [52.0]
Ikka
   Creature in: "Steak for Supper" [C112].
"Indomitables"
   Oahspe High School football team, whose players are all named Seuss,
   in: "The Strangest Game I Ever Refereed" [C114].
Iota
   Blue-haired animal from North Dakota in: *If I Ran the Zoo* [9.0].
Island of Gwark
   Habitat of the world's biggest bird, the Fizza-ma-Wizza-ma-Dill, in: *If I
   Ran the Zoo* [9.0].
Island of Sala-ma-Sond
   Setting for the story "Yertle the Turtle" in: *Yertle the Turtle and Other Sto-
   ries* [17.0].
Island of Zort
   Setting for the poem "The Ruckus" [C94].
Isle of Bo-Bo
   Habitat of the Bo-Bobians in: "Who's Who in Bo-Bo" [C128].
Ish
   Creature with a wishing platter called a "Ish wish dish" in: *One Fish, Two
   Fish, Red Fish, Blue Fish* [20.0].
It-Kutch
   Creature from Ka-Troo in: *If I Ran the Zoo* [9.0].

Itch
The letter Itch is for "Itch-a-pods" in: *On Beyond Zebra* [12.0].
Itch-a-pods
Animals who race back and forth on a very high sidewalk in: *On Beyond Zebra* [12.0].

Jake, Dr.
Physician and Gertrude's uncle (named Dr. Dake in the book version) in: "Gertrude McFuzz" [C32].
Jake the turtle
Innocent turtle who gets bopped on the head with a coconut in: *Because a Little Bug Went Ka-CHOO!* [48.0].
Jake the Pillow Snake
I Can Read with My Eyes Shut! [54.0]
Jedd
Creature who sprouts pom-poms in: *Dr. Seuss's Sleep Book* [23.0].
Jertain
Chicken-legged creature behind a curtain in: *There's a Wocket in My Pocket!* [46.0].
Jibboo
Scraggly beast in: *Oh, the Thinks You Can Think!* [49.0].
Jigger-Rock Snatchem
Weapon contraption devised to combat the Tripple-Sling Jigger in: *The Butter Battle Book* [59.0].
Jill-ikka-Jast
Fleet-footed beast whose long ears serve as reins in: *Scrambled Eggs Super!* [10.0].
Jim
Daddy who likes to swim in: *Oh Say Can You Say?* [55.0].
Jivvanese
Language characterized by graphic symbols and taught to ducks by Prof. de Breeze in: *Did I Ever Tell You How Lucky You Are?* [42.0].
Joats
Goat-like creatures in: *If I Ran the Zoo* [9.0].
Joe Crow
Clothed bird in: *Fox in Socks* [27.0].
Jogg
The letter Jogg is for "Jogg-oons" in: *On Beyond Zebra* [12.0].
Jogg-oons
Desert-dune-dwelling, sad-tune-crooning blue-eyed creatures in: *On Beyond Zebra* [12.0].

Jones, Jimbo
   Toothless jellyfish who can't play the trombone in: *The Tooth Book* [57.0].
Jordan, Jerry
   Dr. Seuss's ABC [24.0]
Josiah
   Ukariah's grandpa in: *Halloween Is Grinch Night* [D23.0].
Jott [*see* Juggling Jott]
Judson
   One of the "Boys with the Siamese Beards" (the other is Whitney) in: *The 5,000 Fingers of Mr. T* [D2.0].
Juggling Jot
   Creature who juggles punctuation marks in: *If I Ran the Circus* [13.0].
Jungle of Nool
   Setting for the story in: *Horton Hears a Who!* [11.0].
Jungles of Hipp-no-Hungus
   Habitat for wild birds in: *If I Ran the Zoo* [9.0].
Jungles of Jorn
   Habitat for the horn-tooting apes in: *If I Ran the Circus* [13.0].

K.K. Kats
   Band that plays at the party in: *Hooper Humperdink–? Not Him!* [52.0].
Ka-Troo
   Habitat for exotic animals in: *If I Ran the Zoo* [9.0].
Katroo
   Setting for the story *Happy Birthday to You!* [18.0].
Katroo Birthday Pet Reservation
   Place where pets are arranged by height in: *Happy Birthday to You!* [18.0].
Katta-ma-Side
   Arctic canoe-like boat made of sea-leopard hide in: *Scrambled Eggs Super!* [10.0].
Katz, Mr.
   Science teacher in: *Hooray for Diffendoofer Day!* [65.0].
Katzen-bein, Zooie [*see* Zooie Katzen-bein]
Katzen-stein
   Kingdom, and setting for the story, in: *I Can Lick 30 Tigers Today! and Other Stories*: "King Looie Katz" [34.0].
Kaverns of Krock
   Scary caves in: *Did I Ever Tell You How Lucky You Are?* [42.0].
Keck, County of [*see* County of Keck]
Key-Slapping Slippard
   Green creature, which it is bad luck to kill, that lives in the keyhole and prevents its use in: *I Had Trouble in Getting to Solla Sollew* [28.0].

Kick-a-Poo Kid
   Weapon loaded with Poo-a-Doo powder and mounted on Daniel, a Kick-a-Poo spaniel, in: *The Butter Battle Book* [59.0].
King Abdulla Bullah Bull Bull Ben-eer
   Ruler of Casbahmopolis in: *Pontoffel Pock, Where Are You?* [D39.0].
King Birtram
   King of the Kingdom of Binn in: *The King's Stilts* [4.0].
King Bruce
   Temporarily psychotic Scottish king who finds false inspiration in a spider who is trying to make a lemon-meringue pie in: "If at First You Don't Succeed — Quit!" [C53].
King Derwin
   King of the Kingdom of Didd in: *The 500 Hats of Bartholomew Cubbins* [2.0]; *Bartholomew and the Oobleck* [8.0]; "The Royal Housefly and Bartholomew Cubbins" [C93].
King Grimalken
   Greedy king of the Kingdom of Didd in: "King Grimalken and the Wishbones" [C60].
King Looie Katz
   King of Katzen-stein (and the Cat in the Hat's great great great great grandpa) in: *I Can Lick 30 Tigers Today! and Other Stories*: "King Looie Katz" [34.0].
King Yertle [*see* Yertle the Turtle]
Kingdom of Binn
   Setting for the story *The King's Stilts* [4.0].
Kingdom of Didd
   Setting for the stories: *The 500 Hats of Bartholomew Cubbins* [2.0]; *Bartholomew and the Oobleck* [8.0]; "King Grimalken and the Wishbones" [C60]; "The Royal Housefly and Bartholomew Cubbins" [C93].
Kleezer, Frederick Van Klunk (Sir)
   Historical figure in: *The Hoober-Bloob Highway* [D25.0].
Klopps, Katy
   Dumb girl who chews off bottle caps in: *The Tooth Book* [57.0].
Klotz
   Goat-like creature with black dots in: *Oh Say Can You Say?* [55.0].
Knox, Mr.
   Foil to the fox in: *Fox in Socks* [27.0].
Knox, Nixie
   Dr. Seuss's ABC [24.0]
Kooie Katz
   Fooie Katz's tail-bearer in: *I Can Lick 30 Tigers Today! and Other Stories*: "King Looie Katz" [34.0].

Kratchmuks [*see* Pastoolas]

Kraus, Kitty O'Sullivan
  Girl who has a balloon swimming pool in: *Oh, the Thinks You Can Think!* [49.0].

Krox, J. Michael (Mr. and Mrs.)
  Couple whose clock has three hands in: *Dr. Seuss's Sleep Book* [23.0].

Kweet
  Bird with the world's sweetest eggs in: *Scrambled Eggs Super!* [10.0].

Kwigger
  Tiny red bird whose eggs are no bigger than a pin head in: *Scrambled Eggs Super!* [10.0].

Kwong [*see* Long-Legger Kwong]

Kwuggerbug
  Pesky bug in: "Horton and the Kwuggerbug" [C45].

Lake Winna-Bango
  Locale for the story: *Thidwick, the Big-Hearted Moose* [7.0].

Lapp, Little Lola
  Dr. Seuss's ABC [24.0]

Lass-a-lack
  Eggless bird in: *Scrambled Eggs Super!* [10.0].

Leaping Louella
  Winner of the snail race in: *The Hoober-Bloob Highway* [D25.0]

Lerkim
  Hideout where the Once-ler stays in: *The Lorax* [39.0].

Life-Risking-Track
  Race track in: *If I Ran the Circus* [13.0].

Linnix
  Bobtailed cat in: "The Royal Housefly and Bartholomew Cubbins" [C93].

Little Cat A, B and C
  Miniature "Cats-in-the-Hat" that come out of the Cat's hat, in shell sequence, to help clean up the mess in: *The Cat in the Hat Comes Back!* [16.0].

Little Cat D, E, F, and G
  Miniature "Cats-in-the-Hat" that pop out of the Little Cat C's hat in sequence to help clean up the outside mess in: *The Cat in the Hat Comes Back!* [16.0].

Little Cat H-V
  Miniature "Cats-in-the-Hat" that appear stacked under Little Cat G's hat in: *The Cat in the Hat Comes Back!* [16.0].

Little Cat W, X, Y, and Z
    Miniature "Cats-in-the-Hat" that appear on the head of Little Cat V in: *The Cat in the Hat Comes Back!* [16.0].
Lolla-Lee-Lou, Miss
    Pretty girl-bird in: *Yertle the Turtle and Other Stories*: "Gertrude McFuzz" [17.0].
Long-Legger Kwong
    Long-legged bird who lays her eggs from twenty feet in the air in: *Scrambled Eggs Super!* [10.0].
Looie Katz [*see* King Looie Katz]
Loon, Miss
    School librarian, who shouts "LOUDER!" in: *Hooray for Diffendoofer Day!* [65.0].
Lorax
    Personified voice of reason in: *The Lorax* [39.0].
Lord Droon
    King Birtram's chancellor, who didn't like fun, in: *The King's Stilts* [4.0].
Lord Godiva [*see* Godiva family]
Louella [*see* Leaping Louella]
Lowe, Mr.
    Sad, worrisome school principal in: *Hooray for Diffendoofer Day!* [65.0].
Luck, Luke
    Man who, along with his duck, likes lakes in: *Fox in Socks* [27.0].
Lulu
    One of the seven Lady Godivas in: *The Seven Lady Godivas* [3.0].
Lunk, Sgt.
    One of Dr. Terwilliker's minions in: *The 5,000 Fingers of Mr. T* [D2.0].
Lunks
    Creatures from the Wilds of Nantucket in: *If I Ran the Zoo* [9.0].
Lurch
    Tiny creature in a pail in: *If I Ran the Circus* [13.0].

Mack
    Turtle at the bottom of the pile, representing the oppressed "common man," in: *Yertle the Turtle and Other Stories*: "Yertle the Turtle" [17.0].
Malone, Dr.
    Physician who is called on to treat the verbal afflications of Gerald McCloy in: *Gerald McBoing Boing* [D19.0].
Marco
    Boy protagonist in: *And to Think That I Saw It on Mulberry Street* [1.0]; *McElligot's Pool* [6.0]; "Marco Comes Late" [C68].

Mariah
    Ukariah's grandma in: *Halloween Is Grinch Night* [D23.0].
Marshmallow Dip
    Enticing treat in: *I Am NOT Going to Get Up Today!* [61.0].
Mary Lou
    Boat with a big hole in: *Because a Little Bug Went Ka-CHOO!* [48.0].
Matilda, the Elephant
    Nurturing elephant (and precursor of the character Horton) in: "Matilda, the Elephant with a Mother Complex" [C69].
Max
    The Grinch's dog in: *How the Grinch Stole Christmas* [15.0]; *The Grinch Grinches the Cat in the Hat* [D22.0]; *Halloween Is Grinch Night* [D23.0].
Mayzie
    Lazy bird who laid the Egg and then abandons it in: *Horton Hatches the Egg* [5.0] [*see also* McGrew, Mayzie].
Mazurka [*see* Tufted Mazurka]
McBean, Sylvester McMonkey
    Huckster "Fix-it-Up Chappie" who plays on the fears and prejudices of Sneetches in: *The Sneetches and Other Stories*: "The Sneetches" [21.0].
McBoing Boing, Gerald [*see* McCloy, Gerald]
McBride, Henry
    Boy character who daydreams about career choices in: "The Great Henry McBride" [C36].
McCave, Mrs.
    Mother of twenty-three sons, all named Dave, in: *The Sneetches and Other Stories*: "Too Many Daves" [21.0].
McCloy, Gerald
    Title character, a first-grader who only utters noises such as "boing, boing," in: *Gerald McBoing Boing* [D19.0].
McCluck
    Greedy duck in: "The Bippolo Seed" [C9].
McCobb, Mike
    Trapeze artist in: *The Tooth Book* [57.0].
McElligot's Pool
    Setting for the story *McElligot's Pool* [6.0].
McFuzz, Gertrude
    Vain, jealous girl-bird in: *Yertle the Turtle and Other Stories*: "Gertrude McFuzz" [17.0].
McGann, Patrolman
    Police officer in: *Wacky Wednesday* [47.0].

McGillicuddy, Mac
> The principal do-gooding fairy who helps Pock in: *Pontoffel Pock, Where Are You?* [D39.0].

McGrew, Dr.
> One of a group of physicians, including McGuire, McPherson, Blinn, Ballew, Timpkins, Tompkins, Diller, and Drew, all of whom are consulted in: *You're Only Old Once!* [60.0].

McGrew, Gerald.
> Boy protagonist who imagines fantastic creatures and schemes in: *If I Ran the Zoo* [9.0]; "The Great McGrew Milk Farm" [C37]; "How Gerald McGrew Caught the Filla-ma-Zokk" [C48]; "If I Ran the Circus" [C54].

McGrew, Liz
> Gerald's sister in: "The Great McGrew Milk Farm" [C37].

McGrew, Mayzie
> Girl protagonist in: *Daisy-Head Mayzie* [D6.0; 63.0].

McGrew, Mr.
> Bearded man in: *I Can Draw It Myself: By Me, Myself* [36.0].

McGrew Milk Farm
> Gerald McGrew's imaginary get-rich enterprise in: "The Great McGrew Milk Farm" [C37].

McGrew Zoo
> Gerald McGrew's imaginary zoo, also referred to as "McGrew's Zoo," in: *If I Ran the Zoo* [9.0].

McGuff
> Greedy, demanding small bird in: "The Kindly Snather" [C61].

McGurk, Morris
> Boy protagonist who conjurs up his "Circus McGurkus" in: *If I Ran the Circus* [13.0].

McMunch
> Three school cooks who share the same name in: *Hooray for Diffendoofer Day!* [65.0].

McPhail, Snorter
> Loudest participant in the Snore-a-Snort Band in: *Dr. Seuss's Sleep Book* [23.0].

McPhee, Gus and Phoebe
> Married birds who separate because of Phoebe's obsessive cleaning in: "Wife up a Tree" [C129].

McPhee, Phillip and Phoebe
> Married birds who live in "Tree Number 3" [C121].

McPherson, Samuel S., Sgt.
> Grinch alarm warden in: *Halloween Is Grinch Night* [D23.0].

Mercedd
  Town whose residents include the Hinkle-Horn Honking Club in: *Dr. Seuss's Sleep Book* [23.0].

Merry Christmas Mush
  Unpopular green Christmas dish in: *Oh Say Can You Say?* [55.0].

Meyers, Butch
  Busdriver of the Happy Way Bus in: *I Had Trouble in Getting to Solla Sollew* [28.0].

Midwinter Jicker
  Inclement weather cycle, causing downpours, in: *I Had Trouble in Getting to Solla Sollew* [28.0].

Miff-muffered moof
  Substance that the Once-ler uses to make his clothes in: *The Lorax* [39.0].

Mike
  Bear-like creature who rides downhill on a bike made for three and pushes it uphill in: *One Fish, Two Fish, Red Fish, Blue Fish* [20.0].

Mini-Moons
  Cratered habitat for Bloop-Bleepers in: *The Hoober-Bloob Highway* [D25.0].

Mirabelle, the Elephant
  Formerly the mascot on the Wellesley College crew team, now a "professional drinking-elephantess," in: "Quaffing with the Pachyderms" [C90].

Miss ... [see ..., Miss]

Mitzi
  One of the seven Lady Godivas in: *The Seven Lady Godivas* [3.0].

Mokk [see Mountains of Mokk]

Mooney, Marvin K.
  Main pup-like character in: *Marvin K. Mooney, Will You Please Go Now!* [41.0].

Mop-Noodled Finch
  Eggless bird in: *Scrambled Eggs Super!* [10.0].

Morton, the Elephant [see Horton, the Elephant]

Moth-Watching Sneth
  Huge scary bird who lays red eggs in: *Scrambled Eggs Super!* [10.0].

Motta-fa-Potta-fa-Pell
  Country with exotic beasts in: *If I Ran the Zoo* [9.0].

Mountain Neeka-tave
  Mystic mountain and magicians' haunt in: *Bartholomew and the Oobleck* [8.0]; "King Grimalken and the Wishbones" [C60].

Mountains of Mokk
  Habitat for the Filla-ma-Zokk in: "How Gerald McGrew Caught the Filla-ma-Zokk" [C48].

Mountains of Tobsk
  Habitat of Obsks in: *If I Ran the Zoo* [9.0].
Mt. Crumpit
  Mountain where the Grinch plans to dump stolen gifts in: *How the Grinch Stole Christmas* [15.0].
  Mountain habitat of the Grinch, which looms above Who-ville, in: *Halloween Is Grinch Night* [D23.0].
Mt. Dill-ma-dilts
  Locale for mountain climbing in: *Great Day for Up!* [45.0].
Mt. Strookoo
  Mountain habitat of the tiny Mt. Strookoo Cuckoo in: *Scrambled Eggs Super!* [10.0].
Mt. Zorn
  Place where the birthday horn is sounded in: *Happy Birthday to You!* [18.0].
Mulberry Street
  Marco's route to school in: *And to Think That I Saw It on Mulberry Street* [1.0]; "Marco Comes Late" [C68].
  Officer Pat's beat in: "How Officer Pat Saved the Whole Town" [C49].
  Setting for the stories: "Latest News from Mulberry Street" [C62]; "Steak for Supper" [C112].
  The school locale in: *Gerald McBoing Boing* [D19.0].
  (Mulberry Street exists in Geisel's home town, Springfield, Mass.)
Mulcahey's Gazelles
  "Bring 'em Buck Alive!" [C12]
Mulligatawny
  Scraggle-foot desert creature in: *If I Ran the Zoo* [9.0].
Mullik, Mr.
  Inventor in: "Mr. Mullik Begs to Introduce His Three Checks to Matrimony" [C73].
Munkits
  Rock-hopping creatures in: "The Munkits" [C75].
Murgatroyd
  Horned beast in: "Bring 'em Buck Alive!" [C12].
Music-Fix [*see* Smell-Fix]
Mustard Pools
  Ponds used to clean up after lunch in: *Happy Birthday to You!* [18.0].

Na-Nupp
  Night-time locale with three moons in: *Oh, the Thinks You Can Think!* [49.0].
Nadd, Sir [*see* Sir Nadd]

Nantasket
  Wild habitat in: *If I Ran the Zoo* [9.0].
Nantucket [*see* Wilds of Nantucket]
Natch
  Cave-dwelling beast from Kartoom in: *If I Ran the Zoo* [9.0].
Nathan
  Lord Godiva's war horse in: *The Seven Lady Godivas* [3.0].
Ned
  Dog too long for his bed in: *One Fish, Two Fish, Red Fish, Blue Fish* [20.0].
Neefa Feefa
  Famous eye-ball dancer who captivates Pock in: *Pontoffel Pock, Where Are You?* [D39.0].
Neeka-tave [*see* Mountain Neeka-tave]
Nellar
  Cellar dweller in: *There's a Wocket in My Pocket!* [46.0].
Nerd
  Grumpy creature from Ka-Troo in: *If I Ran the Zoo* [9.0].
Nerkle
  Needle-nosed creature from Ka-Troo in: *If I Ran the Zoo* [9.0].
Nesselrode
  Long-necked creature in: "Bring 'em Buck Alive!" [C12].
New-Cow-McGrew Cow
  Cow with one head and 100 "machines" (*i.e.* udders; *cf.* below: Umbus) in: "The Great McGrew Milk Farm" [C37].
Nink
  Yellow creature floating in the sink in: *There's a Wocket in My Pocket!* [46.0].
Nitches
  Small caves where Nutches dwell in: *On Beyond Zebra* [12.0].
Nizzards
  Giant blackbirds who attack the Dike Trees and become Lord Droon's diet in: *The King's Stilts* [4.0].
Nobsk [*see* River of Nobsk]
Nolster
  Creature who plays a One-Nozzled Noozer in: *If I Ran the Circus* [13.0].
Nook
  Dog-like creature in a pink hat, on which is hooked a cook book, in: *One Fish, Two Fish, Red Fish, Blue Fish* [20.0].
Nook Gase
  Banana-munching creature in the book case in: *There's a Wocket in My Pocket!* [46.0].

Nool [*see* Jungle of Nool]
Nooth Brush
    Rainbow-colored bird on the toothbrush in: *There's a Wocket in My Pocket!*
    [46.0].
North Ninza-Skrinza-Bo
    Arctic locale in: *The Hoober-Bloob Highway* [D25.0].
Norton, the Elephant [*see* Horton, the Elephant]
Norval
    Sympathetic waiting room fish in: *You're Only Old Once!* [60.0].
Nuh
    The letter Nuh is for "Nutches" in: *On Beyond Zebra* [12.0].
Nupboards
    Little yellow creature in the cupboards in: *There's a Wocket in My Pocket!*
    [46.0].
Nupper
    Creature in: "Steak for Supper" [C112].
Nureau
    Blue creature in a bureau in: *There's a Wocket in My Pocket!* [46.0].
Nutches
    Creatures who live in small caves called Nitches in: *On Beyond Zebra*
    [12.0].

Oahspe High School
    School whose football team, the "Indomitables," plays Harvard in: "The
    Strangest Game I Ever Refereed" [C114].
Obsk
    Red-haired "sort of a Thing-a-ma-Bobsk" in: *If I Ran the Zoo* [9.0].
Ocean of Olf
    Habitat of a walrus named Rolf in: *If I Ran the Circus* [13.0].
October
    Month when wishes come true in: *Please Try to Remember the First of
    Octember!* [53.0].
o'Dell, Conrad Cornelius o'Donald
    Little boy who is learning to spell in: *On Beyond Zebra* [12.0].
Officer Pat [*see* Pat (Officer)]
Officer Thatcher [*see* Thatcher (Officer)]
Offt
    Creatures so light that they weigh "minus one pound" in: *Dr. Seuss's Sleep
    Book* [23.0].
Ogelthorpe, Oliver (Sir)
    Historical figure in: *The Hoober-Bloob Highway* [D25.0].

Ogler
  Medical clinician-technician in: *You're Only Old Once!* [60.0].
o'Grunth
  Horned, valve-bellowed instrument used: to capture the Filla-ma-Zokk
  in "How Gerald McGrew Caught the Filla-ma-Zokk" [C48]; to draw out
  the Flunnel in *On Beyond Zebra* [12.0].
Once-ler
  Sole survivor, narrator and antagonist personifying greed in: *The Lorax*
  [39.0].
One-Nozzled Noozer
  Horned instrument in: *If I Ran the Circus* [13.0].
One-Wheeler Wubble
  Monowheel carriage pulled by a camel in: *I Had Trouble in Getting to
  Solla Sollew* [28.0].
Oobleck
  New strange green substance that comes down from the sky and almost
  wrecks the Kingdom of Didd in: *Bartholomew and the Oobleck* [8.0].
Oppenbeem, Olivetta
  Chubby guest at the party in: *Hooper Humperdink–? Not Him!* [52.0].
Organ-McOrgan-McGurkus
  Calliope-like contraption that Morris McGurk plays in: *If I Ran the Cir-
  cus* [13.0].
Oscar the Ostrich
  Dr. Seuss's ABC [24.0]
O'Shea, Mordecai Ali Van Allen
  Oh, the Places You'll Go! [62.0]

Palooski [*see* Russian Palooski]
Pam the clam
  The Tooth Book [57.0]
Parsifal
  Hedwig's last horse in: *The Seven Lady Godivas* [3.0].
Pastoolas
  Unit of currency (absurdly smaller units include: drakmids, zlobeks and
  kratchmuks) used at the Terwilliker Institute in: *The 5,000 Fingers of Mr.
  T* [D2.0].
Pat (Officer)
  Policeman in: "How Officer Pat Saved the Whole Town" [C49].
Patrol Cats
  Cats, organized as Day Cats and Night Cats, trained to chase away the
  Nizzards in: *The King's Stilts* [4.0].

Peeping Brothers
  Peeping Tom, Peeping Dick, Peeping Harry, Peeping Jack, Peeping Drexel,
  Peeping Sylvester, and Peeping Frelinghuysen are the marital prospects of
  the Ladies Godiva in: *The Seven Lady Godivas* [3.0].
Peeping Jack (and Peeping Jack II)
  Mitzi's horse-propelled rowboats in: *The Seven Lady Godivas* [3.0].
Pelf
  Bird who lays blue eggs three times as big as herself in: *Scrambled Eggs
  Super!* [10.0].
Pepper, Peter
  Dr. Seuss's ABC [24.0]
Perilous Poozer of Pompelmoose Pass
  Leader of the Poozers and enemy of General Genghis Kahn Schmitz in:
  I Had Trouble in Getting to Solla Sollew [28.0].
Pete
  Boy without feet in: *I Can Draw It Myself: By Me, Myself* [36.0].
Pete's Pizza Palace
  Goal in a maze game in: *The Cat's Quizzer* [51.0].
Peter the Postman
  Skiing mailman who crosses the ice in: *Oh, the Thinks You Can Think!* [49.0].
Pickle Juice Machine
  The 5,000 Fingers of Mr. T [D2.0]
Pill-berry vine
  Source of pink magic pill-berries in: *Yertle the Turtle and Other Stories*:
  "Gertrude McFuzz" [17.0].
Pineapple Butterscotch Ding Dang Doo
  Enticing treat in: *I Am NOT Going to Get Up Today!* [61.0].
Pipulated Pink Weed
  The Hoober-Bloob Highway [D25.0]
Pitzu
  Unique bird with a prized tail plume in: "Hejji" [C42].
Plain-Belly Sneetch [*see* Sneetches]
Plunger, Mr.
  School custodian in: *Hooray for Diffendoofer Day!* [65.0].
Pock, Pontoffel
  Irresponsible boy protagonist and bungling pickle factory worker in:
  Pontoffel Pock, Where Are You? [D39.0].
Pollen, Dr.
  Allergy physician in: *You're Only Old Once!* [60.0].
Pommefritte, Jacques
  Contestant in: "The Great Diet Derby" [C35].

Pontoffel Pock [*see* Pock, Pontoffel]

Poo-Booken, Prince of [*see* Prince of Poo-Booken]

Poogle-Horn Players
Musicians who wake up the Prince of Poo-Booken in: *Did I Ever Tell You How Lucky You Are?* [42.0].

Poozers
Tiger-like creatures, led by Perilous Poozer of Pompelmoose Pass, in: *I Had Trouble in Getting to Solla Sollew* [28.0].

Potter, Mr.
T-crosser and I-dotter at an I-and-T factory in Van Nuys in: *Did I Ever Tell You How Lucky You Are?* [42.0].

Prairie of Prak
Setting for the poem "The Zaks" [C133].

Prairie of Prax [*see* Prax]

Prak [*see* Prairie of Prak]

Prax
Prairie setting for the story "The Zax" in: *The Sneetches and Other Stories*: "The Zax" [21.0].

Preep
Creature from Ka-Troo in: *If I Ran the Zoo* [9.0].

Prince of Poo-Booken
Did I Ever Tell You How Lucky You Are? [42.0]

Private SNAFU [*see* S.N.A.F.U., Pvt.]

Proo
Creature with heart-shaped hair from Ka-Troo in: *If I Ran the Zoo* [9.0].

Prooie Katz
Blooie Katz's tail-bearer in: *I Can Lick 30 Tigers Today! and Other Stories*: "King Looie Katz" [34.0].

Prune Picker's Plight
Ailement in: *You're Only Old Once!* [60.0].

Qilq, Qincy
Entrepeneur (and pseudonymous author) who solicits public donations to himself so that, once rich, he can become a philanthropist in: "Wanted, $1,000,000 for Qincy Qilq" [C126].

Quacking Quackeroo
Dr. Seuss's ABC [24.0]

Quan
The letter Quan is for "Quandry" in: *On Beyond Zebra* [12.0].

Quandry
Small red aquatic creature who lives by himself and worries constantly in: *On Beyond Zebra* [12.0].

Queek, Quincy
   News broadcaster in: *The Tooth Book* [57.0].
Queen of Quincy
   Dr. Seuss's ABC [24.0]
Queen of Qumland
   Warty-nosed historical figure in: *The Hoober-Bloob Highway* [D25.0].
Quibble, Miss
   Yelling teacher in: *Hooray for Diffendoofer Day!* [65.0].
Quiffer Quax
   The Hoober-Bloob Highway [D25.0]
Quilligan Quail
   I Had Trouble in Getting to Solla Sollew [28.0]
Quimney
   Swift unidentified creature in: *There's a Wocket in My Pocket!* [46.0].

Redd-Zoff, Jo and Mo
   Two world-champion sleep talkers in: *Dr. Seuss's Sleep Book* [23.0].
Revere, Paul (horse of)
   "Paul's horse," in "Happy Birthday to Sally ...:" *The Cat in the Hat Song Book* [31.0].
Rink-Rinker-Fink
   Rock-like beast in: *Oh, the Thinks You Can Think!* [49.0].
River of Nobsk
   Nearby the habitat of Obsks, in: *If I Ran the Zoo* [9.0].
River Wah-Hoo
   Beautiful river that runs by the city of Solla-Sollew in: *I Had Trouble in Getting to Solla Sollew* [28.0].
River Woo-Wall
   Beautiful river that runs by the city of Boola Boo Ball in: *I Had Trouble in Getting to Solla Sollew* [28.0].
Rolf
   Walrus who can balance on one whisker in: *If I Ran the Circus* [13.0].
Roller-Skate-Skiis
   If I Ran the Circus [13.0]
Rooshian Palooski [*see* Russian Palooski]
Roover River
   Habitat of Doubt-trout in: *The Sneetches and Other Stories*: "What Was I Scared Of?" [21.0].
Ross, Rosy Robin
   Dr. Seuss's ABC [24.0]
Ruckus
   Bird who makes noise, but without substance, in: "The Ruckus" [C94].

Ruins of Runk
    Dark, run-down place where Gucky Gown lives in: *Did I Ever Tell You How Lucky You Are?* [42.0].
Rumfa-Ramfa Rinko-Dinko Pod-u-lotta Pike-us
    "Brontosaurus" type dinosaur skeleton (similar in appearance to Dinn, *q.v.*) in: *The Hoober-Bloob Highway* [D25.0].
Russian Palooski
    Red-headed blue-bellied bird in: *If I Ran the Zoo* [9.0]; *The Hoober-Bloob Highway* [D25.0] (where it is named the "Rooshian Palooski" and its appearance is modifiied slightly).
Ruth
    Chickadee hussy, unkempt and uncouth, whom Gus McPhee takes up with in: "Wife up a Tree" [C129].

S.N.A.F.U., Pvt.
    Bungling U.S. Army private (*SNAFU* is an acronym for "Situation Normal All Fouled Up") in: *Private S.N.A.F.U.* [D40.0].
Sala-ma-goox
    Ruffle-necked hen who lays special red eggs in: *Scrambled Eggs Super!* [10.0].
Sala-ma-Sond [*see* Island of Sala-ma-Sond]
Sally
    Sister (her brother is unnamed) in: *The Cat in the Hat* [14.0]; *The Cat in the Hat Comes Back!* [16.0].
Salubrian Snipe [*see* Tizzle-Top Tufted Salubrian Snipe]
Sam
    Child protagonist, also referred to as "Sam-I-am," who pesters an unnamed grouchy adult character into trying green eggs and ham in: *Green Eggs and Ham* [19.0].
Sard, Sali
    Boy who has to mow a huge yard in: *Did I Ever Tell You How Lucky You Are?* [42.0].
Saw Fish
    McElligot's Pool [6.0]
Schleswigh, Gustaav, 3rd
    Cartesian well-digger and inventor of the earth-boring "Warbler" in: "Gustaav Schleswigh, 3rd, 'Hops Off'" [C38].
Schlopmicle Three-O
    String trio of musicians in the restaurant in: *The Grinch Grinches the Cat in the Hat* [D22.0].

Schlopp
Sundae-like dessert with a cherry on top in: *Oh, the Thinks You Can Think!* [49.0].

Schloppity-Schlopp
Toxic liquid by-product of the Thneed factory in: *The Lorax* [39.0].

Schlottz
Goatish creature with a long knotted tail in: *Did I Ever Tell You How Lucky You Are?* [42.0].

Schmitz, Genghis Kahn, Gen.
Mounted knight in armor in: *I Had Trouble in Getting to Solla Sollew* [28.0].

Schnack
Purple bird in: *Oh Say Can You Say?* [55.0].

Schneeloch, Miss
Marco's teacher, mentioned in a newspaper article promoting *Horton Hatches the Egg* [see F1].

Schnopp [*see* Ham-ikka-Schnim-ikka-Schnam-ikka Schnopp]

Schnorkin
Huge tank-tracked mechanical contraption that falls apart in: *The Hoober-Bloob Highway* [D25.0].

Schnutz-berry
Substitute for raspberries in the Glunker Stew recipe in: *I Can Lick 30 Tigers Today! and Other Stories*: "The Glunk That Got Thunk" [34.0].

Schultz, Fannie
Gerald's first grade teacher in: *Gerald McBoing Boing* [D19.0].

Schwinn, Gretchen von
Berlinner who has a "blue-footed ..." mandolin in: *Oh Say Can You Say?* [55.0] (her "Schwinn mandolin" appears as the "Self-Strumming Celestial Guitar" in *The Hoober-Bloob Highway* [D25.0]).

Sea Horse
McElligot's Pool [6.0]

Seersucker [*see also* Wild Seersucker]
Creature from Ka-Troo in: *If I Ran the Zoo* [9.0].

Self-Strumming Celestial Guitar
The Hoober-Bloob Highway [D25.0] (the same insturment appears as the "Schwinn mandolin" in *Oh Say Can You Say?* [55.0])

Sennacherib
Dog-like nymph of all good sons of Hooey in: "Hooeyana — A Reverie" [C44].

Seuss, Stanbridge, *et al.*
Teammates, all named Seuss, who play on the Oahspe High School

"Indomitables" football team in: "The Strangest Game I Ever Refereed" [C114].

Shade-Roosting Quail
Eggless bird in: *Scrambled Eggs Super!* [10.0].

Sheik Ali ben Giseh
Greatest of desert bird hunters, who captures a Sudanese Humming Bird, in: "Quality" [C91].

Single-File Zummzian Zuks
Ducks who carry their red eggs on their thumbs in: *Scrambled Eggs Super!* [10.0].

Sir Alaric
Keeper of Records in the Kingdom of Didd in: *The 500 Hats of Bartholomew Cubbins* [2.0].

Sir Nadd
Wise man in: *The 500 Hats of Bartholomew Cubbins* [2.0]; "King Grimalken and the Wishbones" [C60]; "The Royal Housefly and Bartholomew Cubbins" [C93].

Sir Snipps
Hat maker in: *The 500 Hats of Bartholomew Cubbins* [2.0].

Six-footed Foddle [*see* Foddle]

Skeegle-mobile
Vehicle used while hunting for arctic beasts in: *If I Ran the Zoo* [9.0].

Skipper Zipp's Clipper Ship Chip Chop Shop
Oh Say Can You Say? [55.0]

Skirtz
Mosquito-like bug in: *I Had Trouble in Getting to Solla Sollew* [28.0].

Skrink
Prairie dog-like creature in: *I Had Trouble in Getting to Solla Sollew* [28.0].

Skrope
Cleaning agent that cleans soup off of rope in: *Oh Say Can You Say?* [55.0].

Slick, Sammy
Dr. Seuss's ABC [24.0]

Slim Jim Swim Fins
Oh Say Can You Say? [55.0]

Slippard [*see* Key-Slapping Slippard]

Smell-Fix
Bottled magical deodorizer, which Bart adapts as a "Music-Fix" music-capturing device, in: *The 5,000 Fingers of Mr. T* [D2.0].

Smiling Sam
Toothy crocodile in: *The Tooth Book* [57.0].

Smorgasbord
Creature who carries delectibles in: *Happy Birthday to You!* [18.0].

Snarp [*see* Harp-Twanging Snarp]

Snather
Kindhearted, large-beaked bird who provides cooling shade in: "The Kindly Snather" [C61].

Snafu, Pvt. [*see* S.N.A.F.U., Pvt.]

Snee
The letter Snee is for "Sneedle" in: *On Beyond Zebra* [12.0].

Sneecher, Miss
Mayzie's teacher in Room Number 8 in: *Daisy-Head Mayzie* [D6.0; 63.0].

Sneeden's Hotel
McElligot's Pool [6.0]

Sneedle
Ferocious mos-keedle (a mosquito-like bug; *cf. above*: Ann) who can only be killed with a kerosene-soaked navy bean in: *On Beyond Zebra* [12.0].

Sneelock, Mr.
Store owner on whom Morris McGurk is relying for help, including being the drum major and others, in: *If I Ran the Circus* [13.0].

Sneelock's Store
Locale, owned by Mr. Sneelock, behind which is the vacant lot for the circus in: *If I Ran the Circus* [13.0].

Sneetches
"Sort-of-a-birds" in two kinds (Star-Belly and Plain-Belly) in: *The Sneetches and Other Stories*: "The Sneetches" [21.0].

Sneeth, Simon
Toothless snail in: *The Tooth Book* [57.0].

Sneggs
Bug in: *I Can Draw It Myself: By Me, Myself* [36.0].

Snell, Sam, Dr.
Physician who attends the camel in: *I Had Trouble in Getting to Solla Sollew* [28.0].

Sneth [*see* Moth-Watching Sneth]

Snick-Berry Switch
Three-branched stick used as a weapon in: *The Butter Battle Book* [59.0].

Snide bush
Berry-bearing woody plant in: *The Sneetches and Other Stories*: "What Was I Scared Of?" [21.0].

Snipps, Sir [*see* Sir Snipps]

Snookers and Snookers
"The Official Katroo Happy Birthday Cake Cookers" in: *Happy Birthday to You!* [18.0].

Snore-a-Snort Band
Snoring band in: *Dr. Seuss's Sleep Book* [23.0].

Snumm [*see* Drum-Tummied Snumm]

Snuvv

Once-ler's secret strange hole in his glove in: *The Lorax* [39.0].

Gloved creatures in: *Oh, the Thinks You Can Think!* [49.0].

Soapy Cooper's Super Soup-Off-Hoops Soak Suds

Oh Say Can You Say? [55.0]

Soggy Toast

Racing snail in: *The Hoober-Bloob Highway* [D25.0].

Solla Sollew

Idyllic city and destination of the unnamed protagonist in: *I Had Trouble in Getting to Solla Sollew* [28.0].

Soobrian Snipe

Birds in: *If I Ran the Circus* [13.0].

Sour-Sweet Wind

Wind that signals the approach of the Grinch in: *Halloween Is Grinch Night* [D23.0].

South Bookend, Minn.

Site of Zilch Zoo in: "Bring 'em Buck Alive!" [C12].

South-West-Facing Cranes

Scrambled Eggs Super! [10.0]

Spazz

The letter Spazz is for "Spazzim" in: *On Beyond Zebra* [12.0].

Spazzim

Horned beast handy for traveling in: *On Beyond Zebra* [12.0].

Spingel-Spungel-Sporn, Sally

The Cat in the Hat Song Book [31.0]

Spotted Atrocious

Ferocious caged beast with teeth weighing sixty pounds each in: *If I Ran the Circus* [13.0].

Spreckles, Dr.

Physician specializing in "footsies, fungus and freckles" in: *You're Only Old Once!* [60.0].

Springlebucks

Horned creatures resembling mountain goats in: *Pontoffel Pock, Where Are You?* [D39.0].

Spritz

Eggless bird in: *Scrambled Eggs Super!* [10.0].

Squitsch

Scissored tool for grabbing Grice eggs in: *Scrambled Eggs Super!* [10.0].

Star-Belly Sneetch [*see* Sneetches]

Star-Off Machine
McBean's contraption that removes star-bellies for $10 each in: *The Sneetches and Other Stories*: "The Sneetches" [21.0].

Star-On Machine
McBean's contraption that applies star-bellies for $3 each in: *The Sneetches and Other Stories*: "The Sneetches" [21.0].

State Highway Two-Hundred-and-Three
McElligot's Pool [6.0]

State Street
Biking locale in: *I Wish That I Had Duck Feet* [29.0].

Stethoscope Row
Doctors' offices hallway in: *You're Only Old Once!* [60.0].

Stickle-Bush Trees
Cacti in: *If I Ran the Circus* [13.0].

Stine, Stan
Bald-headed man in need of green hair in: *I Can Draw It Myself: By Me, Myself* [36.0].

Stipulated Stink-Weed
The Hoober-Bloob Highway [D25.0]

Stoopnagel
Name of an adolescent Murgatroyd in: "Bring 'em Buck Alive!" [C12].

Strawberry Flip
Enticing treat in: *I Am NOT Going to Get Up Today!* [61.0].

Street of the Lifted Lorax
Setting for the story *The Lorax* [39.0].

Stroodle
Sort of a stork, but with yellow fur like a poodle, in: *Scrambled Eggs Super!* [10.0].

Stroodle, Herman (Butch)
Classmate in: *Daisy-Head Mayzie* [D6.0; 63.0].

Stroogle, Maestro
Floogle horn maker in: *Pontoffel Pock, Where Are You?* [D39.0].

Stroogo
Ugly blue-green dungeon guard in: *The 5,000 Fingers of Mr. T* [D2.0].

Squeers, Grandmother
Modern granny in: "To My Grandmother, My 'Buddy'" [C118].

Sudanese Humming Bird
Nearly extinct bird captured at an expense of 10,000 pounds of gold in: "Quality" [C91].

Sue
Girl who sews socks, among other things, in: *Fox in Socks* [27.0].

Super-Axe-Hacker
  Truffula Tree-felling contraption in: *The Lorax* [39.0].
Super-zooper-flooper-do
  Mr. Plunger's janitorial machine, which keeps the whole school clean, in: *Hooray for Diffendoofer Day!* [65.0].
Sutherland sisters
  Three wacky girls in: *Wacky Wednesday* [47.0].
Swak
  Eel-like creature in: "Bring 'em Buck Alive!" [C12].
Sweet, Horace P.
  Happy Way Bus Line president in: *I Had Trouble in Getting to Solla Sollew* [28.0].
Swomee-Swans
  The Lorax [39.0]

Tadd

  Todd's twin in: "Tadd and Todd" [C115].
Teenie [*see* Clementina]
Tellar
  Cellar dweller in: *There's a Wocket in My Pocket!* [46.0].
Terwilliger, Uncle
  Dr. Seuss's make-believe uncle in: *The Cat in the Hat Song Book* [31.0]; "My Uncle Terwilliger on the Art of Eating Popovers" [C77].
Terwilliker, Dr.
  The piano teacher (named "Terwilliger" in early drafts of the screenplay) who runs the Terwilliker Institute and has a grandiose teaching method in: *The 5,000 Fingers of Mr. T* [D2.0].
Terwilliker Institute
  Evil locale run by Dr. Terwilliker in: *The 5,000 Fingers of Mr. T* [D2.0].
Thatcher (Officer)
  Policeman in: *Daisy-Head Mayzie* [D6.0; 63.0].
Thidwick
  Moose who is kind to a fault in: *Thidwick, the Big-Hearted Moose* [7.0]; *see also* Heironimus, Thidwick.
Thing-a-ma-Bobsk [*see* Obsk]
Thing One and Thing Two
  Blue-haired child-like creatures who spring out of the Cat in the Hat's Fun-In-A-Box and wreak havoc in the house in: *The Cat in the Hat* [14.0].
Thinker-Upper
  The personified imagination of the unnamed sister (the Cat in the Hat's daughter) in: *I Can Lick 30 Tigers Today! and Other Stories*: "The Glunk That Got Thunk" [34.0].

Thnad
  The letter Thnad is for "Thnadners" in: *On Beyond Zebra* [12.0].
Thnadners
  Creatures whose shadows are inversely proportional to their size in: *On Beyond Zebra* [12.0].
Thneed
  Useless all-purpose garment that the Once-ler knits from Truffula Tree tuft in: *The Lorax* [39.0].
Three-Nozzled Bloozer
  Horned instrument in: *If I Ran the Circus* [13.0].
Three-Seater Zatz-it Nose-Patting Extension
  Monocycle contraption used for patting the nose of the Zatz-it in: *On Beyond Zebra* [12.0].
Throm-dim-bu-lator
  Complex machine with clocks and gears, all scattered apart in pieces, in: *Did I Ever Tell You How Lucky You Are?* [42.0].
Through-Horns-Jumping-Deer
  Acrobatic deer in: *If I Ran the Circus* [13.0].
Thwerll
  Bug with snarled legs in: *If I Ran the Zoo* [9.0].
Tick-Tack-Toe
  Wild beast with the game patterned on his belly in: *If I Ran the Zoo* [9.0].
Time-Telling Fish
  Happy Birthday to You! [18.0]
Tizzle-Top Tufted Salubrian Snipe
  Feather-headed bird in: *The Hoober-Bloob Highway* [D25.0]
Tizzle-Topped Grouse
  Tree dweller whose red egg mixes with that of the Sala-ma-goox's in: *Scrambled Eggs Super!* [10.0].
Tizzle-topped Tufted Mazurka [*see* Tufted Mazurka]
Tizzy
  Three-eyelashed bird with blue eggs in: *Scrambled Eggs Super!* [10.0].
To-an-Fro Marchers
  Fros and Tos, who march on top of each other in five layers, in: *If I Ran the Circus* [13.0].
Tobsk [*see* Mountains of Tobsk]
Todd
  Tadd's twin in: "Tadd and Todd" [C115].
Toney, Jr.
  Infant who speculates about the arrival of his new baby brother in: "Somebody's a-Comin' to Our House" [C107].

Tos [*see* To-an-Fro Marchers]

Tournament Knights
Boxing glove jousters (Sirs Hector, Vector, Bopps, Beers, Hawkins, Dawkins, Jawks, and Jeers) in: *If I Ran the Circus* [13.0].

Tree Number 3
McPhee domicile in: "Tree Number 3" [C121].

Tree-Spider
Bug who spins his web in Thidwick's antlers in: *Thidwick, the Big-Hearted Moose* [7.0].

Tri-Motored Bird-Transport
Airplane contraption in: "Quality" [C91].

Triple-Sling Jigger
Weapon contraption aimed at VanItch in: *The Butter Battle Book* [59.0].

Truffle
Fluff-muffled creature in: *If I Ran the Circus* [13.0].

Truffula Trees
Bright-colored trees that bear Truffula Fruits and have soft tuft, which is used to make Thneed, in: *The Lorax* [39.0].

Tufted Mazurka
Tizzle-topped, long-throated canary from Yerka in: *If I Ran the Zoo* [9.0].

Turnbull triplets
"The Tragic Tale of the Turnbull Triplets" [C120]

Tutt-a-Tutt Tree
Source of nuts that, when chewed, give strength to teeth and length to hair in: *You're Only Old Once!* [60.0].

Tuttle-Tuttle Tree
Haunt for tired turtles in: *Dr. Seuss's ABC* [24.0].

Tweetle-Beetles
Tiny pink bugs that battle each other in bottled puddles in: *The Hoober-Bloob Highway* [D25.0].

Twiddler Owls
Owls with inferior, dusty-tasting eggs in: *Scrambled Eggs Super!* [10.0].

Twining, Miss
Teacher of knot tying, among other skills, in: *Hooray for Diffendoofer Day!* [65.0].

Ubb, Uncle
Dr. Seuss's ABC [24.0]

Ukariah
Boy Who who stands up to the evil Grinch in: *Halloween Is Grinch Night* [D23.0].

Um
   The letter Um is for "Umbus" in: *On Beyond Zebra* [12.0].
Umbroso, Mrs.
   McElligot's Pool [6.0]
Umbus
   Cow with one head and infinite sets of udders and feet (*cf.* above: New-Cow-McGrew Cow) in: *On Beyond Zebra* [12.0].
Uncle ... [*see* ..., Uncle]
Uppers
   Birds who represent positive economic trends, except on alternate Thursdays, in: "The Economic Situation Clarified" [C22].
Utterly Sputter
   Flying contraption that sprinkles Blue Goo; both the Yooks and the Zooks have this weapon, causing a temporary stand-off in: *The Butter Battle Book* [59.0].

Vacu-Sound Sweeper [*see* Acoustical Anti Audial Bleeper]
Vale of Va-Vode
   Locale in: *Dr. Seuss's Sleep Book* [23.0].
Valley of Vail
   Locale of the Chippendale Mupp in: *Dr. Seuss's Sleep Book* [23.0].
Valley of Vung
   Locale in: *I Had Trouble in Getting to Solla Sollew* [28.0].
Van Ness, Dr.
   Physician engaged in the study of stress in: *You're Only Old Once!* [60.0].
Van Tass, Einstein
   Brightest boy in Mayzie's class in: *Daisy-Head Mayzie* [D6.0; 63.0].
Van Vleck
   Bug whose yawn starts everyone else's yawning in: *Dr. Seuss's Sleep Book* [23.0].
VanBuss, Mr.
   Man who sold Gustav the Goldfish in: "Gustav, the Goldfish" [C39].
VanItch
   Zook who fights against Grandpa Yook in: *The Butter Battle Book* [59.0].
Vina, Vera Violet
   Dr. Seuss's ABC [24.0]
Vining, Miss
   Teacher who peppers pigeons and puts saddles on lizards and leopards in: *Hooray for Diffendoofer Day!* [65.0].
Vipp
   Habitat of the Vipper of Vipp in: *Oh, the Thinks You Can Think!* [49.0].

Vipper of Vipp
    Regal bird in: *Oh, the Thinks You Can Think!* [49.0].
Vlad Vlad-i-koff
    Black-bottomed eagle who disposes of Horton's clover in: *Horton Hears a Who!* [11.0].
Von Crandall, Dr.
    Ear doctor in: *You're Only Old Once!* [60.0].
Von Eiffel, Dr.
    Dietician in: *You're Only Old Once!* [60.0].
Voom
    Essence in Little Cat Z's hat that cleans up everything in: *The Cat in the Hat Comes Back!* [16.0].
Vroo
    The letter Vroo is for "Vrooms" in: *On Beyond Zebra* [12.0].
Vrooms
    Two brothers, built like brooms, who take turns sweeping using each other, in: *On Beyond Zebra* [12.0].
Vudds
    Creatures in: "Bring 'em Buck Alive!" [C12].
Vug
    Unidentified beast lying under the rug in: *There's a Wocket in My Pocket!* [46.0].

WQUACK
    Radio call letters in: *The Tooth Book* [57.0].
Wah-Hoo, River [*see* River Wah-Hoo]
Warbler
    Contraption designed to bore and transport a passenger through the center of the earth in: "Gustaav Schleswigh, 3rd, 'Hops Off'" [C38].
Wasket
    Purple creature in a waste basket in: *There's a Wocket in My Pocket!* [46.0].
Waterloo, Willy
    Dr. Seuss's ABC [24.0]
Wellar
    Cellar dweller in: *There's a Wocket in My Pocket!* [46.0].
West Beast
    Best beast on the beach in: *Oh Say Can You Say?* [55.0].
West Gee-Hossa-Flat
    Locale with a dead-end road in: *Hunches in Bunches* [58.0].
West Upper Ben-Deezing
    Home of the Zoom-a-Zoom Troupe in: *If I Ran the Circus* [13.0].

West Watch-A-Ka-Tella
Baby's ("Bub's") earthly destination, where there are rules and chores but also delights, in: *The Hoober-Bloob Highway* [D25.0].

Wheef
Creature in: "Steak for Supper" [C112].

Whelden the Wheeler
Orderly in: *You're Only Old Once!* [60.0].

Which-What-Who
Combined imaginary attributes (duck feet, antlers, long tail, spouting hat) of the boy in: *I Wish That I Had Duck Feet* [29.0].

Whisper-ma-Phone
Once-ler's audio-phone contraption in: *The Lorax* [39.0].

Whitney
One of the "Boys with the Siamese Beards" (the other is Judson) in: *The 5,000 Fingers of Mr. T* [D2.0].

Who, Cindy-Lou [*see* Cindy-Lou]

Who-Bups
Creatures who clip tasty treats from foliage in Birthday Flower Jungle in: *Happy Birthday to You!* [18.0].

Who-hash
Canned food in: *How the Grinch Stole Christmas* [15.0].

Who-pudding
Christmas dish in: *How the Grinch Stole Christmas* [15.0].

Who-roast-beast
Christmas dish in: *How the Grinch Stole Christmas* [15.0].

Who-ville [also sometimes: Whoville]
Residence of Whos in: *Horton Hears a Who!* [11.0]; *How the Grinch Stole Christmas* [15.0]; *Halloween Is Grinch Night* [D23.0].

Whos
Small creatures from Who-ville in: *Horton Hears a Who!* [11.0]; *How the Grinch Stole Christmas* [15.0]; *Halloween Is Grinch Night* [D23.0].

Whoville [*see* Who-ville]

Whyllis, Phyllis
Three-time graduate of Smith College and secretary to Colonel Gimbel in: "The Clock Strikes 13!" [C16].

Wickersham Brothers
Three big jungle monkeys who, with their extended family, harass Horton in: *Horton Hears a Who!* [11.0].

Wienerschnitzel
Flying bird in: "Bring 'em Buck Alive!" [C12].

Wiggins, Warren
Dr. Seuss's ABC [24.0]

Wilberforce, Waldo
  The Cat in the Hat Song Book [31.0]
Wild Seersucker
  Fish-like beast in: "Bring 'em Buck Alive!" [C12].
Wilds of Nantucket
  Habitat of Lunks in: *If I Ran the Zoo* [9.0].
Wilfred
  Grand Duke and nephew of King Derwin in: *The 500 Hats of Bartholomew Cubbins* [2.0].
Wily Walloo
  Creature who can throw his long tail like a lassoo in: *If I Ran the Circus* [13.0].
Witzel Birds
  Whistling birds in: *The Grinch Grinches the Cat in the Hat* [D22.0].
Wobble, Miss
  Smelling teacher in: *Hooray for Diffendoofer Day!* [65.0].
Wocket
  Small furry green creature with light brown hair, who peeks out of the boy's hip pocket in: *There's a Wocket in My Pocket!* [46.0].
Wogs
  World's sweetest frogs, which Kweet eat, in: *Scrambled Eggs Super!* [10.0].
Wolgasts
  Man-eating herd animals in: "Bring 'em Buck Alive!" [C12].
Woo, Waldo
  Dr. Seuss's ABC [24.0]
Woo-Wall, River [*see* River Woo-Wall]
Woozo [*see* Wuzzy Woozo]
Woset
  Long-eared yellow creature in a closet in: *There's a Wocket in My Pocket!* [46.0].
Wubble [*see* One-Wheeler Wubble]
Wuff-Whiffer
  "Diet-Devising Computerized Sniffer" in: *You're Only Old Once!* [60.0].
Wum
  The letter Wum is for "Wumbus" in: *On Beyond Zebra* [12.0].
Wumbus
  Whale-like mountain dweller in: *On Beyond Zebra* [12.0].
  Color-changing monster in: *Halloween Is Grinch Night* [D23.0].
Wump
  Camel-like creature, in one-hump and seven-hump versions, in: *One Fish, Two Fish, Red Fish, Blue Fish* [20.0].

Wuzzy Woozo
  Fuzzy creature in: *Halloween Is Grinch Night* [D23.0].

Yekk
  The letter Yekk is for "Yekko" in: *On Beyond Zebra* [12.0].
Yekko
  Mustached creature who howls in an underground grotto in: *On Beyond Zebra* [12.0].
Yellow-Green Penguin
  Rare arctic bird, captured at a cost of $300,000, in: "Quality" [C91].
Yeps
  Friendly green creatures who sit on the steps in: *There's a Wocket in My Pocket!* [46.0].
Yerka
  African island in: *If I Ran the Zoo* [9.0].
Yertle the Turtle
  Despotic king of the pond (for Dr. Seuss the character represented Adolph Hitler) on the Island Sala-ma-Sond in: *Yertle the Turtle and Other Stories*: "Yertle the Turtle" [17.0].
Yill-iga-yakk
  Front-halfed yakk in: *I Can Draw It Myself* [36.0].
Ying
  Creature who sings in the bath in: *One Fish, Two Fish, Red Fish, Blue Fish* [20.0].
Yink
  Pink-tufted creature who likes to wink and drink pink ink in: *One Fish, Two Fish, Red Fish, Blue Fish* [20.0].
Yookery
  Bomb shelter in: *The Butter Battle Book* [59.0].
Yookie-Ann Sue
  Chief drum majorette of the Butter-Up Band in: *The Butter Battle Book* [59.0].
Yooks
  People who live on "this side" of the Wall and eat their bread with the butter-side up in: *The Butter Battle Book* [59.0].
Yopp
  Tiny blue creature who likes to hop from finger to finger in: *One Fish, Two Fish, Red Fish, Blue Fish* [20.0].
Yorgenson, Yolanda
  Dr. Seuss's ABC [24.0]
Yot
  Pink-frilled creature in a pot in: *There's a Wocket in My Pocket!* [46.0].

Yottle
  Striped straw-spewing creature in a bottle in: *There's a Wocket in My Pocket!* [46.0].
Yuzz
  The letter Yuzz is for "Yuzz-a-ma-Tuzz" in: *On Beyond Zebra* [12.0].
Yuzz-a-ma-Tuzz
  Blue-eyed creature in: *On Beyond Zebra* [12.0].

Zabladowski, August
  The plumber in: *The 5,000 Fingers of Mr. T* [D2.0].
Zable
  Hot-dog eater on the table in: *There's a Wocket in My Pocket!* [46.0].
Zaks
  Confrontational obstinate creatures (*cf.* Zax) in: "The Zaks" [C133].
Zall
  Swift unidentified creature that scoots down the hall in: *There's a Wocket in My Pocket!* [46.0].
Zamp
  Orange creature in the lamp in: *There's a Wocket in My Pocket!* [46.0].
Zans
  Large creature whose horns are useful for opening cans in: *One Fish, Two Fish, Red Fish, Blue Fish* [20.0].
Zanzibar Zidd
  Caged bird in: *I Can Draw It Myself: By Me, Myself* [36.0].
Zatz
  The letter Zatz is for "Zatz-it" in: *On Beyond Zebra* [12.0].
Zatz-it
  Giraffe-like creature whose nose is too high to pet, except by using the Three-Seater Zatz-it Nose-Patting Extension, in: *On Beyond Zebra* [12.0].
Zax
  Singular and plural for confrontational, obstinate creatures, named "Zaks" in an earlier version of the story, in: *The Sneetches and Other Stories*: "The Zax" [21.0].
Zaxx
  Cave man retailer and Guss's competitor in: *Signs of Civil-iz-ation* [A15.0].
Zaxx-ma-Taxx
  Zaxx's product that competes with the Guss-ma-Tuss in: *Signs of Civil-iz-ation* [A15.0].
Zeds
  Yellow pets, each with one fast-growing hair on its head, in: *One Fish, Two Fish, Red Fish, Blue Fish* [20.0].

Zeep
Pet long-tailed bear-like creature in: *One Fish, Two Fish, Red Fish, Blue Fish* [20.0].

Zelf
Purple creature lying on the top shelf in: *There's a Wocket in My Pocket!* [46.0].

Zellar
Cellar dweller in: *There's a Wocket in My Pocket!* [46.0].

Zenobia
Queen of the spelling bees in: *Spelling Bees* [A10.0].

Ziffer-Zoof Seeds
Seeds "which nobody wants because nobody needs" in: *Dr. Seuss's Sleep Book* [23.0].

Ziffs
Birds just like Zuffs, but living on cliffs, in: *Scrambled Eggs Super!* [10.0].

Zifft
Fluff-footed, frizzle-topped, three-fingered creature who makes the perfect Christmas gift in: "Perfect Present" [C84].

Zike-Bike
Three-wheeled in-line bicycle in: *Marvin K. Mooney, Will You Please Go Now!* [41.0].

Zilch Zoo
Mr. Buck's zoo, with celophane cages, in South Bookend, Minn., in: "Bring 'em Buck Alive!" [C12].

Zillow
Friendly mustached creature on the pillow in: *There's a Wocket in My Pocket!* [46.0].

Zinn-a-zu Birds
Family of birds, including a woodpecker uncle, who nest in Thidwick's antlers in: *Thidwick, the Big-Hearted Moose* [7.0].

Zinniga-Zanniga Tree
Tree, the flowers of which produce wonderful medicinal juices, in: "The Rabbit, the Bear and the Zinniga-Zanniga" [C92].

Zinzibar-Zanzibar trees
Habitat of birds whose eggs taste like the air in the holes of Swiss cheese in: *Scrambled Eggs Super!* [10.0].

Zip-Around Flynn
Fast-flying blue jay who flies *too* fast in: "Speedy Boy" [C110].

Zizzer-Zazza-Zuzz
Creature with pink-and-white checkered fur in: *Dr. Seuss's ABC* [24.0].

Zlobeks [*see* Pastoolas]

Zlock
   Striped creature behind the clock in: *There's a Wocket in My Pocket!* [46.0].
Zobbel
   Midget creature in: "Bring 'em Buck Alive!" [C12].
Zode
   Creature who approaches life too cautiously and ends up with nothing but split pants in: "Did I Ever Tell You …?" [C18].
Zomba-ma-Tant
   Mountainous oriental region in: *If I Ran the Zoo* [9.0].
Zong
   Long-tailed creature in: *Oh, the Thinks You Can Think!* [49.0].
Zooie Katzen-bein
   Cat who has no one to carry his tail in: *I Can Lick 30 Tigers Today! and Other Stories*: "King Looie Katz" [34.0].
Zooks
   People who live on "the other side" of the Wall and eat their bread with the butter-side down in: *The Butter Battle Book* [59.0].
Zoom-a-Zoop Troupe
   Trapeeze artists in: *If I Ran the Circus* [13.0].
Zort [*see* Island of Zort]
Zossfossel, Ziggy and Zizzy
   Siblings who got every answer wrong in: *The Cat's Quizzer* [51.0].
Zower
   Large dog-like creature in the shower in: *There's a Wocket in My Pocket!* [46.0].
Zuffs
   Birds just like Ziffs, but bluff-dwellers, in: *Scrambled Eggs Super!* [10.0].
Zuks [*see* Single-File Zummzian Zuks]
Zumble-Zay
   Umbrellaed three-wheeled sulky pulled by an elephant in: *Marvin K. Mooney, Will You Please Go Now!* [41.0].
Zummers
   Creatures who hum "with heads in their plumming" in: *Happy Birthday to You!* [18.0].
Zumms
   Mountain habitat, also spelled "Zummz," of the Single-File Zummzian Zuks in: *Scrambled Eggs Super!* [10.0].
Zwicker-Fogels
   Monster birds in: *Halloween Is Grinch Night* [D23.0].
Zwieback Motel
   Locale in: *Dr. Seuss's Sleep Book* [23.0].

INDEX OF BOOKS
AND FILMS

This index provides an alphabetical listing of the books, animated shorts/ features and motion pictures (but not contributions to magazines, animated adaptations or sound recordings) described in the above bibliography, together with titles in translation and related titles (such as story titles that differ from the title of the work in which they originally appeared) that are associated with the original works. Titles representing works authored under pseudonyms other than "Dr. Seuss," or released in other than book format, are noted parenthetically. Citation numbers in brackets [ ] refer to item numbers in the bibliography.

INDEX OF TRANSLATIONS

This index groups, by non–English language, the books, sound recordings and animated versions that have been published in translation. Citation numbers in brackets [ ] refer to item numbers in the bibliography, where translated titles and other bibliographical information may be found.

NAME INDEX

This listing indexes the personal and corporate names associated with the creation, collaboration, translation, performance, and adaptation of Dr. Seuss's works. Also included are names of dedicatees and of authors writing about Geisel and his work. Citations refer to item numbers in the bibliography. For a listing of fictional names created by Dr. Seuss, please consult Part III, "A Dr. Seuss Iconography."